ANOKA COUNTY

1. Crooked Lake
2. Lake George

CARVER COUNTY

3. Lakes Ann & Lucy
4. Auburn Lake
5. Lake Bavaria
6. Courthouse Pond
7. Eagle Lake
8. Hydes Lake
9. Lotus Lake
10. Lakes Minnewashta
    & St. Joe
11. Parley Lake
12. Pierson Lake
13. Steiger Lake
14. Lake Waconia
15. Zumbra &
    Schutz Lakes

HENNEPIN COUNTY

16. Bryant Lake
17. Bush Lake
18. Lakes Calhoun
    & Brownie
19. Cedar Lake
20. Christmas Lake
21. Crystal Lake

22. Eagle Lake
23. Fish Lake
24. Haften Lake
25. Lake Harriet
26. Hyland Lake
27. Lake Independence
28. Lake of the Isles
29. Little Long Lake
30. Long Lake
31. Medicine Lake
32. Lake Minnetonka
33. Lakes Nokomis
    & Hiawatha
34. Parkers Lake
35. Lake Rebecca
36. Lake Riley
37. Lake Sarah
38. Spurzem Lake
39. Staring Lake
40. Twin Lakes
41. Weaver Lake
42. Whaletail Lake
43. Wirth Lake

SCOTT COUNTY

44. Cedar Lake
45. Fish Lake
46. McMahon Lake
47. O'Dowd Lake
48. Prior Lake
49. Spring Lake
50. Thole Lake

ISBN 0-961522-3-5

9 780961 522131

Printed in the United States of America.

Library of Congress Catalog Number: 90-080825

Single copies of this book may be ordered directly from the publisher at $12.95 per copy plus $0.84 Minnesota sales tax and $2.00 postage and handling charges. Send $15.79 by check or money order to:

FINS Publications
P.O. Box 130005
Roseville, MN 55113-0505

Multiple copies are available at 40 percent discount ($7.77 per copy) when purchased in quantities of 6 or more. Include 6.5 percent Minnesota Sales Tax and $3.00 UPS charges. Fishing clubs and other organizations are encouraged to take advantage of this offer as a fund raiser.

The *Twin Cities Fishing Guide* was first published in 1982 and revised in 1993.

Other books by Sybil Smith: *Brainerd-Whitefish Area Fishing Guide.*

ISBN 09615221-3-5

Printed by Sentinel Printing Company, Inc., St. Cloud, MN

Twin Cities
FISHING GUIDE

by
Sybil Smith

Cover Design
by
Villager Graphics

Cover Art
by
Cindy Berglund

Maps
by
Sharon & Joe Kadlec,
Kathy Overby, &
Sybil Smith

FINS PUBLICATIONS

Acknowledgments

The author acknowledges a debt of gratitude to the many people who donated their time and expertise to make this book possible.

I am constantly awed by the dedication, knowledge, and willingness to help demonstrated by Duane Shodeen, Regional Fisheries Supervisor, Metro Region, Minnesota Department of Natural Resources; Bruce Gilbertson and Dave Zappetillo, Area Fisheries Managers; and the DNR staff. Their assistance was invaluable during my many phone calls and visits to the Metro Region headquarters to get information on interpreting the data on the fish management programs and latest survey data on the various lakes and rivers in the Twin Cities.

The staff of the Regional Trails and Waterways program, Del Barber (past coordinator), Larry Killien, and Martha Regler worked with me on the status of all the public boat launches listed in the book. Martha also assisted in the identification and location of fishing docks accessible to handicapped anglers.

Dick Trombley, former Area Fisheries Manager, and Jack Lauer, Hinckley Fisheries Specialist, provided data for the Chisago lakes. Dan Dieterman and Larry Gates, Fisheries Specialists in Lake City, supplied information for Lake Byllesby.

John Daily, DNR aquaculture specialist and expert angler, helped update the seasonal pattern charts and reviewed the book to make certain all the information and techniques were technically sound and made good fishing sense. Ilo Howard, consultant for the DNR, suggested sources of shore fishing information.

The DNR topographical maps were invaluable reference material as I worked with the fishing experts to develop up-to-date and precise fishing maps.

I received valuable information regarding park facilities and plans for future development from the staffs of the Hennepin County Regional Parks, Minneapolis Parks, each county in the metro area, and many other units of government.

Many thanks to those involved in the Herculean effort to drag me into the 20th century computer world and teach me how the dang things work: Gary Harpster and Susan Nesbitt from Bold Eagle Enterprises, Kathy and Bob Overby, and Pat Bell. Sharon and Joe Kadlec from Kadlec Associates provided good instruction and electronic illustration for most of the maps. Kathy Overby's computer talents and suggestions helped me make the maps look professional.

Bravo to Cindy Berglund, Bob Roller, Jim Rickard from J. Rickard Visuals, Tom Iten from Sentinel Printing, Don Leper from Stanton Publication Services, and Linda Bryan from Your Blue Pencil for their advice on graphics, production, and printing. Also thanks to LaVonne Olberg, Beth Hutchinson, Lee Frielinger, and B.J. Reed for their help with data entry and proofreading.

A warm word of appreciation to Marion and Larry Hudah for the use of their lakeside cabin to get away from the telephone and concentrate on this project.

And finally, a special tribute to that army of expert anglers who answered my endless questions, gave me information about their favorite fishing holes, and showed great patience when I went back to them again and again to clarify fish locations and make sure their advice would be understood by the reader.

Contents

FISHING IN
THE TWIN CITIES

WHY FISH METRO LAKES AND RIVERS?

The Twin Cities offers a vast smorgasbord of fishing opportunities. The 7-county metro area has more than 60,000 acres of water in lakes as well as 21,000 acres of water in rivers — and most of it is accessible to anglers.

Fishing close to home has many advantages. It takes less travel time, costs less money, and requires less equipment. A small boat with an inexpensive gas or electric motor will put you within easy reach of most of the best hotspots. You can go fishing more frequently, stay on the water longer, and learn more about the areas you fish. Experts all agree that the better you know each lake you fish the better chance you have of catching fish in all seasons.

Here are some of the reasons metro lakes continue to be a favorite for anglers.

- There are now over 200 bodies of water in the 7-county area that are accessible to the public. Many boat launches have been upgraded, and parking facilities have been enhanced.

- Aeration devices have been installed on 45 Twin Cities lakes that have frequent winterkill, and more are being added each year.

- Fishing piers that are accessible to handicapped anglers have been added on 32 lakes. Regional, county, and city parks have been opened or expanded. Shore fishing areas are a priority.

- This incredible wealth of fishable water contains nearly every species of game-fish known to the Midwest. In addition, the DNR stocks walleyes in 40 lakes; muskies in 28 lakes; and trout and/or salmon in 6 lakes.

- In an attempt to increase the size of largemouth bass and sunfish, 14 lakes now have slot limits, minimum length restrictions, or Catch & Release requirements. Tournament statistics for largemouth bass show that anglers are catching more bass on some of these lakes and that the average size has increased in recent years.

- Because of improved sewage treatment facilities on the lower Mississippi River, the PCB levels decreased about 85 percent from 1976 to 1987, and the game fish have returned.

ABOUT THE BOOK

The *Twin Cities Fishing Guide* represents the accumulated wisdom of many of the area's top experts — tournament anglers, guides, bait and tackle shop dealers, DNR staff, lakeside homeowners, and old-timers who have fished these waters for a lifetime.

We asked them to select their favorite water, mark the hotspots on a contour map, and tell us how to fish those spots. Our contributors took great care in correcting (and in some cases, totally redrawing) the lake maps to make them as accurate as possible. They added details such as sunken islands, humps, bars, reefs, stumps, and boating hazards that are not marked on other maps.

This book is not intended to be a training manual for basic fishing skills. Although some "how-to" information is included, the primary purpose of the book is to show you where to find fish and to share with you some of the techniques the experts use to catch them. A Glossary section is included.

We also consulted government agencies for the latest information on the development of public accesses, shoreline parks, and camping facilities.

This guide identifies shorefishing sites that have the best track record for consistently producing fish. We made a special effort to include the location of fishing piers and other shoreline facilities that are accessible to handicapped anglers.

In this edition, we have included most of the smaller neighborhood lakes that are prime panfish waters because the majority of anglers fish primarily for panfish such as crappie, sunfish, and perch.

For each lake, we have included information about the population and average size of each species of fish. Here are the criteria we used. The sizes indicated for each species pertain only to the average sizes in the metro area and may not be valid for other parts of the state.

SPECIES	SMALL	MEDIUM	LARGE
Largemouth Bass	up to 1-1/2 lbs.	1-1/2 to 3 lbs.	over 3 lbs.
Smallmouth Bass	up to 1 lb.	1 to 2 lbs.	over 2 lbs.
Muskie	up to 6-1/2 lbs.	6-1/2 to 15 lbs.	over 15 lbs.
Northern Pike	up to 3 lbs.	3 to 6 lbs.	over 6 lbs.
Walleye	up to 1-1/2 lbs.	1-1/2 to 3 lbs.	over 3 lbs.
Crappie	up to 1/4 lb.	1/4 to 3/4 lbs.	over 3/4 lbs.
Sunfish	up to 1/4 lb.	1/4 to 1/2 lbs.	over 1/2 lbs.

SELECTING THE RIGHT LAKE

The wise angler should concentrate on selecting the right lake for a variety of fishing conditions. Here are some of the factors that should be considered.

SPECIES OF FISH For each lake described in this book, we have provided a chart that indicates the average size and population of each major species. Select a lake that has an abundant supply of the species you prefer.

For big walleyes, try the larger, deeper lakes or the rivers. For fast action rather than size, check the population charts.

The largest northern pike will be found in the multi-species lakes stocked with trout. Young trout provide a food source rich in fat and protein that gives an extra boost to the growth rate of the northern pike.

Good bass and sunfish lakes abound throughout this area. The most consistently productive lakes are the smaller ones with thick weed beds. Rivers are the best bet for a consistent supply of smallmouth bass.

For the best crappies, fish the better bass and sunfish lakes. Lakes with darker water are more consistently productive. On clear-water lakes, the crappie locations are less predictable and the fish will drive you crazy with a feast-or-famine pattern.

SIZE OF FISH Even if a lake has plenty of game fish, it may not produce many lunkers. A lake will usually have good numbers of smaller fish or a few large fish of a given species, but rarely both. If you're looking for a trophy, consider the history of the lake. Does it have a reputation for large fish? A lake that is subject to frequent severe winterkill is not likely to produce trophy-sized bass, northern pike, or walleyes. Crappies and sunfish, on the other hand, often benefit from a partial winterkill because it reduces the overpopulation and offers more food for the remaining supply.

SEASON OF THE YEAR To determine the seasonal fish movements of the species you're looking for and the type of bottom structure preferred by that species, consult the Seasonal Patterns section of this book. The shallow back bays where crappies were so abundant in the spring are rarely the place to look for them in the summer.

In the early spring, water temperature is the crucial factor. Small, shallow lakes with murky water warm up fast and provide the earliest spring fishing. Long, narrow lakes offer more shoreline area for warm runoff water than round lakes.

On hot summer days, the fish will usually prefer deeper water away from the shoreline. Look for lakes that have lots of sunken islands, humps, saddles, and weedy points extending into deep water. River fishing can also be terrific.

In late fall, try the large deep lakes with clear water. They will usually have plenty of healthy weeds long after the weeds have died off in the shallow, murky lakes. Look for lakes with steep drop-offs near the shallow "foodshelves". The fish will make short vertical movements up these steep drop-offs for feeding.

WATER CLARITY Biologists from the DNR measure water clarity by lowering an 8-inch black and white disc (Secchi disc) into the water and measuring the depth at which the disc is no longer visible. We have included these Secchi Disc readings on the map of each lake.

In *Walleye Fishing* by Dick Sternberg (The Hunting & Fishing Library), the author suggests using the Secchi disc readings to determine the time of day when walleye fishing will be best. "If the reading is a foot or less, chances are walleyes will feed intermittently from midmorning through midafternoon. If the reading is 10 feet or more, walleyes may feed only at night. Your best choice is a lake where the reading is between 3 and 8 feet. Here walleyes feed heavily around dusk and dawn with occasional feeding periods during the day."

Dark, murky, or stained lakes are usually better bass lakes than are lakes with clear water. They are also the best bet right after a cold front when the skies are bright and cloudless, or for midday fishing or very calm days. The dark water reduces light penetration and allows the fish to stay in the shallows where they're easier to catch. Night fishing is seldom productive on these lakes.

Fish the deep, clear lakes during low-light periods. Dusk and dawn can be productive and night fishing can be phenomenal. Clouds or wind will reduce light penetration and may spark a daytime feeding spree. Clear-water lakes warm up and cool down slowly and the oxygen levels will be deeper. Fish relate more to the deep-water structure and are easily spooked when in the shallows.

The water clarity ratings provided in this book apply to normal conditions. However, temporary conditions (such as high winds, rainstorms, midsummer algae growth, and heavy boat traffic) can sometimes reduce the clarity.

FISH MANAGEMENT PROGRAMS

DNR fish stocking programs are carefully planned and monitored to maintain the proper balance in the food chain. State law prohibits the DNR from stocking fish in lakes that do not provide free access to the public. The major species that are managed or stocked in area lakes and rivers are bass, crappie, sunfish, northern pike, walleye, muskie, and trout.

LARGEMOUTH BASS, CRAPPIE, AND SUNFISH Most lakes in the metro area have sufficient spawning areas and natural habitat to produce an abundance of these species, and they are usually not stocked unless a lake has suffered a severe winterkill, undergone chemical rehabilitation, or is maintained as a Children's Pond. On 5 lakes, the DNR has initiated an experimental "slot limit" for bass. On these lakes, all bass between 12 and 16 inches long must be returned to the water unharmed. Bass of this size consume large quantities of small sunfish, reducing the overpopulation and allowing the remaining sunfish to grow larger. On 7 lakes, there is now a minimum size limit of 16 inches for largemouth bass. On Lake Waconia, all bass between 17 and 21 inches long must be released. On Lake Steiger, all fish except panfish must be released. Check the "Regulations" section of the maps to see if your favorite lake has restrictions. However, these regulations may change from year to year, so be sure to also check the current *Minnesota Fishing Regulations* booklet you received with your fishing license.

SMALLMOUTH BASS You'll find smallmouth bass in White Bear Lake, Lake Minnetonka, and the Mississippi and St. Croix Rivers. These reproduce naturally; this species is not stocked in metro area lakes.

NORTHERN PIKE The continuing loss of wetlands and marsh areas to urban development hampers the natural reproduction of northern pike on many lakes. The DNR maintains several spawning areas for stocking lakes that do not have an abundant natural supply of northerns. Many lakes are also stocked with winter-rescued northern pike yearlings or adults.

WALLEYE Lakes chosen for walleye stocking are usually those with a below-average population of northern pike because northerns are very efficient predators who make no distinction between perch (their favorite food) and young walleyes. The walleye stocking program now includes regular stocking of 26 lakes. Latest reports indicate that Waconia, Minnetonka, Harriet, Forest, Green, South Center, Prior, White Bear, Spring, Big Marine, Nokomis, and Phalen now have an exceptional supply. Some are as large as 11 pounds. Look for Lakes Independence, Bald Eagle, and Centerville to join this list in a few years.

MUSKIE To add a real challenge for anglers, pure strain muskies have been stocked in 9 lakes and some now weigh more than 25 pounds. Hybrid tiger muskies, a cross between muskies and northerns, have been stocked in 18 lakes. In Lake Calhoun in the summer of 1991, a 33-1/2 pound hybrid muskie was caught that broke that state record. For size limits, check the "Special Regulations" section on the maps.

TROUT You'll find trout and/or salmon in 6 lakes: Courthouse Pond, Square, Little Long, Cenaiko (Coon Rapids Dam), Christmas, and Lac Lavon (Burnsville). Brown's Creek, a mile and a half of stream located near the junction of Hwy. 95 and Hwy. 96 north of Stillwater, is stocked with brown trout yearlings annually.

CATCH AND RELEASE

Anglers are learning that hauling in big stringers of fish is no longer acceptable, and Catch and Release is necessary to ensure an adequate supply of decent sized fish for future trips. Yes, you can take some home to eat, and the smaller ones are the best tasting. Release the medium-sized fish to catch later when they're larger. For more information or tips for successful release, ask the DNR for their free pamphlet, *An Angler's Guide to Catch and Release.*

EURASIAN WATER MILFOIL

Yeah, this weed's now growing in numerous metro lakes and it's spreading. It can grow up to 2 inches a day and will crowd out native weeds. Because most of it floats on the surface as thick brown mats, boating and fishing are very difficult. A cure is being developed, but for now, control is the key.

Here's what you can do to help.

- Call the DNR Information Center (296-6699) and order their free pamphlet that shows how to identify this weed.

- Carry the pamphlet with you in your tackle box, and check your boat, motor, and trailer for pieces of milfoil whenever you leave the water. It only takes a small fragment to infect a new lake or a different section of a lake.

But take heart. Those thick, brown masses of matted vegetation don't have to signal the end of your fishing success. Tournament anglers on Lake Minnetonka have found that by adapting techniques and patterns they are catching bass that are larger than ever. The theory is that the dense growth of this weed on the surface of the water and the sparse stems underneath allow the bass to do a better job of ambushing the smaller baitfish. Here are a few tips from Lake Minnetonka tournament winners.

In the early season before the weeds grow to the surface, cast a large-blade spinnerbait or a buzzbait across the tops of the weeds. Engage the reel just before the lure hits the water. Or try twitching a shallow-running crankbait. Soft-body topwater lures are more buoyant.

When the weeds are on the surface, the trick is to pitch your lure into the holes between patches of milfoil. You'll need to fine tune your concentration, and you'll have to work harder to feel the strike. A sensitive rod is a must.

Flipping a jig and pig (pork rind) is a favorite technique. Use a large jig (3/4 to 1 oz.) so it can drop through the thick matting. Lighter jigs will get hung up. You may have to jiggle or shake your rod to help the jig fall through the weeds. Let it sit there for at least 30 seconds before beginning the retrieve. Cone-shaped jigs (needle nose) are more efficient. A metal flake design on the jig skirt is more visible in darker water.

There is no such thing as a truly weedless lure in milfoil, but try the super weedless lures invented in the South where milfoil is widely prevalent. The Johnson Silver Minnow or Moss Boss or the Blue Fox Flipping Fool are good choices. Watch for new lures now being developed that will be even more effective.

Also try casting a lightweight, weedless, topwater lure onto the weedy mat and retrieve it across the openings of the weeds.

Unlike other types of weeds, the outside weedlines of milfoil don't produce the big fish except in late summer. For the rest of the season, most of the fish you catch here are small northerns. Make certain you always check the inside weedline too. Spinnerbaits and crankbaits are good weedline lures. Cast parallel to the weeds. Rocky areas surrounded by milfoil can also be real hotspots. A good fishing map will show these.

ABOUT THE MAPS

Contour maps allow you to pinpoint the areas where the fish are most likely to be. They show the shape and depth of the lake bottoms by using contour lines representing the change in depth at 5 or 10 foot intervals. A rapid change in depth such as a steep slope is represented by contour lines that are very close together. Widely spaced contour lines indicate a gradually sloping bottom. Good maps will indicate the location of large structures such as points, bars, steep drop-offs, sunken islands, extended flats, reefs, inlets, creek channels, and submerged road beds. Fish will frequent these areas during part or all of the season.

All of the larger species of fish are identified on the maps, but there are so many varieties of sunfish that we have lumped them all together. Therefore the sunfish category includes bluegills, pumpkinseed, and other members of the sunfish family.

To help you find fish more consistently, we have also included on each map the depth of the thermocline and the Secchi disc measurement.

- The depth of the thermocline is essential information for summer fishing because the fish will not be comfortable below that depth. In most metro lakes, the thermocline forms about mid-June and lasts until fall turnover in mid-September. Murky lakes tend to form a thermocline faster than clear lakes.

Shallow lakes (less than 25 feet deep) with plenty of wave action from prevailing winds will not form a thermocline because the wave action continually circulates the water from top to bottom.

- The Secchi disc measurement indicates water clarity — 0 to 2 feet indicates muddy or murky water; 2 to 4 feet indicates stained water; and more than 4 feet indicates clear water. For tips on when to fish each type of water, see the "Water Clarity" section of this chapter.

CHANGES ARE INEVITABLE

In this book, we have presented the most up-to-date information available about fish populations, lake characteristics, and lakeside fishing facilities. But changes occur from season to season and year to year. Fish populations are affected by stocking programs, winterkill, water pollution, inadequate reproduction, fluctuations in forage populations, increased populations of predator species, fishing pressure, and depletion of fish habitat and spawning areas. Some species, notably the crappie, are notoriously cyclical in abundance.

Sometimes anglers will find fewer weeds during the summer following a winter of heavy snowfall and will need to adapt to new fish locations. Eurasian milfoil weed infestations can alter fishing locations, patterns, and techniques.

Significant changes in the water level can also affect the location of the fish. In 1986, for example, Minnesota anglers were plagued with the wettest season in recorded history and the highest lake levels in the century. On many lakes, fish moved from their traditional locations. The next year was the beginning of a three-year drought, and lake levels plummeted. In 1991 and 1992, extremely heavy rains rapidly brought most of the lake levels back to normal. Unless anglers were alert to these changes and could adapt to them, their catch was apt to be very limited.

Heavy rains cause many changes. When high water floods new areas, the abundance of food draws bait fish into the shallows — with the game fish not far behind. Heavy rains increase the amount of runoff water, bringing nutrients and causing an overabundance of plankton that increase the murkiness of the water. The darker water encourages the fish to stay in the shallows longer.

In shallow lakes with low water levels, the greatest threat to fish is winterkill. If the volume of water is decreased, a lake has less capacity for storage of dissolved oxygen to last through the winter.

Changing water levels also affect the accuracy of contour maps drawn to reflect the depth of the lake bottom when water levels are normal. The condition of public boat accesses can change drastically too. Unusually high or low water levels can make the launch areas unusable. Frost heave can destroy a paved boat launch, and a heavy rain can cause deep ruts in sand or gravel.

Centerville is becoming one of the prime walleye lakes in the metro area. A partial winterkill in 1985 wiped out a portion of the game fish population. Then an aerator was installed and walleyes have been stocked each year. Centerville's high population of decent-sized perch provides the walleyes with plenty of food for optimum growth. The low population of northern pike increases the walleyes' chances of survival.

Centerville, located below Peltier Lake in the city of Centerville, is a bowl-shaped lake without a lot of structure. The experts say you'll have to work harder to find the fish here than on Peltier but it will be worth your time. Use caution around the pump house. There are shallow rocks here. In the winter, springs in this area weaken the ice.

SPECIES	POPULATION	AVERAGE SIZE
Bass	Fair	Medium
Northern Pike	Poor to Fair	Medium
Walleye	Fair to Good	Medium
Crappie	Good	Medium
Sunfish	Fair	Small

BASS In all seasons, you'll find the bass at the south end of the lake from the public access east to the houses on the eastern shoreline. Cast to the fallen trees and shallow cabbage weeds.

NORTHERN PIKE In the early season, work the shoreline from the public access east to the pump house and up the eastern side of the lake. Also try the backwater areas and the north side of the boggy islands on the southeast corner. Troll the outside edge of the weeds in 4 to 8 feet of water with red and white spoons, sucker minnows, or strip-ons. Summer northerns are in the same areas, but move down to the 10 to 15 foot depths. In the fall, concentrate on the remaining green weeds in these areas. In the winter, fish the area from the pump house west to the square land point on the south side of the lake.

WALLEYE For early-season walleyes, try back-trolling in 4 to 10 feet of water between the two land points on the south end of the lake. Use a jig and leech or shallow-running minnow crankbait. In spring and winter, the rocky 10-foot hole at the north end of the lake is a good bet. An all-season spot is the east side of the hook-shaped land point on the southeast corner. Start shallow (3 to 10 feet) in the spring, and move down to the 6 to 11 foot depths in the summer. Anchor here and use leeches with slip bobbers. Try the 15-foot depths in the winter.

CRAPPIE & SUNFISH The 4-foot hole at the north end of the lake is one of the best all-season crappie spots in the lake, especially during low-water years. You can cast from shore, wade, or use a boat. Come early: it's a crowded spot. An ice jig or a small (1/32 oz.) white or chartreuse feather jig with a crappie minnow will do the job. The rocky area around the pump house on the lower east side is another good all-season location. Also try drifting or trolling on the breaks from the pump house up the east side to the northeast corner. In all seasons, you'll find a good supply of sunfish around the pump house or in the backwater area around the islands with the bass.

This information was provided by Terry Dillard, Dave Genz, and Mike Ring.

CENTERVILLE LAKE
455 acres

1. **RICE CREEK CHAIN OF LAKES PARK RESERVE** (Entrance to boat launch) — camping; beach. Hours: 7:30 a.m. to 9:30 p.m. Phone: 757-3920.

2. **SHORE FISH AREA**

3. **PUBLIC ACCESS** (Use Rice Creek Park entrance) concrete boat ramp; 29 trailer spaces (fee). Ramp will be closed if parking lot is full.

Shoal Water Soils:
Sand — 90%
Muck — 9%
Rubble — 1%

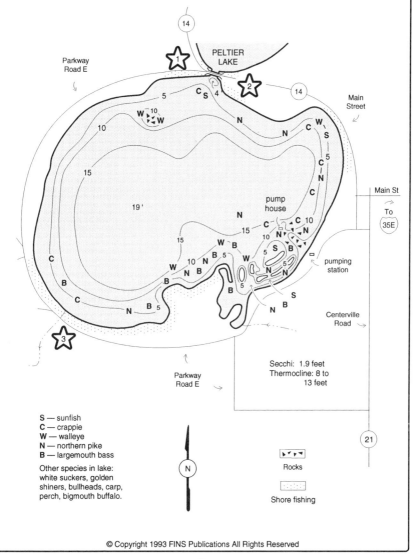

Secchi: 1.9 feet
Thermocline: 8 to 13 feet

S — sunfish
C — crappie
W — walleye
N — northern pike
B — largemouth bass

Other species in lake: white suckers, golden shiners, bullheads, carp, perch, bigmouth buffalo.

Rocks

Shore fishing

Coon Lake has a reputation for producing big crappies that break state records. According to the experts, "The bass have come back bigtime since the severe winterkill of 1986". An aerator was installed in 1987 to prevent winterkill, and walleyes have been stocked each year since then.

Coon Lake, located on County Road 22 about 3 miles east of Hwy. 65, is a huge, turbid, shallow, junkweed lake. The biggest and best supply of fish is in the channel area and in the deeper eastern half where the oxygen supply is best.

SPECIES	POPULATION	AVERAGE SIZE
Bass	Good	Medium to Large
Northern Pike	Very Good	Small to Large
Walleye	Poor to Fair	Small
Crappie	Excellent	Small to Large
Sunfish	Very Good	Small to Large

BASS   For early-season bass, the bulrush beds and weeds at the east end of the eastern half of the lake are good locations. Cast a spinnerbait with a big single blade to the edges and inside turns of the weeds. Also work the submerged weeds in 2 to 8 feet of water around the 19-foot hole on the western half of the lake. In the summer, move to the deeper weedlines, points, and the docks that are near deep water. Also try the small bay with the 20-foot hole on the north side of the eastern half of the lake.

NORTHERN PIKE   You'll find early-season northerns in the shallow bays. In mid-summer and fall, troll with a sucker minnow in 10 to 15 feet of water from the Coon Lake County Park on the east end down to the 5-foot hump on the west end before the channel.

WALLEYE   The eastern half of the lake is best throughout the season. In the spring, troll the 6-foot depths along the eastern shoreline with a live-bait rig and a minnow. In the summer and fall, work the 2 sand points on the northern shoreline and the drop-offs on the southern shoreline. In late fall, switch to a jig and minnow. The 15-foot area just east of the larger sand point is a good summer location. Try a slip bobber and minnow here in the late afternoon. In the winter, concentrate on the drop-off on the east side of the larger sand point and the edges of the deeper holes.

CRAPPIE & SUNFISH   Early-season crappies will be in the bulrushes near the dam on the eastern half of the lake. Cover the entire area; you'll find them schooled. In bad weather, move down to the 5-foot break. Watch your depth-finder and move deeper until you find the fish. The small canals and the area below the channel on the south side are also good spring locations. In summer, look for suspended crappies over the 29-foot hole in the eastern half of the lake. In the fall, concentrate on the north side of the lake. The fish will be 5 feet below the surface in 9 feet of water. The most productive winter locations are both beaches, the holes, and the channels. The best time is just before dark. Wax worms and small crappie minnows work best. Look for spring and winter sunfish in the crappie spots. In summer and fall, sunfish will be in all the bass haunts.

Information about this lake was provided by Todd Amenrud, Gary and Pete Erickson, and Dave Sonnenburg.

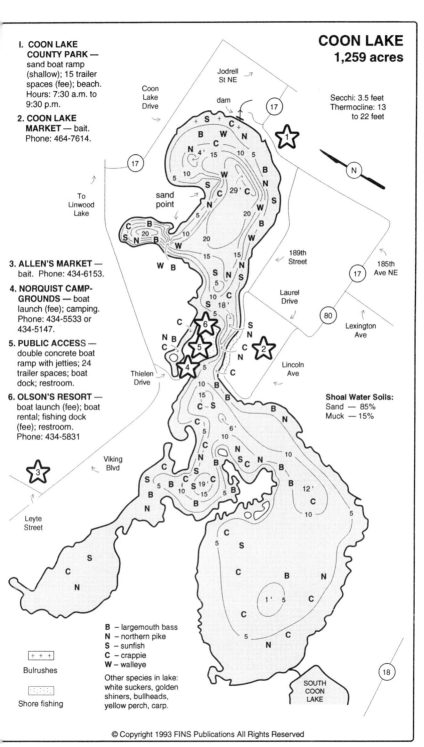

COON LAKE
1,259 acres

I. **COON LAKE COUNTY PARK** — sand boat ramp (shallow); 15 trailer spaces (fee); beach. Hours: 7:30 a.m. to 9:30 p.m.

2. **COON LAKE MARKET** — bait. Phone: 464-7614.

3. **ALLEN'S MARKET** — bait. Phone: 434-6153.

4. **NORQUIST CAMP-GROUNDS** — boat launch (fee); camping. Phone: 434-5533 or 434-5147.

5. **PUBLIC ACCESS** — double concrete boat ramp with jetties; 24 trailer spaces; boat dock; restroom.

6. **OLSON'S RESORT** — boat launch (fee); boat rental; fishing dock (fee); restroom. Phone: 434-5831

Secchi: 3.5 feet
Thermocline: 13 to 22 feet

Shoal Water Soils:
Sand — 85%
Muck — 15%

Jodrell St NE
Coon Lake Drive
dam
To Linwood Lake
sand point
189th Street
185th Ave NE
Laurel Drive
Lexington Ave
Thielen Drive
Lincoln Ave
Viking Blvd
Leyte Street
SOUTH COON LAKE

B – largemouth bass
N – northern pike
S – sunfish
C – crappie
W – walleye

Other species in lake: white suckers, golden shiners, bullheads, yellow perch, carp.

Bulrushes

Shore fishing

11

There are still huge bass coming out of Lake George. One local bait store owner claims he sees at least one 7-pound fish out of this lake every year. A few years ago, professional angler Randy Amenrud caught a 9-pound 2-ounce beauty here.

Despite the size of the bass, it's the northerns that are really prolific. Most are runts, but a 22-pound monster was hauled out of this lake in the winter of 1988/89. In addition, the supply of crappies and sunfish just won't quit.

Lake George, located 9 miles north of Anoka on County Road 9, is one of the clearest lakes in the county.

SPECIES	POPULATION	AVERAGE SIZE
Bass	Good	Medium to Large
Northern Pike	Excellent	Small
Crappie	Good	Small to Medium
Sunfish	Excellent	Small to Medium

BASS In the early season, the cabbage weeds around the entire lake are productive, especially on the north side of the lake. The best spots are on the west, north, and northeast sides and the dual underwater points (bars) on the south side of the lake. From mid-June through September, the weedlines will produce most of the bass. Work both the inside and outside edges of the weeds with a purple or black plastic worm or a crawfish-pattern, shallow-running crankbait. Cast a green or white spinnerbait over the top of the weeds. Trophy-sized bass are often caught at night. In the fall, switch to large lures and work all the weedy points, especially the dual underwater points in the southern section of the lake. A black or brown jig and pork frog worked on the outside edge of the weeds can be productive.

NORTHERN PIKE You'll find a good supply of northerns on the weedy edges in the bass areas. The two underwater points (bars) are good all-season locations. Try a black spinnerbait or sucker minnow. In the fall, switch to larger lures. Perch-pattern crankbaits are a good bet. The underwater points on the south side of the lake are good fall locations. In the winter, work the weedy edges in 12 to 15 feet of water all over the lake, especially on the northern side of the lake.

CRAPPIE & SUNFISH Look for spring crappies and sunfish in the shallow weeds at the north end of the lake where the water warms up first. The small bay at the southwest corner of the lake is another good spring location. You can paddle a small boat through the channel from the main lake if water levels are normal. Ice ants or teardrop jigs tipped with minnows or wax worms are popular. In the summer, the fish will be in the deeper cabbage weedbeds or on the outer edges of them. In late fall and winter, crappies will be suspended in 20 to 30 feet of water in the middle of the lake. Look for the blips on your depthfinder. Use a pink jig head with a white body or an orange jig head with a chartreuse body. Fall sunfish will stay on the outside edge of the remaining green weeds. In the winter, they'll be in the same areas but at the 15 to 17 foot depths.

Information about this lake was provided by Larry Bollig, Steve Larson, Bob McLean, and Lee Schoneman.

LAKE GEORGE
495 acres

1. **LAKE GEORGE REGIONAL PARK** — beach; restroom.
2. **PUBLIC ACCESS** — double concrete boat ramp with jetties; 30 trailer spaces; restroom.

Shoal Water Soils:
Sand — 95%
Muck — 5%

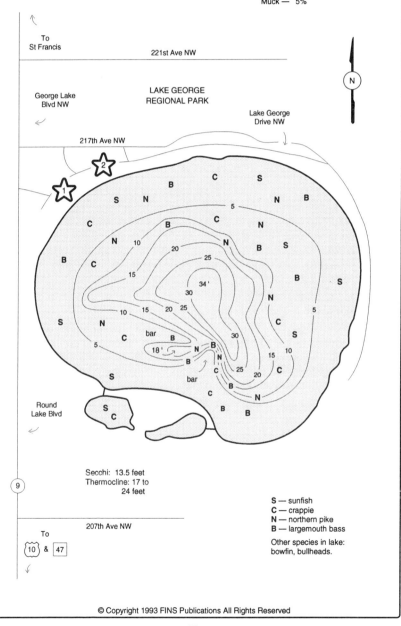

S — sunfish
C — crappie
N — northern pike
B — largemouth bass

Other species in lake: bowfin, bullheads.

Secchi: 13.5 feet
Thermocline: 17 to 24 feet

Linwood, located on Hwy. 22 about 5 miles west of Wyoming, is considered an easy lake to fish, has never had a winterkill, and is crammed full of fish. There's even a decent supply of walleyes, which have been stocked sporadically since 1984. Every once in a while, Linwood is listed in the "Big Fish" section of the Sunday newspapers for yielding a 2 or 3 pound crappie.

SPECIES	POPULATION	AVERAGE SIZE
Bass	Excellent	Medium to Large
Northern Pike	Very Good	Medium
Walleye	Fair	Medium
Crappie	Excellent	Small to Medium
Sunfish	Excellent	Small to Medium

BASS   In June, you'll find a good supply of bass on the shallow flats in the southeast section of the lake, especially at the inlet from Boot Lake. Start at the 1 to 2 foot depths and work down to the weedline as the water warms. The inside weedline will be productive during low-light periods. Use a white spinnerbait with a white twister tail attached to the hook. The underwater point (bar) on the east side of the lake and the bar on the northwest side are prime spring and summer locations. Also try the weedline in front of the dam on the northeast corner. This is also a good fall location.

NORTHERN PIKE   The early-season northerns will be roaming all over the flats in the southeast side of the lake. Use a weedless silver spoon here. In the summer, there will still be a supply in the shallows — but for the big ones, try trolling the weedline around the bar on the northwest side of the lake, below it on the southwest side, and in front of the dam. Stay here in the fall. Winter northerns are in front of the outlet and on the flat on the southeast side of the lake.

WALLEYE   Early-season walleyes will be in front of the dam. Stay in 11 to 12 feet of water. About the second week of June, the bullheads will take over this area. Then move to the long bar on the north side of the lake and the shoreline below this bar. For summer walleyes, troll the west end of the lake with orange stickbaits. Look for the clumps of weeds. In the winter, move back to the dam. Also try the flats on the southeast side of the lake. Stay in 10 to 15 feet of water.

CRAPPIE & SUNFISH   In the spring, the best crappie locations are the spawning areas in front of the dam and the southwest corner. Start shallow and work down to 6 to 7 feet. In the summer, some will stay in front of the dam, and others will be suspended in deep water. In the winter, you'll find them in 12 feet of water in the center of the lake during the day. At night, look for them near the edges of both holes. Use your depthfinder to determine the depth. The bar on the east side of the lake also attracts winter crappies. Sunfish can be found in the bass locations throughout the open-water season. In spring and summer, you'll catch the biggest sunfish by wading with a fly rod in front of the park on the east side of the lake. In the winter, look for them in the crappie locations. The bigger ones are on the edge of the 24-foot hole in 12 to 15 feet of water.

Information about this lake was provided by Todd Amenrud, Larry Bollig, Gary Erickson, and Axel Lind.

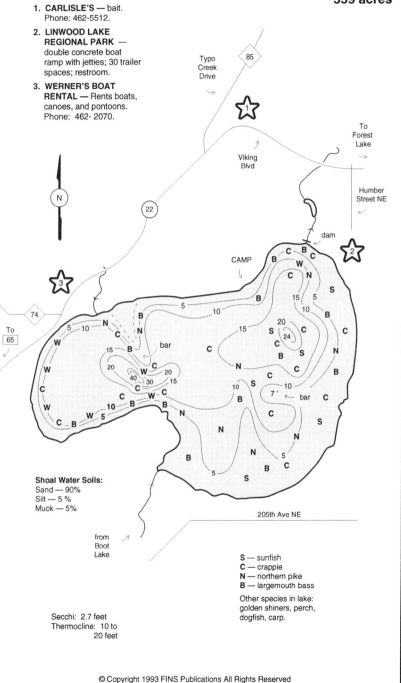

LINWOOD LAKE
559 acres

1. **CARLISLE'S** — bait.
   Phone: 462-5512.

2. **LINWOOD LAKE REGIONAL PARK** — double concrete boat ramp with jetties; 30 trailer spaces; restroom.

3. **WERNER'S BOAT RENTAL** — Rents boats, canoes, and pontoons. Phone: 462- 2070.

Typo Creek Drive

85

To Forest Lake

Viking Blvd

N

22

Humber Street NE

dam

CAMP

2

74

To 65

bar

bar

7'

Shoal Water Soils:
Sand — 90%
Silt — 5 %
Muck — 5%

205th Ave NE

from Boot Lake

S — sunfish
C — crappie
N — northern pike
B — largemouth bass

Other species in lake: golden shiners, perch, dogfish, carp.

Secchi: 2.7 feet
Thermocline: 10 to 20 feet

Big northern pike are the attraction on this lake in southeastern Anoka County. Local experts claim that the average size is 4 pounds, and a few 15 to 18 pound monsters are caught here every winter. Peltier also holds lots of sunfish, crappies, and perch. Since Peltier Lake is part of the Rice Creek chain of lakes, you might even find a rare walleye that strayed in from Centerville Lake or a muskie that wandered in from Bald Eagle Lake.

Peltier is not overfished and is an easier lake to learn than nearby Centerville Lake. It's a shallow, dishpan-shaped lake with simple shoreline structure. An aerator was installed in 1988 to prevent winterkill.

SPECIES	POPULATION	AVERAGE SIZE
Bass	Fair	Medium
Northern Pike	Good	Medium to Large
Crappie	Good	Medium
Sunfish	Good	Medium

BASS   Look for spring bass along the south side of the tree island and by the fence posts on the east and west sides of the tree island. Use a white or chartreuse spinnerbait here. In the summer and fall, you'll find the bass on the weedline at the southwest end of the lake from the dam down the shoreline to the nightclub. You can fish this area from shore or from a boat. In the fall, also try the far north end of the lake and the west shoreline above the dam.

NORTHERN PIKE   In the early season, you'll find a good supply of northerns at the middle of the east side of the lake from the last house down to the farm area. Stay in 5 to 10 feet of water and use spoons, crankbaits, floating minnow lures, or a bobber with sucker minnows. Trolling is effective here too. Check out the shore fishing areas at the dam and the nightclub. Trolling the southern shoreline is effective until early July. Then move to the east, west, and northwest shorelines. Stay in the 10 to 15 foot depths. In the fall, try the 5 to 10 foot depths in front of the dam, the nightclub, and the middle of the east side. The northeast corner below the tree island is another fall hotspot. Winter northerns can be found on the east and west sides of the lake in 5 to 9 feet of water.

CRAPPIE AND SUNFISH   As soon as the ice is out, you can get large sunfish and crappies in the shallow backwater area at the far north end of the lake. Also try the 5 to 10 foot depths below the tree island or around the boat launch area. The middle of the west side of the lake is a good all-season location for both sunfish and crappies. In the summer, the sunfish will be on the weedline in the same areas as the bass. For fall crappies and sunfish, check out the area from the dam down to the nightclub. The north side of the 16-foot hole is a good fall and winter location. The west side of the lake is a good area in early winter (first ice). In mid-winter, the fish will be roaming the deepest parts of the lake. In late winter (until March), you'll find them on the northeast and northwest corners of the main lake (below the island). They'll be on their way up to the spawning areas in the northern bays.

Information about this lake was provided by Terry Dillard, Dave Genz, Mike Ring, and Brad Stanius.

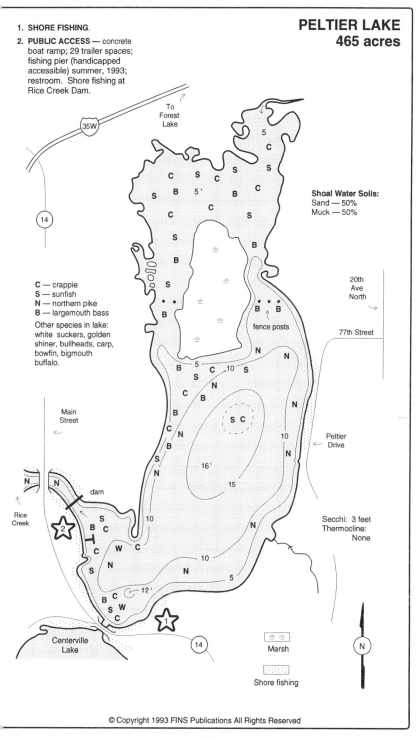

1. **SHORE FISHING**.
2. **PUBLIC ACCESS** — concrete boat ramp; 29 trailer spaces; fishing pier (handicapped accessible) summer, 1993; restroom. Shore fishing at Rice Creek Dam.

PELTIER LAKE
465 acres

To Forest Lake

35W

14

Shoal Water Soils:
Sand — 50%
Muck — 50%

C — crappie
S — sunfish
N — northern pike
B — largemouth bass
Other species in lake: white suckers, golden shiner, bullheads, carp, bowfin, bigmouth buffalo.

C   S   C
S   5'   B
C   B
C   S
S
B
S
B

B   B   B
fence posts

20th Ave North

77th Street

Main Street

Peltier Drive

N   N

dam

Rice Creek

Secchi: 3 feet
Thermocline: None

Centerville Lake

14

Marsh

Shore fishing

N

Ann is part of the Lucy-Ann-Susan chain of lakes located a half mile west of Chanhassen on Hwy. 5 in eastern Carver County. Ann Lake is known for providing an excellent supply of big bass as well as plenty of northern pike, crappies, and sunfish.

There is no public boat launch on Lake Lucy but you can walk in with a small boat. Lucy has a history of frequent winterkill; a partial winterkill occurred in the winter of 1991/1992. You can find a fair supply of northerns, sunfish, and crappies as well as a few bass. Winter anglers drive to the creek and walk through to Lake Lucy. The best locations for all species are the deeper holes. In the winter, start at the deepest area and work up and around the weedy edges of the holes. Sunfish will spread out along the break.

SPECIES	POPULATION	AVERAGE SIZE
Bass	Excellent	Medium
Northern Pike	Good	Small to Medium
Crappie	Good	Medium
Sunfish	Very Good	Small to Medium

BASS For early-season action, work the edges and pockets of the cattails on the northeast side of the lake. Also work the weeds in this area from the shallows out to the drop-offs (2 to 20 feet) with a good weedless lure. The best times are early morning and late evening. As the water warms, move out to the breaks in front of the deep holes. Stay with the drop-offs in the summer. In low-light periods, use noisy surface lures such as jitterbugs, hulapoppers, or floating minnows. A plastic worm or jig and pig will work on sunny days. In the fall, go back to the spring pattern. The bigger fish will be right on the weedline and breaks. Be prepared to lose lures in the thick weeds.

NORTHERN PIKE For early-season northerns, fish the 8 to 12 foot drop-offs. Start at the fishing pier and work the drop-offs along the east and north sides of the lake to the underwater point on the northwest side. Spoons, spinners, and live-bait rigs are the traditional favorites. In the summer, move down to the 16 to 22 foot depths in the same areas. Move back to the shallow depths (6 to 15 feet) in the fall. You'll find the winter northerns on the breaks in 8 to 20 feet of water around the holes.

CRAPPIE For spring crappies, start at the fishing pier and work up and around the north side of the lake to the underwater shoreline bar. In early spring, concentrate on the 10 to 12 foot depths. As the water warms, move up to the 2 foot depths. Summer crappies will be suspended 15 to 20 feet below the surface in 20 to 25 feet of water. Try a feather jig or a small Colorado spinner with a crappie minnow or wax worm. Fall crappies will be schooled in 15 to 20 feet of water. In the winter, you'll find them suspended over the holes 12 to 15 feet below the surface in 22 to 24 feet of water.

SUNFISH Throughout most of the season, sunfish can be found in the weeds in 2 to 6 feet of water around the entire lake. The bigger fish will be in the bass locations. In the winter, work the east side of the lake.

Information about this lake was provided by Phil Gossard.

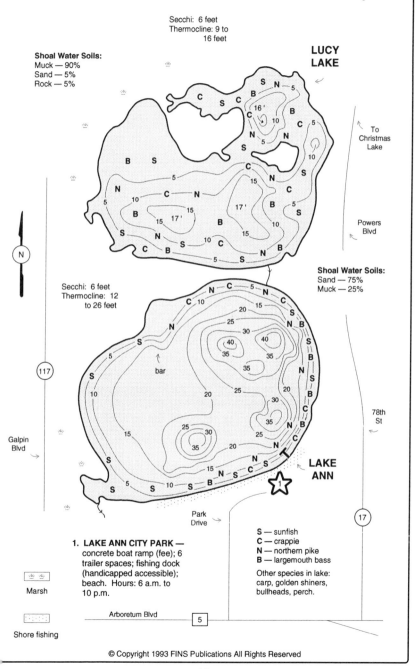

ANN & LUCY LAKES
120 acres — Ann Lake
91 acres — Lucy Lake

SPECIAL REGULATIONS
Electric motors only.

Secchi: 6 feet
Thermocline: 9 to 16 feet

LUCY LAKE

Shoal Water Soils:
Muck — 90%
Sand — 5%
Rock — 5%

To Christmas Lake

Powers Blvd

Shoal Water Soils:
Sand — 75%
Muck — 25%

Secchi: 6 feet
Thermocline: 12 to 26 feet

bar

78th St

Galpin Blvd

LAKE ANN

Park Drive

1. **LAKE ANN CITY PARK —** concrete boat ramp (fee); 6 trailer spaces; fishing dock (handicapped accessible); beach. Hours: 6 a.m. to 10 p.m.

S — sunfish
C — crappie
N — northern pike
B — largemouth bass

Other species in lake: carp, golden shiners, bullheads, perch.

Marsh

Shore fishing

Arboretum Blvd

19

Good populations of sunfish, crappies, bass, and northern pike are what attract metro anglers to this lake. DNR test nettings indicate that the crappie population in the east basin is 3 times the regional average. Located one mile west of the town of Victoria off County Road 11, Auburn is one of the few metro lakes with campsites, a handicapped accessible fishing pier, and a good chance of catching decent-sized fish.

You'll find a much better supply of big fish in the west basin than in the east basin. The channel between the two lakes is so shallow that larger boats will find it impossible to get through except in high water years. The east lake is also subject to occasional winterkill, which results in a boom or bust fishery. Any walleyes caught in Auburn have migrated in from a rearing pond upstream.

This is also a good wading lake for most species, especially when the water level is normal. It has a firm sand bottom and a gap in the weeds at the 3 to 4 foot depths that allows anglers to walk between the 2 weedy areas and cast to both weedlines. Start at the boat access and work down and around past the channel or from the northwest corner down to the southwest corner. You'll also find lots of fish-attracting overhanging brush and trees on the shoreline.

SPECIES	POPULATION	AVERAGE SIZE
Bass	Good	Medium to Large
Northern Pike	Very Good	Medium
Crappie	Very Good	Medium
Sunfish	Very Good	Medium

BASS   The southwest corner of the west basin is the best spot for June bass. This is also good wading territory. Roger Stein, naturalist at the Carver Nature Center, advises casting a purple plastic worm to the weedy edges on both sides of the gap. Use a retrieve and pause technique. Wind the reel slowly 3 times, and then pause before repeating the pattern. This technique works especially well an hour before sunset. On cloudy days, use plastic worms with metal flecks. The same methods are successful in the summer. But because of the heavy weed growth, cast to the pockets and the edge of the weedy openings. You'll need accurate casting here to be successful. In the fall, concentrate on the remaining green weeds in the same areas.

NORTHERN PIKE   In the spring and fall, troll with red and white spoons in 8 to 10 feet of water from the swimming beach down to the fishing pier. You'll also find some small northerns off the fishing pier. Summer and winter northerns will be in about 12 to 14 feet of water on the west side of the lake.

CRAPPIE & SUNFISH   The marshy areas in the east basin are good sunfish and crappie locations from early spring through the spawning period, especially in front of the channel and on the south side. You'll find sunfish in 1 to 2 feet of water and crappies in 3 to 4 feet of water. The area in front of the outlet to Six Mile Creek is a good location in late spring. In the summer, both basins hold sunfish and crappies. The sunfish will be in 10 to 12 feet of water off the edge of the weeds. Crappies will be suspended in about 20 feet of water during the day and move up to the weed beds to feed in low-light periods.

Information about this lake was provided by Roger Stein and Tiny Thomas.

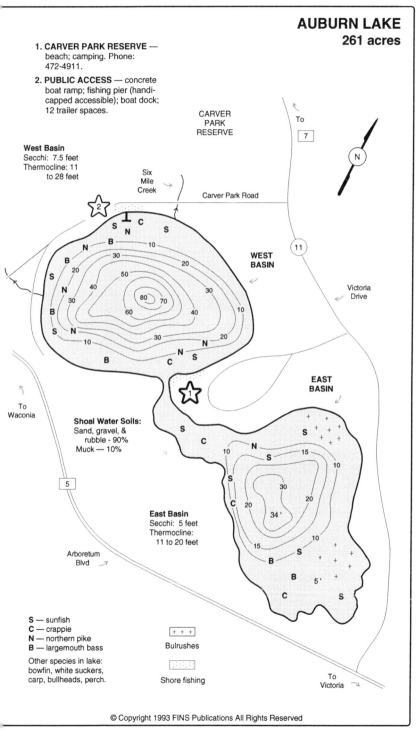

AUBURN LAKE
261 acres

1. **CARVER PARK RESERVE** — beach; camping. Phone: 472-4911.
2. **PUBLIC ACCESS** — concrete boat ramp; fishing pier (handicapped accessible); boat dock; 12 trailer spaces.

CARVER PARK RESERVE

To 7

N

West Basin
Secchi: 7.5 feet
Thermocline: 11 to 28 feet

Six Mile Creek

Carver Park Road

WEST BASIN

10
30
20
20
50
40
30
30
80 70
60
40
10
10
20
30
B C N S

11

Victoria Drive

To Waconia

EAST BASIN

Shoal Water Soils:
Sand, gravel, & rubble - 90%
Muck — 10%

5

+ + +
S + +
+ +
10
N
15
S
10
10
30
20
34'
20
C
15
10
15 S
B S +
B 5' +
C S

East Basin
Secchi: 5 feet
Thermocline: 11 to 20 feet

Arboretum Blvd

S — sunfish
C — crappie
N — northern pike
B — largemouth bass

Other species in lake: bowfin, white suckers, carp, bullheads, perch.

+ + +
Bulrushes

:::::
Shore fishing

To Victoria

21

BAVARIA LAKE

Bavaria is an underfished farm lake located 2 miles south of Victoria on County Road 11 in eastern Carver County. It's noted for its good population of nice-sized bass and overabundance of small northerns. Prior to 1985, northern pike fingerlings and adults were stocked most years. Now the stocking has been curtailed to reduce the surplus and increase the average size. This lake is also chock full of very small sunfish.

SPECIES	POPULATION	AVERAGE SIZE
Bass	Good	Medium to Large
Northern Pike	Very Good	Small to Medium
Crappie	Fair	Small
Sunfish	Good	Small

BASS In early June, look for the bass on the west and northwest sides of the lake in 2 to 8 feet of water. These areas warm up first and contain the best supply of weeds. If the water temperature is cooler than normal (mid 60's), use a jig and pig and slow down your presentation. When the water is warmer, use a buzzbait or white spinnerbait with a pumping retrieve. In the summer, fish the southeast corner of the lake. Because of the heavy speedboat traffic and clear water, the best action will be at night. Work a black spinnerbait across the top of the weeds with a steady retrieve. In early fall, cover the 2 to 14 foot depths on the south and west shoreline with a lipless crankbait. As the season progresses, concentrate on the outer edge of the remaining green weeds in 8 to 10 feet of water.

NORTHERN PIKE Early season northerns will be scattered over the entire lake in about 6 feet of water. Try live-bait rigs, spoons, or crankbaits. The east side and the sandy flat on the middle of the south side are the best locations in the summer. The west and east sides of the lake are the fall hotspots. Stay on the outer edge of the weeds. Look for winter northerns in 15 to 30 feet of water or the southeast and northwest areas of the lake.

CRAPPIE You'll find spring crappies on the western end of the lake. Also try the deeper drop-offs in 15 feet of water on the east side of the lake from the northeast corner down to the southeast corner. Use a small pink and white feather jig with a crappie minnow or a very small spinner. In the summer, start at the northeast corner and work west to the northwest corner. The crappies will be suspended in 20 to 30 feet of water. Fall crappies will be scattered or in small schools on the north and northeast sides of the lake in 10 to 60 feet of water. In the winter, work the northwest and southeast sections of the lake in 15 to 20 feet of water.

SUNFISH Early-season sunfish are plentiful in the western end of the lake. Use a small jig (1/32 or 1/64 oz.) tipped with a night crawler, or use a slip bobber with a #12 Kahle hook and a Eurolarva or night crawler. In the summer, you'll find a good supply in the heavy vegetation in 8 to 12 feet of water at the west end of the lake. Fall sunfish will stay in the same locations in 8 to 10 feet of water. In the winter, look for sunfish in the northwest and southeast sections of the lake in 15 to 20 feet of water.

This information was provided by Jeff Byrne, John Daily, and Terry Hennon.

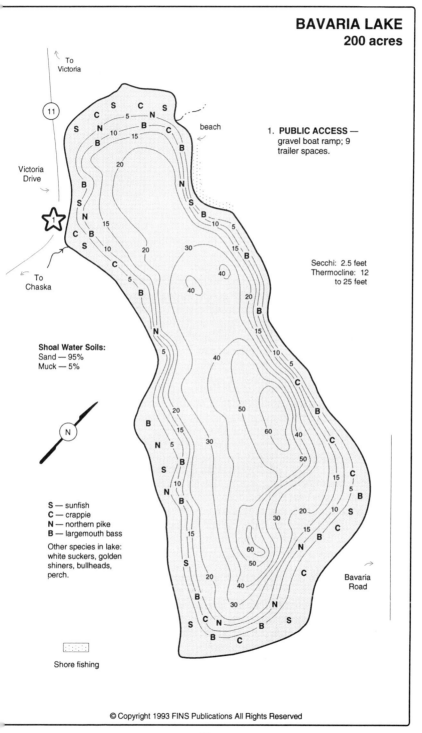

BAVARIA LAKE
200 acres

To
Victoria

(11)

Victoria
Drive

To
Chaska

beach

1. **PUBLIC ACCESS** —
   gravel boat ramp; 9
   trailer spaces.

Secchi: 2.5 feet
Thermocline: 12
to 25 feet

Shoal Water Soils:
Sand — 95%
Muck — 5%

N

S — sunfish
C — crappie
N — northern pike
B — largemouth bass

Other species in lake:
white suckers, golden
shiners, bullheads,
perch.

Bavaria
Road

Shore fishing

Lotus has a reputation as one of the best bass lakes in the area. In addition, several 3-pound crappies and many in the 1 to 1-1/2 pound range have been caught here in recent years. Walleyes were first stocked in 1977, and stocking has continued every 3 years since 1986. A good supply of perch provides plenty of forage for optimum growth. Located in the northeast corner of Carver County, Lotus has lots of good fish-holding structure — points, inlets and outlets, good backwater areas, and nice weedlines. A fish barrier was installed at the outlet of Purgatory Creek in 1991 to prevent undesirable species from entering the lake.

SPECIES	POPULATION	AVERAGE SIZE
Bass	Very Good	Medium
Northern Pike	Poor	Large
Walleye	Good	Small to Medium
Crappie	Good	Small to Large
Sunfish	Good	Medium

BASS   In June, start at the lily pads on the point in front of the small 17-foot hole on the west side of the lake. Continue north and work around the northwest bay in 5 to 10 feet of water. Give special attention to inlets, weedy points, and weedlines. Also fish the east side of the large upper eastern section. Cast a 4-inch plastic worm to the shoreline and retrieve slowly back to the inside weed-line; then jig back to the boat. In the summer, fish the same areas but go deeper to the outside edges of the weeds. The west side of the 17-foot hole holds a good summer supply. In the fall, slowly work the weeds, weedlines, and breaks. Weedlines adjacent to drop-offs are best.

NORTHERN PIKE   The inlet below Carver Beach and the large upper eastern section are the early-season hotspots. Live bait works best. In the summer, troll the breaks in 15 to 20 feet of water from the boat launch up to the north end of the lake and around to the rocky point in the middle of the north side. In the fall, cover the 10 to 20 foot depths in the same areas. The 12 to 17 foot depths on the points and holes are good winter locations.

WALLEYE   In the early season, fish the inlets and around the holes. Also try the 8 to 12 foot depths on the sand point in the middle of the east side. In the summer, stay in the same areas, and fish the 8 to 20 foot depths. The 10-foot depths in the same area are a good bet in the fall. In the winter, the best locations are the holes. Try the 20-foot depths with a live-bait rig and inflated night crawler or leech. Keep your bait 2 to 5 feet off the bottom.

CRAPPIE & SUNFISH   Immediately after ice-out, you'll find the crappies around the holes in 15 to 18 feet of water. As the water warms, work the 8 to 12 foot depths in the bays. When the crappies start to spawn (May to June), move to the 2 to 6 foot depths. In the summer, start at the 20 to 22 foot depths around the edges of the deep holes. Move shallower until you find the fish. Fall crappies will school in 10 to 15 feet of water around the holes. The 2 holes in the upper eastern section of the lake are popular winter locations. This lake produces winter crappies during the day, unlike most lakes when dawn and dusk are the prime times. Sunfish are in all the weedy bays and the bass locations.

Information about this lake was provided by Jeff Byrne and Phil Gossard.

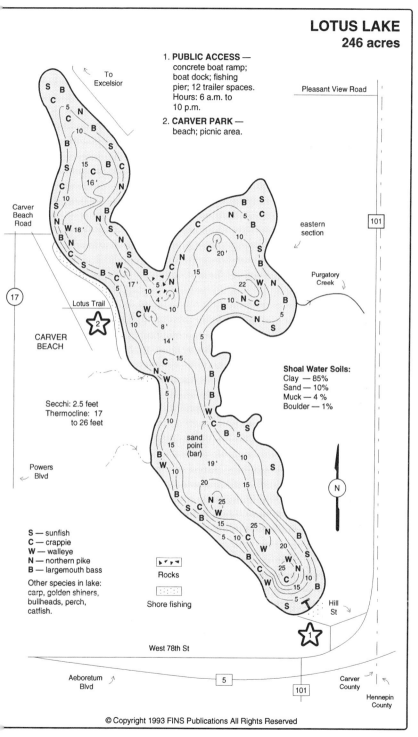

LOTUS LAKE
246 acres

1. **PUBLIC ACCESS** — concrete boat ramp; boat dock; fishing pier; 12 trailer spaces. Hours: 6 a.m. to 10 p.m.

2. **CARVER PARK** — beach; picnic area.

To Excelsior

Pleasant View Road

Carver Beach Road

eastern section

101

Purgatory Creek

Lotus Trail

CARVER BEACH

Shoal Water Soils:
Clay — 85%
Sand — 10%
Muck — 4 %
Boulder — 1%

Secchi: 2.5 feet
Thermocline: 17 to 26 feet

Powers Blvd

sand point (bar)

N

S — sunfish
C — crappie
W — walleye
N — northern pike
B — largemouth bass

Other species in lake: carp, golden shiners, bullheads, perch, catfish.

Rocks

Shore fishing

West 78th St

Hill St

Aeboretum Blvd

5

101

Carver County

Hennepin County

Minnewashta is touted as one of the best multi-species lakes in the area. Located 3 miles southwest of Excelsior in eastern Carver County, this lake has very clear water; lots of healthy, deep bulrush beds; and plenty of points, bars, bays, sunken islands, rock piles, and holes. You can catch fish anywhere in this lake, but the edge of the holes will yield the largest fish.

SPECIES	POPULATION	AVERAGE SIZE
Bass	Very Good	Medium to Large
Northern Pike	Very Good	Small to Medium
Crappie	Fair	Medium
Sunfish	Very Good	Medium to Large

BASS Start the season in Little Minnie Bay. The area above and below the boat launch on the middle lake is also productive. Look for little indentations in the weeds in front of the 3 small bays here. Try a white spinnerbait retrieved slowly over the top of the weeds. The same spots will produce in the summer but drop down to the weedline in 15 to 20 feet of water. Don't pass up the edges of the bulrush beds between the upper and middle lakes; the east side of the middle lake; and the deep weedline on the south side of Red Cedar Point. Night anglers do well on this lake. In the fall, work the 10-foot depths.

NORTHERN PIKE The 21-foot hole in Little Minnie Bay is the best all-season location for big fish. Look for early-season northerns in the weeds on the 11-foot sunken island in the middle of the lake and in front of the old resort on the southwest corner of the middle lake. Troll the drop-offs with a red and white spoon. In the summer, work the weedlines in the same areas. The deep weedline around the southern end is a big fish producer. In mid-summer, drift or troll a sucker minnow in 25 to 35 feet of water from the 44-foot hole in the middle lake down to the 62-foot hole. In the fall, work the weedline in 6 to 7 feet of water around the entire lake. Use a large minnow lure or sucker minnow on a strip-on. The bulrush bed between the upper and lower lakes is productive in the winter.

CRAPPIE Work the spring sunfish locations. Summer crappies will hold just off the weedy edges around most of the lake. The 11-foot sunken island is also good. In the winter, try the 30 to 40 foot depths above the 65-foot hole on the south end of the lake. They will be suspended about 24 feet below the surface. The 25-foot depths on the south side of the 50-foot hole in the upper lake are also productive.

SUNFISH You'll find early-season sunfish in the 2 small bays at the south end of the lake off Hwy. 5. Use a 1/64 ounce feather jig about a foot below the bobber; cast to the 2 to 3 foot depths and retrieve slowly. Little Minnie Bay is a good all season location. Later in the spring, look for spawning sunfish on the sandbar just above the bulrushes between the upper and middle lakes. In the summer, try the weedy edges of the 11-foot sunken island in the middle of the lake. Also fish the 18-foot depths off the western shoreline on the upper lake. Move down to the 10 to 12 foot depths in the fall. Winter sunfish are in the sandy areas below the bulrush beds between the upper and middle lakes. The eastern shoreline here is a good late winter location.

Information about this lake was provided by Randy Barkley, Jeff Byrne, Phil Gossard, and Tiny Thomas.

MINNEWASHTA & ST. JOE LAKES
742 acres — Minnewashta
14 acres — St. Joe

S — sunfish
C — crappie
N — northern pike
B — largemouth bass

Other species in lake:
bullheads, bowfin.

Secchi: 8.5 feet
Thermocline: 19
to 27 feet

Little
Minnie
Bay

7

41

Shoal Water Soils:
Sand — 84%
Muck — 14%
Rubble — 1%

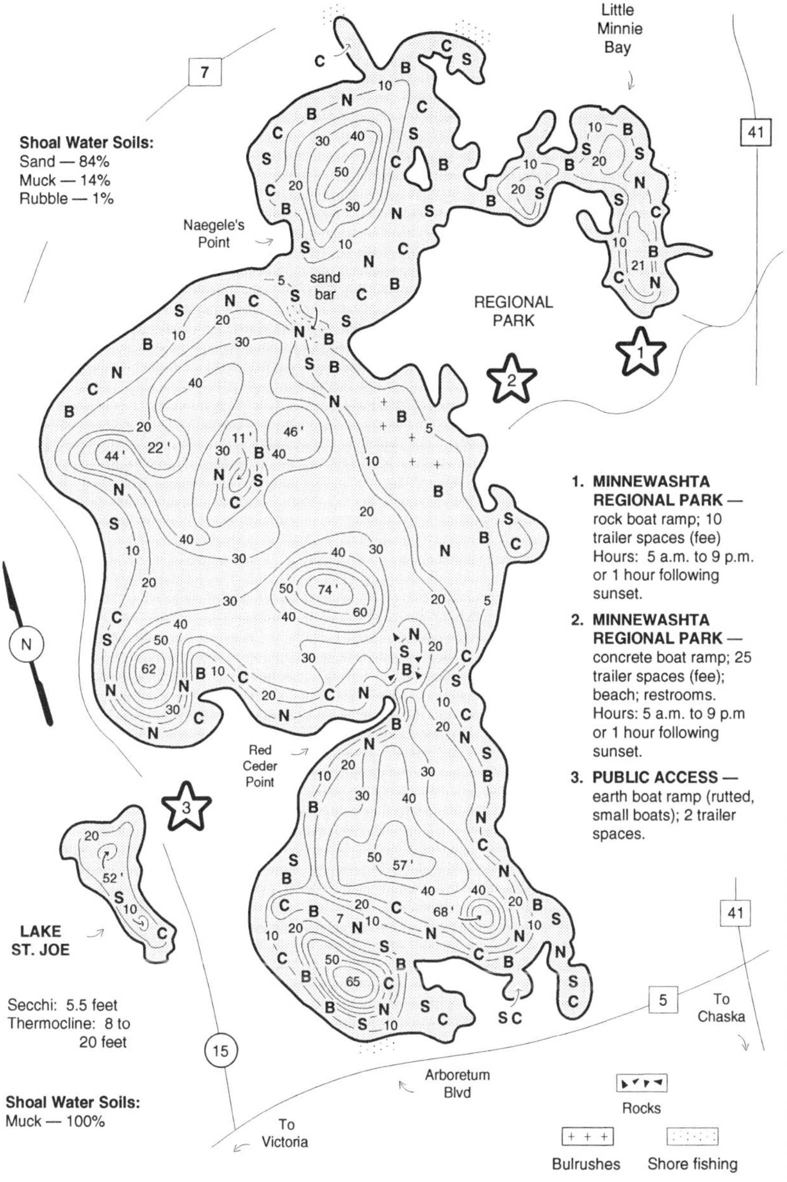

Naegele's
Point

sand
bar

REGIONAL
PARK

1

2

46'

44' 22'

11'

74'

62

Red
Ceder
Point

N

1. **MINNEWASHTA
   REGIONAL PARK** —
   rock boat ramp; 10
   trailer spaces (fee)
   Hours: 5 a.m. to 9 p.m.
   or 1 hour following
   sunset.

2. **MINNEWASHTA
   REGIONAL PARK** —
   concrete boat ramp; 25
   trailer spaces (fee);
   beach; restrooms.
   Hours: 5 a.m. to 9 p.m
   or 1 hour following
   sunset.

3. **PUBLIC ACCESS** —
   earth boat ramp (rutted,
   small boats); 2 trailer
   spaces.

3

52'

57'

68'

65

**LAKE
ST. JOE**

Secchi: 5.5 feet
Thermocline: 8 to
20 feet

Shoal Water Soils:
Muck — 100%

15

41

5

To
Chaska

Arboretum
Blvd

To
Victoria

Rocks

Bulrushes

Shore fishing

Pierson Lake is a favorite with local anglers looking for huge bass, unlimited quantities of northern pike, and a never-ending supply of sunfish. Hybrid tiger muskie fingerlings were stocked in 1984, and stocking will continue every three years.

Located about 2 miles south of Victoria, Pierson is considered an easy lake to fish because there are just so many places the fish can be. According to the experts, "You'll find every species on the weedline." Pierson is also a good trolling lake with a defined weedline and sharp breaks.

SPECIES	POPULATION	AVERAGE SIZE
Bass	Fair	Medium to Large
Northern Pike	Good to Excellent	Medium
Muskie	Poor to Fair	Medium
Crappie	Poor	Small to Medium
Sunfish	Very Good	Small to Medium

BASS   The long land point on the lower western side of the lake is a popular early season location. Also try the bays on the north and south ends of the lake. Spinnerbaits and weedless silver spoons worked slowly over the tops and in the pockets of the shallow weeds is the best technique. In the summer, stay on the two major points, the inside and outside turns of the points, and the fast-dropping weedlines around the lake. Be alert for weedy fingers jutting out from the weedline. About mid to late summer, try vertical jigging on the steep drop-offs at the mouth of the trough on the south end of the lake. The local experts claim that red jigs and red plastic worms work best on this lake. A jig and pig is also effective here.

NORTHERN PIKE & MUSKIE   One of the best all-season hotspots is the 15-foot trough on the south end of the lake. Try trolling in it or across it in 14 feet of water with a red and white spoon or live-bait rig. Also work the bass areas. The little shoreline point above the public access on the west side is a dependable summer location. Use a sucker minnow with a bobber. In the fall, stay on the weedline and troll with a deep-diving lure from this point down to the boat launch. This location really shines during Indian Summer. The best trolling area is the shoreline from the middle of the east side up to the underwater point on the upper east side. The lower side of this point is a productive winter spot. The summer locations work well in the winter too. Muskies can be found in the same locations as the northerns.

CRAPPIE & SUNFISH   For spring sunfish and crappies, the best locations are the edges of the floating bog on the west side of the southern bay, especially the southeast edge of the bog. Stay in 3 to 4 feet of water. Use a bobber and a chartreuse, white, or yellow hair jig with a pink head and a crappie minnow. In the summer, you'll find the crappies suspended off the weeds in 15 to 18 feet of water and over the first drop-off into deep water. Try drifting over the 20 to 25 foot depths with ice flies or jigs with crappie minnows. The best location for winter crappies is the 44-foot hole in the center of the lake. Set your bobber so that the bait is 30 to 35 feet below the surface. For all-season sunfish action, stay in the bays and in the bass locations.

Information about this lake was provided by Jeff Byrne and Gary Lake.

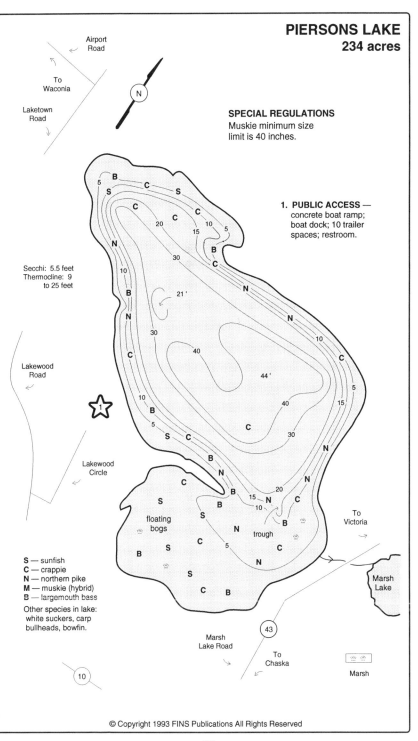

PIERSONS LAKE
234 acres

Airport Road

To Waconia

Laketown Road

N

SPECIAL REGULATIONS
Muskie minimum size
limit is 40 inches.

1. PUBLIC ACCESS —
concrete boat ramp;
boat dock; 10 trailer
spaces; restroom.

Secchi: 5.5 feet
Thermocline: 9
to 25 feet

Lakewood Road

Lakewood Circle

S — sunfish
C — crappie
N — northern pike
M — muskie (hybrid)
B — largemouth bass
Other species in lake:
white suckers, carp
bullheads, bowfin.

floating bogs

trough

To Victoria

Marsh Lake

Marsh Lake Road

To Chaska

Marsh

43

10

STEIGER LAKE

Steiger Lake, located in the town of Victoria, has been designated by the DNR as an experimental Catch & Release lake. All fish except panfish must be returned to the water. But in a few years, you can get your "bragging" photos here of the trophies that didn't get away. In 1988 and 1989, the DNR stocked 15 muskies from 12 to 20 pounds each and more than 250 walleyes averaging 2-1/2 pounds. A 1989 DNR test netting revealed a few 6-pound bass, and it is rumored that an 8 3/4-pound beauty was released. No further stocking is planned for the next 10 years; but with no harvesting permitted, anglers will be catching much larger fish. By 1995, walleyes could be over 10 pounds and muskies up to 30 pounds.

SPECIES	POPULATION	AVERAGE SIZE
Bass	Good	Medium to Large
Walleye	Fair	Medium
Muskie	Fair	Medium
Northern Pike	Very Good	Small to Medium
Crappie	Good	Small
Sunfish	Good	Small

BASS In early June, start on the northwest side of the lake. Cast a lightly weighted plastic worm in 3 to 4 feet of water. Also try both sides of the boat launch before the weeds get too thick, and the far southern end of the lake. As the season progresses, stay in the same areas but move out to the 10 to 15 foot depths. Work a crankbait over the top of the weeds or a plastic worm on the weedy edges. The south side of the bar on the east side of the lake is good in July and August. Stay in 15 to 20 feet of water and toss rattling type crankbaits.

WALLEYE The prime early-season location is the point in front of the public access. Troll with a live bait rig and a leech or night crawler. In the summer, try trolling on the west side with spoons. Go back to the public access point in the fall, and drift slowly with a live bait rig and inflated night crawler.

NORTHERN PIKE & MUSKIE The best all-season trolling areas for northerns are on the northeast, east, and southeast sides of the lake. These areas have a healthy supply of weeds and good drop-offs. The bar on the east side is a prime summer location. Look for muskies in the thick weeds from the observation tower down to the south end. Use minnows in June; switch to a jerkbait in early summer; and topwater spinners and bucktails in late summer and fall. Hot and muggy days are best.

CRAPPIE In the spring, the shallow areas around the boat access are prime territory. The best time is around sunset. In the summer, fish the 18 to 22 foot depths on the east side of the public access and up to the bar. In the fall, troll the weedline (15 to 20 feet) in front of the observation tower. The 18 to 25 foot depths on the east side of the bar produce winter crappies.

SUNFISH Sunfish are all over the lake, but in the spring look for the spawning area on the west side of the point in front of the boat launch. In the summer, stay in 12 to 15 feet of water on the north side of the lake. The largest sunfish seem to be caught in front of the observation tower during the hottest part of the summer. Stay here for winter fish.

This information was provided by Jeff Byrne, Gary Lake, and Roger Stein.

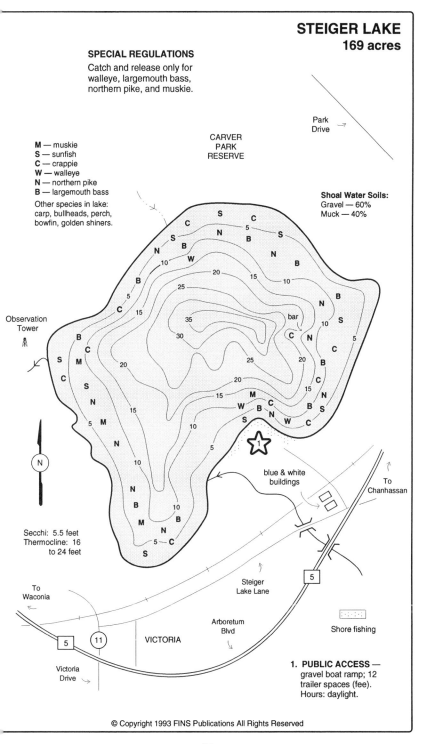

STEIGER LAKE
169 acres

SPECIAL REGULATIONS

Catch and release only for walleye, largemouth bass, northern pike, and muskie.

CARVER PARK RESERVE

Park Drive

M — muskie
S — sunfish
C — crappie
W — walleye
N — northern pike
B — largemouth bass

Other species in lake: carp, bullheads, perch, bowfin, golden shiners.

Shoal Water Soils:
Gravel — 60%
Muck — 40%

Observation Tower

bar

N

Secchi: 5.5 feet
Thermocline: 16 to 24 feet

blue & white buildings

To Chanhassen

To Waconia

Steiger Lake Lane

5

Arboretum Blvd

Shore fishing

VICTORIA

5   11

Victoria Drive

1. PUBLIC ACCESS — gravel boat ramp; 12 trailer spaces (fee). Hours: daylight.

Waconia is touted as one of the best multi-species trophy lakes in the metro area and the regulations on this lake are bound to increase the big-fish potential. (See "Special Regulations" on the map.) Huge numbers of walleye fingerlings are stocked annually, and muskies were added in 1984. It's not uncommon to see 5 to 7 pound bass and 20-pound plus northerns. Located in northern Carver County, this huge, spring-fed lake is loaded with rock, gravel, and sand reefs that attract all species throughout most of the season. Waconia is a good winter lake but use caution in the spring-fed areas.

SPECIES	POPULATION	AVERAGE SIZE
Bass	Good	Medium to Large
Northern Pike	Good	Medium
Walleye	Good	Medium
Muskie	Fair	Medium to Large
Crappie	Very Good	Medium
Sunfish	Excellent	Medium

BASS Start the season in Wagener's Bay; in Waconia Bay; on Reinke's Reef under the trees along the shoreline on the south side of Coney Island; and in the area between the rock jetty and the camp on the west side of the lake. In summer the rock jetty is still productive. Also work Cemetery Reef and the cabbage weeds around the carp trap area and down the western shoreline. In late summer and fall, concentrate on the deep weedlines on Nelson's Flat and North, Pillsbury, Center, Keg's, and Red's Reefs.

NORTHERN PIKE & MUSKIE The best locations throughout the year are Center Reef; Wagener's Bay; from Pillsbury Reef up to Nelson's Flat; and the area between Harm's Point and Waconia Bay. The Whistle Post area on the north side is known for big fish. In the summer, you'll find northerns in 8 to 12 feet of water anywhere on the north side from Reinke's Bay to Nelson's Flat. Stay on the weedline all season and use red and white spoons, sunfish colored crank baits, or sucker minnows. In the winter stay in the 14 to 18 foot depths. Early and late season muskies can be found in Reinke's Bay, on Nelson's Flats, and in Wagener's Bay. In the summer, troll the outside edge of the weedline on the north side of the lake. Also work the drop-offs at Pillsbury, Center, and Reinke's Reefs.

WALLEYE In early season, try drifting over all the reefs in 2 to 8 feet of water with a live-bait rig. Nighttime will be best. In the summer, work the deep weedlines in the same locations. Try night crawlers, minnows, or leeches. In the fall, fish the sharp drop-offs on Red's, Keg's and Cemetery Reefs during the day and the shallows at night. In early winter, fish the 8 to 15 foot depths on all the reefs. Drop down to 16 to 24 feet as the winter progresses.

CRAPPIE & SUNFISH In early spring, crappies and sunfish can be found in Waconia Bay, the rock jetty, and Peterson's Creek. As the water warms, move to Center, Keg's, Anderson's and Pillsbury Reefs. Start at the top of the reef and work down using black, white, or yellow jigs with wax worms. In the summer, also try Red's Reef. You'll find winter crappies on Pillsbury, Cemetery, and Keg's Reefs and sunfish on Pillsbury and Center Reefs.

This information was provided by Tom Hedtke, Cindy and Jim Mase, and Gary Swiers.

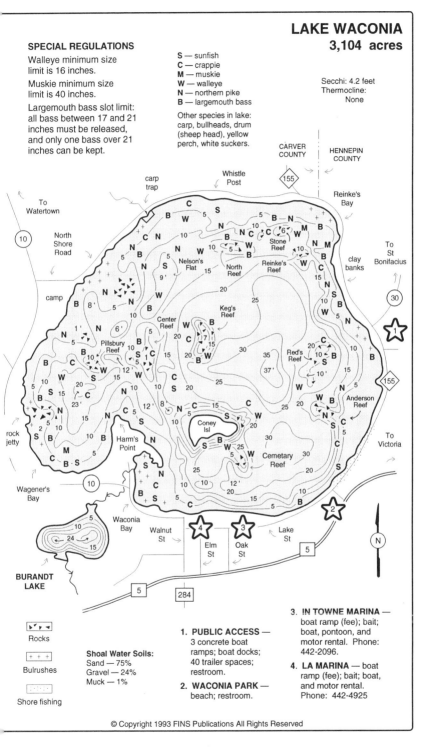

"You're almost guaranteed to get a bass out of Zumbra Lake," claim the experts. The supply of northern pike, sunfish, and crappies isn't shabby either, and the fish are easy to find. This sprawling, clear-water lake is in the Carver County Park Reserve on the northeast border of Carver County.

Schutz Lake has the same mix of fish as Zumbra. It has no public boat launch, but there is a private facility on the lower east side which also offers boat rental. Or you can try wading on the side of the lake adjacent to Carver Park. The sunfish spawning area on the lower west side is a good spring location.

SPECIES	POPULATION	AVERAGE SIZE
Bass	Very Good	Medium
Northern Pike	Very Good	Small to Medium
Crappie	Good	Medium
Sunfish	Very Good	Small to Medium

BASS In June, work the south and southwest shorelines with a white, chartreuse, or black spinnerbait. Or try a night crawler or plastic worm with a weedless hook and small sinker; cast close to shore and jig it slowly back to the boat. There is some good territory here for waders. Start at the boat launch, and work west and up to the point. Stay in about 4 feet of water and cast to the edge and pockets of the lily pads on one side and the inside edge of the weeds on the other. In the summer, you'll find bass concentrated on the deep weedlines. Put your boat in about 15 feet of water and cast toward the weedline with plastic worms or deep-diving lures. The west side of the 8-foot sunken island and the mouth of the long bay on the southwest corner are productive in the spring and fall.

NORTHERN PIKE For early-season northerns, troll across the mouth of the bay on the southwest corner. Use a red and white spoon in 9 to 10 feet of water or try still fishing with a bobber and sucker minnow. In the summer, you'll find northerns around the entire lake, but concentrate on the western side of the eastern arm; down around the peninsula; and around the 8-foot sunken island. A silver spoon or spinnerbait works best. In the fall, work the panfish areas. For winter northerns, try the southwest, west, and northwest sides of the 41-foot hole. Stay on the outside edge and use a big sucker or shiner minnow on a tip-up.

CRAPPIE Spring crappies are in the pads on the northeast end of the eastern arm and in the west, south, and southwest bays. Look for sandy spots in 2 to 2-1/2 feet of water. Use a 1/64 ounce feather jig with a crappie minnow. In the summer, move down to the 12 to 15 foot depths in the same areas. Go back to the 10 foot depths in the fall. Winter crappies are in the 41-foot hole about 30 feet below the surface.

SUNFISH Spring sunfish are in weedy areas in about 3 feet of water. The long bay on the southwest section of the lake is a prime spring producer. Summer sunfish are outside the weeds in 18 to 20 feet of water in the bass spots. Move back to the 8 to 9 foot depths in the fall. For winter sunfish, concentrate on the weedline in the areas where you found northerns in the spring.

Information about this lake was provided by Evie Hedtke, Roger Stein, and Tiny Thomas.

ZUMBRA and SCHUTZ LAKES
162 acres — Zumbra
105 acres — Schultz

1. **ARCHIE'S BOAT RENTAL** — Excelsior. Phone 474-8714.
2. **PUBLIC ACCESS** — sand boat boat ramp; 12 trailer spaces (fee); group camp. Hours: daylight.

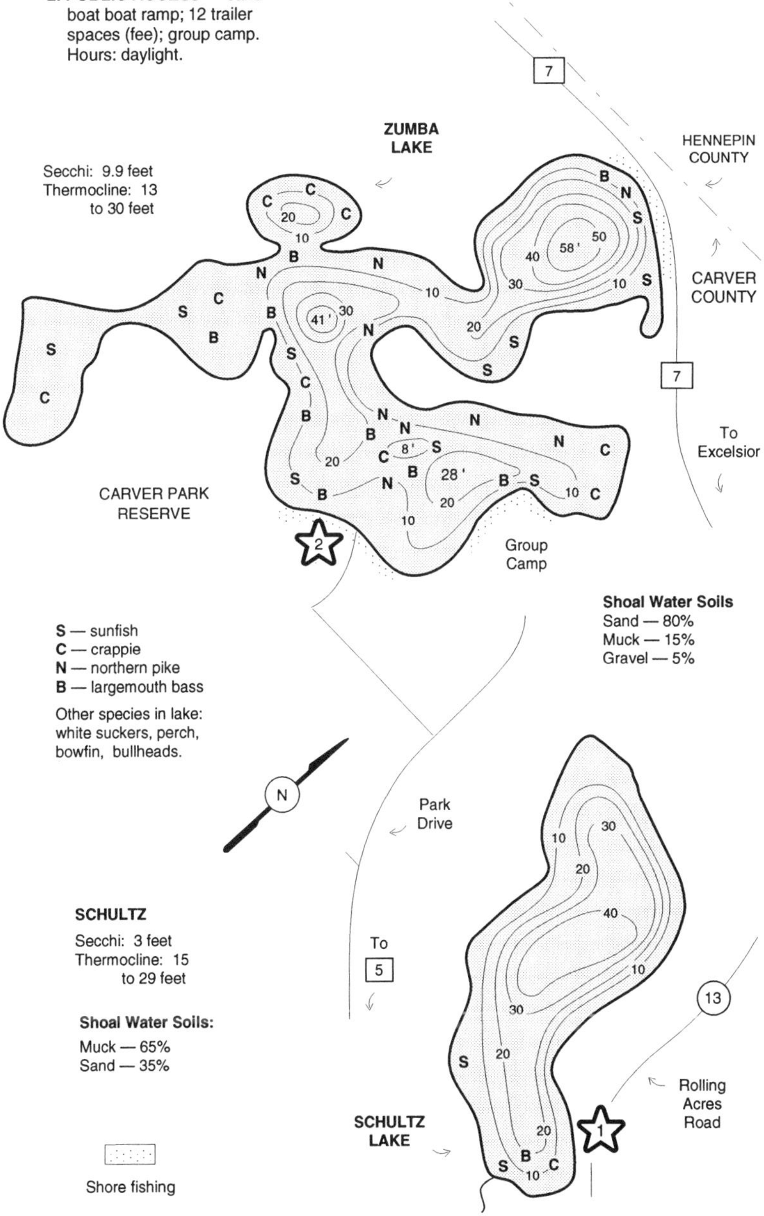

ZUMBA
LAKE
HENNEPIN
COUNTY
CARVER
COUNTY
7
To
Excelsior
CARVER PARK
RESERVE
Group
Camp
41 '
58 '
8 '
28 '
Park
Drive
To
5
13
Rolling
Acres
Road
SCHULTZ
LAKE
N

Secchi: 9.9 feet
Thermocline: 13 to 30 feet

Shoal Water Soils
Sand — 80%
Muck — 15%
Gravel — 5%

S — sunfish
C — crappie
N — northern pike
B — largemouth bass

Other species in lake: white suckers, perch, bowfin, bullheads.

SCHULTZ

Secchi: 3 feet
Thermocline: 15 to 29 feet

Shoal Water Soils:
Muck — 65%
Sand — 35%

Shore fishing

Big Comfort Lake holds lots of decent sized fish. But don't get too cocky; this can be a tough lake to fish. Big Comfort also has a good supply of shiner and silverside minnows that provide plenty of nourishment for the fish. To compete with this natural food supply, you'll have to use some savvy. For instance, work the shady side of a structure where the fish will be shallower and easier to catch.

Walleye stocking started in 1986 and continues about every two years. Big Comfort Lake also receives a limited migration of walleyes from the Sunrise River. Little Comfort is rumored to hold huge winter sunfish.

SPECIES	POPULATION	AVERAGE SIZE
Bass	Fair	Medium
Northern Pike	Good	Medium
Walleye	Good	Medium
Crappie	Good	Medium to Large
Sunfish	Fair	Small to Medium

BASS The weeds and lily pads on both ends of the lake are the best bass locations. Stay here all season. Cast a spinnerbait or buzzbait over the emerging vegetation in June. A jig head with a 4-inch plastic worm is a good lure to use in the holes and edges of the lily pads.

NORTHERN PIKE Early-season northerns will be scattered in the shallow weeds and lily pads on both ends of the lake. Also work the shallow flat in front of the outlet to the Sunrise River. Bright spinnerbaits and spoons are proven winners. In the summer, try the long sandbar on the east side of the lake. Also check out the scattered cabbage and coontail weeds around the lake. Fish the same areas in the fall, especially the sandbar. In the early winter, go back to the flat in front of the outlet. Stay in the 12 to 19 foot depth. The sandbar will also produce.

WALLEYE If spring comes early, try the outlet to the Sunrise River. Walleyes will move in and out of this area depending on the weather. Night fishing can be the key to success here. Work the flat in front of the channel and also move up the channel as far as possible. You'll need a small boat. If this doesn't produce, move back out to the drop-off in front of the channel. Leeches work best on this lake. The sandbar on the mid-eastern side is an all-season hotspot. Also try the sand flat on the upper east side. In the summer, work the 12 to 18 foot breaks on the sandbar. After the fall turnover, try vertical jigging here in 27 to 31 feet of water. Stay on the hard sand bottom, especially where sand and mud meet. For winter walleyes, fish the sandbar and the sharper breaks around the lake.

CRAPPIE AND SUNFISH The channel to Little Comfort and the inlet from the Sunrise River attracts spring crappies. Spring sunfish will be in the shallow, muddy areas in 1 to 2 feet of water and will move out to the deep weeds as the water warms. There is some all-season shore fishing for crappies and sunfish on both sides of the channel to Little Comfort. Summer crappies will move out and suspend at the 10 to 15 foot depths. Look for the blips on your depthfinder. A slip-bobber rig is the best technique. In the fall, the crappies will be hard to find. They will be tightly schooled in the remaining green weeds.

Information about this lake was provided by Frankie Dusenka and Brian Shaw.

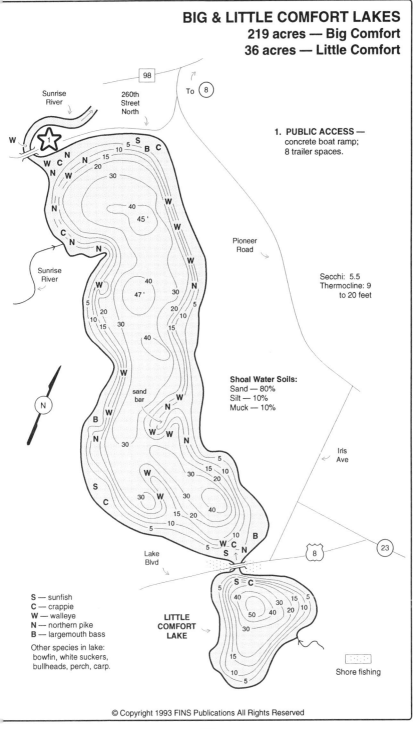

BIG & LITTLE COMFORT LAKES
219 acres — Big Comfort
36 acres — Little Comfort

98

To 8

Sunrise River

260th Street North

1. **PUBLIC ACCESS** —
concrete boat ramp;
8 trailer spaces.

Sunrise River

Pioneer Road

Secchi: 5.5
Thermocline: 9
to 20 feet

N

45'

47'

sand bar

Shoal Water Soils:
Sand — 80%
Silt — 10%
Muck — 10%

Iris Ave

23

8

Lake Blvd

S — sunfish
C — crappie
W — walleye
N — northern pike
B — largemouth bass

Other species in lake:
bowfin, white suckers,
bullheads, perch, carp.

LITTLE COMFORT LAKE

Shore fishing

CHISAGO & SOUTH LINDSTROM LAKES   Chisago County

Chisago and South Lindstrom are excellent spring lakes. The shallow dark-bottom bays on the lower end of Chisago warm up early and offer a smorgasbord of all species. The bass, sunfish, and crappie populations are exceptionally good, and huge numbers of walleye fingerlings are stocked annually.

These lakes used to be the murkiest lakes in the chain, but the receding waters in recent years have reduced the shoreline mud. The supply of healthy weeds has improved and the water is clearer. There's plenty of structure for the ambitious angler — sunken islands, points, bars, bays, brush, and stumps.

SPECIES	POPULATION	AVERAGE SIZE
Bass	Very Good	Small to Medium
Northern Pike	Fair	Medium
Walleye	Good	Small to Medium
Crappie	Good	Small to Medium
Sunfish	Excellent	Small to Medium

BASS   Start the season in Schlimmer's Slough (Bay) from Lake's Point down to the far southern end. Toss a spinnerbait to the shoreline. When the weeds come up, move out to the slop areas in the bays. Drop a silver spoon, spinnerbait, or very weedless lure to the pockets in the thick weeds. The weedline and docks in both lakes are also productive. Other summer hotspots on South Lindstrom Lake are the hooked shoreline bar just east of the beach on the northeast end and the 5-foot bar on the south side. The biggest bass will be in deeper water. In the fall, look for the remaining green weeds.

NORTHERN PIKE   In spring and summer, the northerns will be in the same areas as the bass. When both species are present, the bass will be shallow and the northerns will be on the weedy edges at the 6 to 20 foot depths. You'll find smaller northerns in the slop in the bays and around the islands in the backwaters. The larger fish are in the main body of both lakes. Stay on the main lakes in the fall, and work down to 20 feet. In the winter, try the 6 to 15 foot depths in front of Lake's Point.

WALLEYE   Look for early-season walleyes in South Lindstrom Lake around the 6-foot gravel bar in front of the park and the 5-foot bar on the south side. Also work the 6 to 15 foot depths around the points on the west side of the narrows (by the city of Chisago); around the lower bend of the channel on the east side as you enter Chisago Lake; and the rocky areas and the 10-foot hole in front of the Lake's Point (above Schlimmer's Bay). Summer walleyes will move to the weedy edges in the same areas. Concentrate on the 12 to 20 foot depths. Also try drifting over the weeds and stumps in Schlimmer's Bay and on the northwest corner of Chisago Lake. The summer spots will produce in the fall and winter.

CRAPPIE & SUNFISH   Spring crappies and sunfish are in the shallow dark-bottom bays around the lake. In the summer, the bigger fish will be in the 6 to 15 foot depths in the scattered weeds on the main lake. Fall and early winter fish will be in the remaining weedy areas. In late winter, both crappies and sunfish can be found at the 25-foot depths.

This information was provided by Dave Brandeman, Frankie Dusenka, and Tim Walsh.

CHISAGO & SOUTH LINDSTROM LAKES
450 acres — South Lindstrom
873 acres — Chisago

1. **LONG'S BAIT** — bait. Phone: 1-257-6065.

2. **LINDSTROM BEACH PARK** — sand & gravel boat ramp (closed from June through August); fishing pier; beach; restroom.

SOUTH LINDSTROM
Secchi: 4 feet
Thermocline: 7 to 10 feet

3. **PUBLIC ACCESS** — 2 concrete ramps (to be completed by fall of 1993); 60 trailer spaces; boat dock; restroom.

4. **CHANNEL BOATS** — boat, motor, and pontoon rental; bait; food. Also rents parking spaces. Phone: 1-257-5663.

5. **PUBLIC ACCESS** — concrete boat ramp; parking 2 blocks away on County Road 8 or rent space at Channel Boats.

6. **ROSEHILL RESORT** — boat, motor, pontoon, and canoe rental; cabins. Phone: 1-257-4040.

S — sunfish
C — crappie
W — walleye
N — northern pike
B — largemouth bass
Other species in lake: bowfin, golden shiners, white suckers, perch, bullheads.

CHISAGO
Secchi: 3 feet
Thermocline: 7 to 10 feet

Rocks

Stumps

Shore fishing

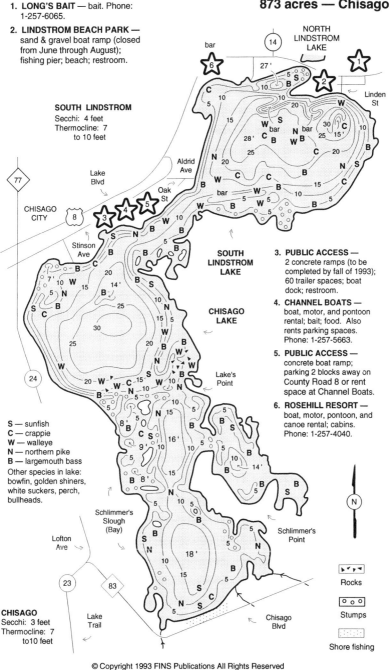

Water levels have receded somewhat since the flooding years of the early and mid-1980's. Gone is much of the fish-holding structure — flooded timber, submerged brush, and floating bogs. But the good news is that since there is less flooded shoreline mud, the water clarity has improved and the healthy green weeds are on the increase. Walleyes, bass, and northern pike populations range from good to excellent, and Green Lake retains its reputation as a panfish factory. A 28-pound northern pike wallhanger was caught on this lake in June of 1990. Walleyes have been stocked most years since 1961

SPECIES	POPULATION	AVERAGE SIZE
Bass	Fair to Good	Medium
Northern Pike	Good	Medium
Walleye	Good	Medium
Crappie	Excellent	Small
Sunfish	Excellent	Small

BASS   You'll find early June bass in Glyer's Bay and in Little Green Lake. Cast a spinnerbait or topwater lure across the top of the emerging weeds. Work all visible structure — wood, weeds, etc. In the summer, there are some good trophy bass in the weedy slop in the same areas. Drop a weedless lure into the pockets of the weeds. Also work the docks on the east shore of the main lake; the scattered vegetation; and any submerged wood. In the fall, there is a good supply of remaining green vegetation on the east shoreline and on Lindberg's Point.

NORTHERN PIKE   Early season northerns will be scattered in Glyer's Bay. In the summer, try Lindberg's Point and the rocky areas below the narrows. Also work the slop in Glyer's Bay. Use a bright-colored spinnerbait rigged with a sucker minnow, and cast it over the cabbage weeds. Let it drop down in the weedy openings. This technique is most effective on calm days. In the fall, the remaining green weeds will be the best locations. Lindberg's Point is a good fall and early winter spot. Also try the spring locations. The camp shoreline on the east side is productive in late winter.

WALLEYE   You'll find early-season walleyes in the rocky areas below the narrows; Lindberg's Point; the boulder area as you enter Glyer's Bay; and the 6-foot sunken island in front of the resort (new public access) on the southeast corner of the main lake. Work the 6 to 20 foot depths on the sharp breaks of the flats in these areas. The same locations will produce in the summer and early fall. The area in front of the camp is also a good fall producer. In the winter, look for walleyes in 12 to 20 feet of water off Lindberg's Point and in front of the camp.

CRAPPIE & SUNFISH   Glyer's Bay and the shallow bays in Little Green Lake will produce a good supply of sunfish and crappies in the early season. In the summer, sunfish will be in the bass locations, and crappies will be suspended in 15 to 25 feet of water in the main lake. The area in front of the camp and Lindberg's Point are crappie hotspots in the summer and fall. Winter crappies can be found in Little Green Lake and in the upper portion of Glyer's Bay in 6 feet of water. Winter sunfish are also in Glyer's Bay in 6 to 10 feet of water.

Information about this lake was provided by Dave Brandeman, Frankie Dusenka, and Tim Walsh.

GREEN & LITTLE GREEN LAKES
178 acres — Little Green
1,715 acres — Green

1. **FRANKIE'S LIVE BAIT** — bait; tackle. Phone: 1-257-6334
2. **FAMILY SPORTS CENTER** — bait; tackle. Phone: 1-257-6143.
3. **LITTLE GREEN PARK** — concrete boat ramp; 10 trailer spaces; restroom.
4. **PUBLIC ACCESS** — cement ramp to be completed 1994; formerly Hackel's Resort.
5. **LINDBERG'S LANDING** — boat launch (fee); boat rental, camping; restroom. Phone: 1-257-2631.

Shoal Water Soils:
Sand - 75%
Boulder - 20%
Gravel - 5%

Secchi: 3.7 feet
Thermocline: 22 to 27 feet

S — sunfish
C — crappie
W — walleye
N — northern pike
B — largemouth bass

Other species in lake: white suckers, bullheads, perch, carp.

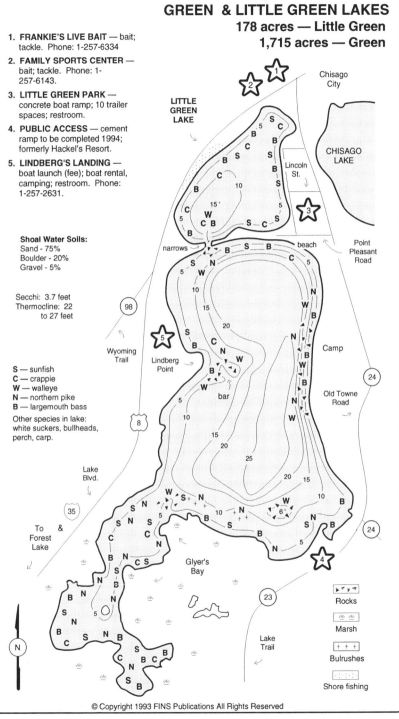

Rocks
Marsh
Bulrushes
Shore fishing

41

Fish locations in North Center Lake have changed since water levels dropped dramatically in the late 1980's. Flooded timber, brush, and stumps are no longer the only fish-holding structures, and it's back to the weeds and mid-lake structures for the serious angler. The lower half of the lake contains more weeds for better bass and panfish success, whereas the upper half of the lake has bars, rocks, and sharper breaks that attract walleyes, perch, and larger northern pike. Walleyes have been stocked annually since the early 1970's, and this lake also contains some native (naturally reproduced) walleyes.

SPECIES	POPULATION	AVERAGE SIZE
Bass	Very Good	Medium
Northern Pike	Good	Medium to Large
Walleye	Good	Medium
Crappie	Excellent	Medium
Sunfish	Excellent	Medium

BASS   In June, start with the bays on the north end of the lake (they may be dry in low water years), and then work all the small bays around the entire lake. For all-season success, try skipping your bait under willow trees and boat docks. In the summer, look for the pure beds of cabbage weeds. A good example is the 5-foot sunken island on the lower end of the lake. Also try the rocky tip of the bar just west of Nelson's Island.

NORTHERN PIKE   Look for spring and summer northerns in the bass spots. The mouth of the inlet in Nelson's Bay attracts the larger fish. This is a tough lake to troll because there is no defined weedline. In the fall, stay on the sharp drop-offs, and cover a lot of water. The small land point below Hillcrest Campgrounds is a good place to start. Stay in 2 to 10 feet of water. In the winter, try the 15 to 20 foot depths around the hole on the southeast corner.

WALLEYE   In the early season, they'll be scattered in the weeds or tightly schooled below the break where the sand bottom ends and the mud bottom begins. Start at the weedline and work down to the edge of the soft bottom. Use a jig with a minnow or leech to find the fish, then put on a slip bobber. The best locations are the tip of the rocky bar west of Nelson's Island and the shoreline points on both the east and west sides of the upper third of the lake. Stay in the 18 to 25 foot depths. In the summer, fish the top of the rocky bar and the points with a shallow-running crankbait, especially at night. The spring locations are also productive in the fall and winter.

CRAPPIE & SUNFISH   In the spring, you'll find crappies and sunfish in all the small bays. The mouth of the inlet in Nelson's Bay attracts panfish through May. In the summer, the bigger sunfish will be deeper in the bass locations. The 5-foot sunken island on the southeast side of the lake is a prime sunfish location. Summer crappies will be suspended in 12 to 20 feet of water on the north end of the lake. In the fall and winter, sunfish will be scattered on the grassy flats south and southwest of Doctor's Island in 8 to 10 feet of water. Winter crappies will be with the walleyes in the upper half of the lake suspended off the sharper breaks in 15 to 25 feet of water.

This information was provided by Dave Brandeman and Frankie Dusenka.

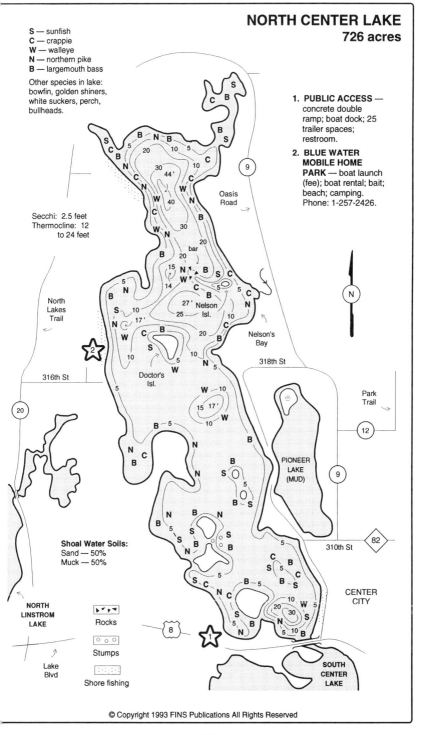

NORTH CENTER LAKE
726 acres

S — sunfish
C — crappie
W — walleye
N — northern pike
B — largemouth bass

Other species in lake:
bowfin, golden shiners,
white suckers, perch,
bullheads.

1. **PUBLIC ACCESS** —
   concrete double
   ramp; boat dock; 25
   trailer spaces;
   restroom.

2. **BLUE WATER
   MOBILE HOME
   PARK** — boat launch
   (fee); boat rental; bait;
   beach; camping.
   Phone: 1-257-2426.

Oasis
Road

Secchi: 2.5 feet
Thermocline: 12
   to 24 feet

North
Lakes
Trail

bar

Nelson
Isl.

Nelson's
Bay

318th St

316th St

Park
Trail

Doctor's
Isl.

PIONEER
LAKE
(MUD)

310th St

82

CENTER
CITY

Shoal Water Soils:
Sand — 50%
Muck — 50%

NORTH
LINSTROM
LAKE

Rocks

8

Stumps

Lake
Blvd

Shore fishing

SOUTH
CENTER
LAKE

NORTH
LINSTROM
LAKE

20

9

12

N

North Lindstrom Lake has many of the advantages of the larger lakes in the Chisago chain without a lot of the hassles. The public boat launch is in such poor shape that it discourages speedboat traffic and heavy fishing pressure. But if you have a small boat or lots of muscle, you'll find decent populations of bass and northern pike as well as some walleyes that migrated in from South Lindstrom.

You won't need a boat to reach the excellent panfish population. North Lindstrom has the most productive early-season shore fishing territory in the entire area. The best location is the channel from Bowl Lake. You can fish from shore on both sides of the channel. The panfish are activated by the warmer water flowing through the channel from shallow, muddy-bottom Bowl Lake.

North Lindstrom Lake has clear water and is better for fall fishing than most of the other lakes in the Chisago chain.

SPECIES	POPULATION	AVERAGE SIZE
Bass	Good	Medium
Northern Pike	Fair	Medium
Walleye	Fair to Good	
		Medium
Crappie	Fair	Small to Medium
Sunfish	Excellent	Small to Medium

BASS June bass will be in the bays on both ends of the lake. Cast a white spinnerbait with a silver blade or a top-water stickbait into the openings in the lily pads and emerging weeds. A slow retrieve is essential at this time of the year. As the water warms, move out to the weedline on the main lake. Start on the north end and work down to about the middle of the east side. The overhanging willows on the west side offer some shady cover. There are also productive docks on this side of the lake. In the fall, stay in the same locations but concentrate on the healthy green weeds. Because this lake has clear water, the weeds will remain green longer into the season.

NORTHERN PIKE In the spring, the northerns will be in the bass locations on both ends of the lake. A black spinnerbait with a chartreuse blade is always a good choice. In the summer, the prime location is the underwater gravel point (bar) on the west side. You'll do better if you work the shady side of this structure. Here's a good tip: the brighter the day, the deeper the fish will be. In the fall, stay in the same locations but concentrate on the 10 to 15 foot depths. In the winter, cover the 10 to 20 foot depths on the upper east side of the lake.

CRAPPIE & SUNFISH The early-season hotspots for both crappies and sunfish are the bays on both ends of the lake, Bowl Lake, and the channel to Bowl Lake. In the summer, you'll find a good crop of crappies and sunfish in the cabbage weeds. The larger fish will be on the deeper weedline and the smaller fish will be in the shallow weeds. In the fall, the best crappie location is the upper east side of the lake. Look for fall sunfish in the remaining green weeds anywhere in the lake. Winter crappies will be suspended in 10 to 20 feet of water in the fall locations, and the sunfish will be near the bottom.

This information was provided by Dave Brandeman and Frankie Dusenka.

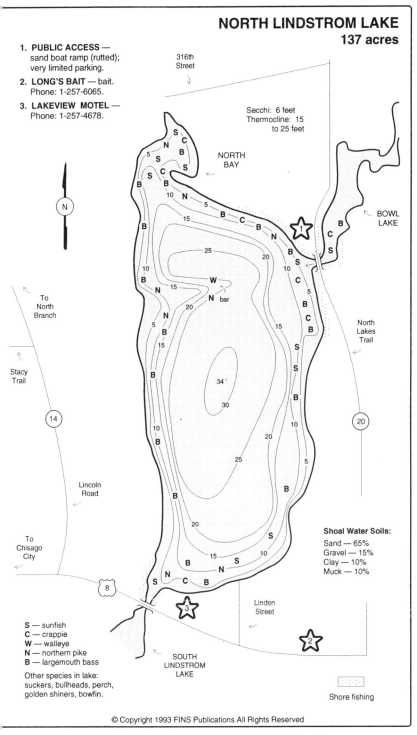

NORTH LINDSTROM LAKE
137 acres

1. **PUBLIC ACCESS** — sand boat ramp (rutted); very limited parking.
2. **LONG'S BAIT** — bait. Phone: 1-257-6065.
3. **LAKEVIEW MOTEL** — Phone: 1-257-4678.

316th Street

Secchi: 6 feet
Thermocline: 15 to 25 feet

NORTH BAY

BOWL LAKE

N

To North Branch

Stacy Trail

14

Lincoln Road

To Chisago City

8

20

North Lakes Trail

Linden Street

Shoal Water Soils:
Sand — 65%
Gravel — 15%
Clay — 10%
Muck — 10%

S — sunfish
C — crappie
W — walleye
N — northern pike
B — largemouth bass

Other species in lake: suckers, bullheads, perch, golden shiners, bowfin.

SOUTH LINDSTROM LAKE

Shore fishing

SOUTH CENTER LAKE   Chisago County

"South Center is the best lake in the Chisago Chain for big bass and northerns, and you'll never run out of spots," says Frankie Dusenka, manager of Frankie's Bait in Chisago City. It's very fertile, crammed full of structure, and has lots of shallow weeds. Walleye fingerlings have been stocked most years since the early 1970's. This lake also has a panfish population that just won't quit. South Center is an excellent spring lake with many sheltered bays that warm up fast to produce some terrific early-season catches. It's also a prime fall lake.

SPECIES	POPULATION	AVERAGE SIZE
Bass	Very Good	Medium
Northern Pike	Very Good	Medium to Large
Walleye	Good	Small to Medium
Crappie	Excellent	Small to Medium
Sunfish	Excellent	Small to Medium

BASS   You'll find June bass in the upper western bays; the eastern section of the lake; and Pancake Island. Toss a spinnerbait or a 4-inch plastic worm to the thickest weeds and lily pads. Look for pockets and points that extend out toward deeper water. In mid-June, the eastern section gets choked with weeds, and you'll have to use a pole to push your boat through them. But this slop can produce big fish throughout the summer. Throw a silver spoon, rubber frog, or very weedless lure into the weedy holes. The western section starts to shine in July. Look for the docks, weedlines, and points. The big boulders on Needle Point and the 4-foot sunken island are prime producers in the summer and fall. Stay with the remaining green weeds. If there's no action, move to the very sharp drop-offs such as the land point on the lower western section.

NORTHERN PIKE   Before the weeds come up in the spring, try trolling a medium-running stickbait in 5 to 6 feet of water on the west side of Sunset Point; along the bolder-strewn bar below the 100-foot hole; and the 4-foot sunken island in front of the bar. These areas are all-season hotspots. In the summer, try spoonplugging at the 10 to 25 foot depths in these same areas. For fall northerns, look for the healthy green weeds or the sharpest drop-offs. Work the land point on the lower west side; the drop-off between the tip of Needle Point and the 100-foot hole; and the saddle between the rocky 4-foot sunken island and the rocky bar. In the winter, fish the 8 to 15 foot depths in the summer locations, especially the west side of Sunset Point.

WALLEYE   The best all-season areas are Needle Point and the rocky bars in the western section of the lake. In the early season, work the 4 to 10 foot depths; in the summer, stay on the deeper breaks; and in the fall, move from shallow to deep, down to the 35-foot depths.

CRAPPIE & SUNFISH   The small dark-bottom bays around the entire lake will be the major spring locations for crappies and sunfish. In the summer, the weedlines hold the best supply. The slop in the eastern section of the lake is also a magnet for summer sunfish. Docks are productive too. The eastern section is also prime territory for sunfish and crappies in the fall and winter. In late winter, Pancake Island is the hotspot.

This information was provided by Dave Brandeman and Frankie Dusenka.

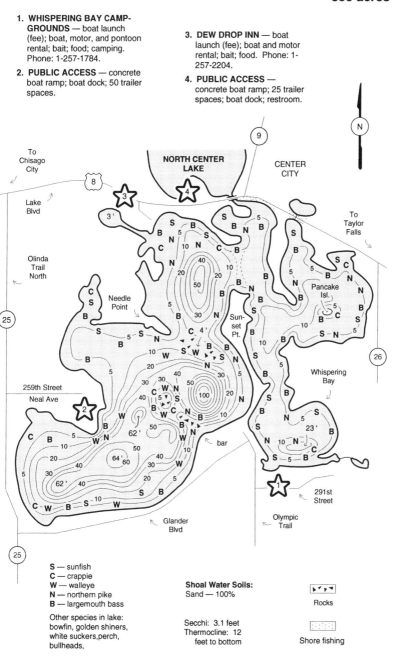

SOUTH CENTER LAKE
836 acres

1. **WHISPERING BAY CAMP-GROUNDS** — boat launch (fee); boat, motor, and pontoon rental; bait; food; camping. Phone: 1-257-1784.

2. **PUBLIC ACCESS** — concrete boat ramp; boat dock; 50 trailer spaces.

3. **DEW DROP INN** — boat launch (fee); boat and motor rental; bait; food. Phone: 1-257-2204.

4. **PUBLIC ACCESS** — concrete boat ramp; 25 trailer spaces; boat dock; restroom.

N

To Chisago City

8

NORTH CENTER LAKE

CENTER CITY

9

Lake Blvd

3

3'

To Taylor Falls

Olinda Trail North

25

Needle Point

Pancake Isl.

Sun-set Pt.

26

Whispering Bay

259th Street
Neal Ave

2

62'

bar

64'
60

62'

23'

291st Street

Glander Blvd

Olympic Trail

1

25

S — sunfish
C — crappie
W — walleye
N — northern pike
B — largemouth bass

Other species in lake: bowfin, golden shiners, white suckers, perch, bullheads,

Shoal Water Soils:
Sand — 100%

Secchi: 3.1 feet
Thermocline: 12
    feet to bottom

Rocks

Shore fishing

LAKE BYLLESBY

Lake Byllesby is a reservoir on the Cannon River located 2 miles west of Cannon Falls. A drawdown in 1987 to aid in dam repairs caused the loss of most of the fish. The lake was restocked with northern pike, smallmouth bass, white bass, crappies, bluegills, and channel catfish. Yellow perch were stocked in the winter of 1991/92. Northern pike and channel catfish populations will be evaluated periodically and restocked accordingly.

There is little natural reproduction of walleyes and northerns in this lake. However, spawning access in the Cannon River immediately upstream and in the tributary streams is adequate to replenish these populations.

Due to the acceleration of the natural sedimentation process caused by intensive agriculture, loss of wetlands, and fertilizer runoff, Byllesby has limited submerged vegetation. It also develops smelly algae blooms in midsummer.

The fun part of this lake is that you never know what you are going to catch. But it's a tough lake to fish. The experts advise anglers looking for big fish to work the old river channel (see map). Stay in the 3 to 15 foot depths. This lake will stratify in the summer, so don't fish any deeper than 10 feet.

SPECIES	POPULATION	AVERAGE SIZE
Smallmouth Bass	Poor	Medium
Largemouth Bass	Good	Medium
Northern Pike	Good	Medium to Large
Walleye	Fair	Medium to Large
Catfish	Good	Medium
Bluegill	Fair	Small to Medium
Crappie	Fair	Small to Medium

WALLEYE Stay on the river channel all season. Slowly drift or back troll across the channel in the 3 to 15 foot depths. Use a small crankbait or a jig tipped with a minnow or nightcrawler. The river channel is also the best winter location.

NORTHERN The river channel is the site for big northerns all season. Drift across with a medium-sized sucker minnow, or troll around the lake with a deep-running fluorescent crankbait or a chartreuse and orange spinnerbait with a fluorescent blade. Look for the patches of weeds. The woody debris on the west side of the lake also attracts a good supply of northerns. Stay in the 2 to 8 foot depths. In the summer, also fish the weedy patches on the west side of the long land point on the east side of the lake. The very sharp shoreline break across the lake from this point is a good fall location.

CRAPPIES & SUNFISH Very early season crappies will be near the edge of the river channel in 4 to 5 feet of water. Use a chartreuse or pink and white jig (1/80 or 1/64 oz.) tipped with a crappie minnow. About mid-May, move to the bulrushes, cattails, and woody debris on the west side of the lake. Go back to the river channel and springs in the winter. A black jig with a small crappie minnow is a winner. Evening is the best time. Sunfish are found in the weedy areas. The bigger ones are deeper on the edge of the weeds.

Information about this lake was provided by John Berendt, Dan Dieterman, Larry Gates, Glen Hallow, and Bill Mosca.

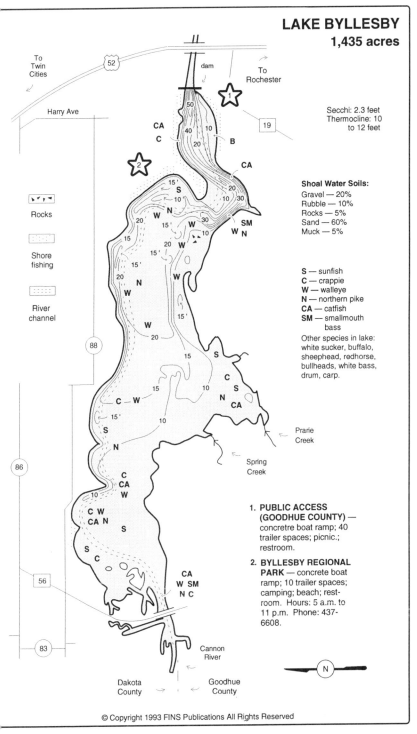

LAKE BYLLESBY
1,435 acres

To Twin Cities

52

dam

To Rochester

Harry Ave

19

Secchi: 2.3 feet
Thermocline: 10 to 12 feet

CA
C
50
40
10
B
CA
15'
S
20
10
W
N
20
30
15'
10
SM
20
W
N
15
W
20
W
15'
15'
N
20
W
W
15'
W
20

Shoal Water Soils:
Gravel — 20%
Rubble — 10%
Rocks — 5%
Sand — 60%
Muck — 5%

S — sunfish
C — crappie
W — walleye
N — northern pike
CA — catfish
SM — smallmouth bass

Other species in lake: white sucker, buffalo, sheephead, redhorse, bullheads, white bass, drum, carp.

Rocks

Shore fishing

River channel

88

86

15
S
C
S
15
10
N
CA
C W
15'
10
S
N
C
CA
W
10
C W
CA N
S
S C

Prarie Creek

Spring Creek

56

CA
W SM
N C

83

Cannon River

Dakota County

Goodhue County

1. **PUBLIC ACCESS (GOODHUE COUNTY)** — concretre boat ramp; 40 trailer spaces; picnic.; restroom.

2. **BYLLESBY REGIONAL PARK** — concrete boat ramp; 10 trailer spaces; camping; beach; restroom. Hours: 5 a.m. to 11 p.m. Phone: 437-6608.

N

Crystal Lake, located in Burnsville just east of I-35W, is a favorite for largemouth bass and northern pike enthusiasts. Hybrid (tiger) muskie fingerlings were stocked in 1984 and 1988, and stocking will continue every 3 years if tests indicate a good survival rate. Some of these muskies are over 20 pounds. There are plenty of islands, points, and sunken islands to challenge structure anglers.

SPECIES	POPULATION	AVERAGE SIZE
Bass	Good	Medium
Northern Pike	Good	Small to Medium
Muskie	Fair	Small to Medium
Crappie	Poor to Fair	Small to Medium
Sunfish	Very Good	Small

BASS In the early season, the bass will be in the small shallow bay on the far west side of the lake and the southeast side of Maple Island. Toss to the emerging weeds with a spinnerbait, buzzbait, plastic worm, or topwater lure. You'll find a good collection of summer bass off the deeper points on the north side of Maple Island; the 8-foot sunken island; and around the small island. These spots also produce in the fall. In addition, work the 10 to 12 foot depths along the shoreline on the west side of the main lake.

NORTHERN PIKE Look for early-season northerns in the shallow bays south and southeast of Maple Island and on the south side of the small island. Also fish the 2 to 6 foot depths along the northern shoreline from the park on the northeast side to the land point in the middle of the north side. This point is also productive in the summer and fall. The north side of Maple Island is good too. Crystal is one of the best trolling lakes in the area. Stay in 12 feet of water and concentrate on the edge of the weedline and the deeper points. In the winter, fish the north and east sides of Maple Island. Muskies will be on the weedy points.

CRAPPIE In the early season, the best crappie spots are the southeast side of Maple Island; the small western bay next to I-35W; and the eastern bay. In the summer, this bay is choked with weeds. Summer crappies will be on the deeper weedy points on the north side of Maple Island. The favorite technique is a small jig with a crappie minnow or wax worm. Also work around the small island on the eastern side of the lake. Look for fall crappies around the sunken islands and the deeper points off of Maple Island. In the winter, fish the weedline between Maple Island and the long land point on the west side of the lake.

SUNFISH In the spring, fish the crappie locations. The southeastern bay holds the largest fish. Big summer sunfish are in the bass areas. Stay on the deep weedlines, breaklines, and points. The west side of the 8-foot sunken island is a good place to start. Work down to 25 feet. In the fall, stay in the deep weedy areas and the shallow points all over the lake. Winter sunfish will be in 10 to 12 feet of water around the 8-foot sunken island and the east side of Maple Island.

Information about this lake was provided by Dave Gardell and Terry Tuma.

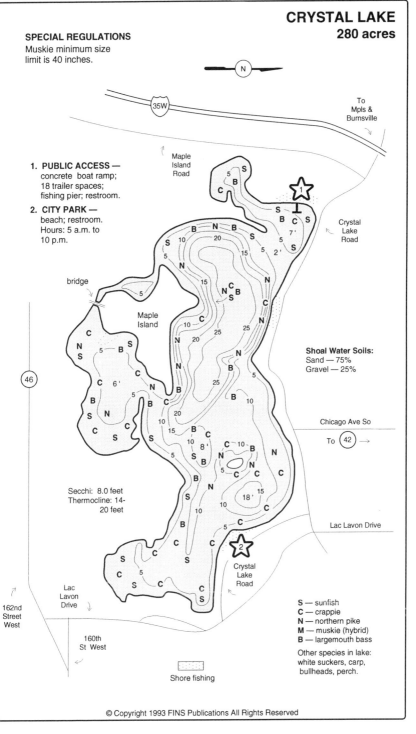

CRYSTAL LAKE
280 acres

SPECIAL REGULATIONS
Muskie minimum size
limit is 40 inches.

To
Mpls &
Burnsville

Maple
Island
Road

1. **PUBLIC ACCESS —**
   concrete boat ramp;
   18 trailer spaces;
   fishing pier; restroom.
2. **CITY PARK —**
   beach; restroom.
   Hours: 5 a.m. to
   10 p.m.

Crystal
Lake
Road

bridge

Maple
Island

Shoal Water Soils:
Sand — 75%
Gravel — 25%

Chicago Ave So

To (42) →

Secchi: 8.0 feet
Thermocline: 14-
20 feet

Lac Lavon Drive

Lac
Lavon
Drive

Crystal
Lake
Road

162nd
Street
West

160th
St West

S — sunfish
C — crappie
N — northern pike
M — muskie (hybrid)
B — largemouth bass

Other species in lake:
white suckers, carp,
bullheads, perch.

Shore fishing

Marion Lake, located in Lakeville just east and west of I-35W, has ample populations of bass, northern pike, crappies, sunfish, and perch. Huge numbers of
walleyes have been stocked every two years since 1979. This is a small, shallow
lake that warms up early and provides excellent spring panfishing. An aeration
system was installed in 1991 to prevent winterkill.

SPECIES	POPULATION	AVERAGE SIZE
Bass	Fair to Good	Small to Medium
Northern Pike	Good	Small to Medium
Walleye	Good	Small to Large
Crappie	Good to Excellent	Small to Medium
Sunfish	Excellent	Small to Medium

BASS For June bass try the east side of the second lake and the bay on the
southwest corner of the first lake. Cast plastic worms and spinnerbaits to the new
emerging weeds. You'll find summer bass on the east side of the second lake and
the west side of the main (first) lake. Use weedless lures and cast to the pockets,
holes and the edges of the weeds. Also work the docks around the entire lake.
In the fall, try the deeper breaklines or weedlines adjacent to deep water.

NORTHERN PIKE In the early season, fish the new weed growth around the
second lake; the weedline on the southwest side of the first (main) lake; above the
point on the east side that separates the first and second lakes; and below the
narrows on the west side of the first lake. Use a bobber, or troll with red and white
spoons or crankbaits. Summer and fall northerns are on the west side of the first
lake where the road (Juno Trail) runs parallel to the lake. In early winter, work the
entire second lake. In mid-winter, move to the upper half of the first lake.

WALLEYE Look for early-season walleyes on the sandbars and weedy areas.
The west side of the first lake where Juno Trail parallels the lake is a good place
to start. At the narrows, look for patches of weeds on a hard bottom of sand,
gravel, or rock. Also fish the drop-offs around the points on the north side of the
first lake. Use a live-bait rig on the edge of the weeds or work a rattling-type
crankbait over the top of the weeds.

CRAPPIE Good springtime areas are the fishing pier, the small shallow bays on
the south side of the lake, the shoreline around the second lake, and most of the
public shore areas. As the water warms, the crappies will suspend off the
weedline on the east side of the first lake, especially by the 20-foot hole. In the
fall, fish the deep breaklines on the upper west and mid-east sides of the first lake.
In the winter, the breaklines and points will be the best area.

SUNFISH In late April, look for the sunfish in the shallow, weedy bays and on
top of the weedy points on the first lake. For summer sunfish, move down to the
weedlines on the first lake. The breaklines and weedlines on the lower half of the
first lake will produce in the fall. Winter sunfish can be found around the entire
second lake during early and late ice and on the middle of the east side of the first
lake during mid-winter ice.

Information about this lake was provided by Dave Gardell and Terry Tuma.

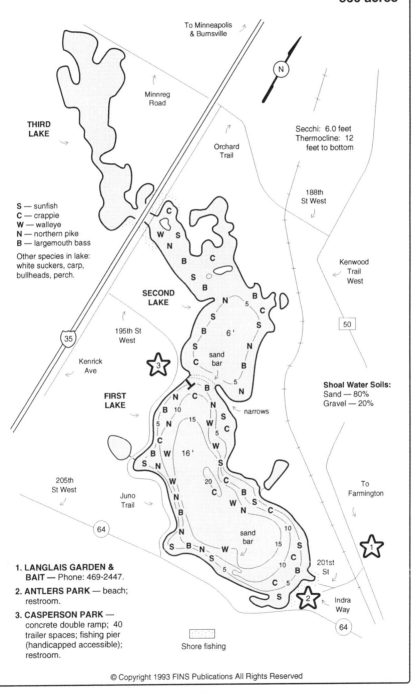

LAKE MARION
560 acres

To Minneapolis & Burnsville

Minnreg Road

THIRD LAKE

Orchard Trail

Secchi: 6.0 feet
Thermocline: 12 feet to bottom

188th St West

S — sunfish
C — crappie
W — walleye
N — northern pike
B — largemouth bass

Other species in lake: white suckers, carp, bullheads, perch.

Kenwood Trail West

SECOND LAKE

195th St West

Kenrick Ave

FIRST LAKE

narrows

Shoal Water Soils:
Sand — 80%
Gravel — 20%

sand bar

205th St West

Juno Trail

To Farmington

sand bar

201st St

Indra Way

1. **LANGLAIS GARDEN & BAIT** — Phone: 469-2447.

2. **ANTLERS PARK** — beach; restroom.

3. **CASPERSON PARK** — concrete double ramp; 40 trailer spaces; fishing pier (handicapped accessible); restroom.

Shore fishing

53

This cozy little lake is located 5 miles west of the city of Lakeville just off I-35W. It offers an abundance of bass, northern pike, crappies, sunfish, and bullheads. Hybrid tiger muskie yearlings were first stocked in 1986, and further stocking is scheduled for every two years.

SPECIES	POPULATION	AVERAGE SIZE
Bass	Good	Small to Medium
Northern Pike	Good	Small to Medium
Muskie	Poor	Small
Crappie	Good	Small
Sunfish	Good	Small

BASS   Look for early-season bass on the large bulrush bed on the east side of the lake. You'll also find them around the weedy land point on the upper east side and on the west shoreline from the beach up to the north end. Use yellow, white or chartreuse spinnerbaits with matching blades. For summer success, fish the weedlines and drop-offs on the small bulrush island on the east side of the lake in front of the round land point. A jig and pig is the favorite lure here, and plastic worms will produce all season. In the early morning, toss spinnerbaits to the shoreline on the west and north sides of the lake. The best docks are on the north side. Fall bass will be on the deeper drop-offs and around the small bulrush island.

NORTHERN PIKE & MUSKIE   In the early season, troll with shiner or sucker minnows in about 10 feet of water on the north and northwest sides of the lake. Summer northerns are on the weedlines and breaklines in the same areas. Cover the 10 to 12 foot depths. The southwest side of the small bulrush island and the north side of the large bulrush bed can also be productive. In the fall, the best locations are the west side of the lake; the southwest side of the small bulrush island; and the round land point on the east side. The same locations produce in the winter. Use sucker or shiner minnows.

CRAPPIE   The west side of the lake is a good location for spring crappies. A small hook and small crappie minnow works best under tough conditions. In the summer, look for the crappies suspended in 10 to 12 feet of water. The west side of the small bulrush bed can be productive. Also try the deep breaklines (drop-offs) on the west side of the lake. At this time of the year, vertical fishing is a good technique. Position the boat over the suspended school and use a light split-shot weight, small hook, and crappie minnow without a bobber. Jigs are effective too. In the fall, try the small bulrush island or work the northwest side of the lake at the 10 to 15 foot depths. In the winter, concentrate on the breaklines.

SUNFISH   Spring sunfish can be found over the weedy, soft-bottom areas on the south and southeast sides of the lake. In the warmer months, move to the edge of the deep weeds. The sunfish will either stay on the weedlines in the fall or move to the shallow areas. In the winter, look for irregularities in the breaklines.

Information about this lake was provided by Dave Gardell and Terry Tuma.

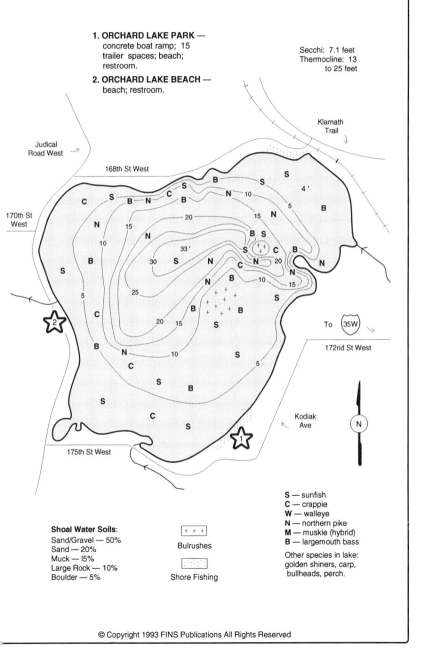

ORCHARD LAKE
250 acres

SPECIAL REGULATIONS
Muskie minimun size
limit is 40 inches.

1. **ORCHARD LAKE PARK** —
   concrete boat ramp; 15
   trailer spaces; beach;
   restroom.
2. **ORCHARD LAKE BEACH** —
   beach; restroom.

Secchi: 7.1 feet
Thermocline: 13
to 25 feet

Klamath Trail

Judical Road West

168th St West

170th St West

172nd St West

175th St West

Kodiak Ave

To 35W

N

S — sunfish
C — crappie
W — walleye
N — northern pike
M — muskie (hybrid)
B — largemouth bass

Other species in lake:
golden shiners, carp,
bullheads, perch.

Shoal Water Soils:
Sand/Gravel — 50%
Sand — 20%
Muck — 15%
Large Rock — 10%
Boulder — 5%

+ + +
Bulrushes

Shore Fishing

55

Bass, northern pike, and panfish are the major attractions on this lake in north eastern Eden Prairie. Hybrid tiger muskies were first stocked in 1985 and will b restocked every 3 years.

SPECIES	POPULATION	AVERAGE SIZE
Bass	Fair to Good	Medium
Northern Pike	Fair	Medium
Muskie	Fair	Small
Crappie	Very Good	Small
Sunfish	Excellent	Small

BASS In June, slowly work the edges of the lily pads around the entire lake. I the early morning, use a black buzzbait with a trailer hook. When the sun hits th water, switch to a white spinnerbait. The bulrushes on the upper and lower wes side are prime early-season locations. The weeds, lily pads, and bulrushes on th lower half of the middle section are especially productive. In the summer, the bes location is the rocky underwater point on the east side of the lake. Toss crankbait over the top of the weedy pockets to locate the school. Then follow u with a black or purple plastic worm. Continue to fish the pads and the good wee growth on the 5 to 6 foot break around the lake. Early fall bass can be found the remaining green weeds on the 8-foot weed break in the summer locations Try a dark-skirted spinnerbait with a single copper or gold blade tipped with po rind. After turnover, move back to the early-season locations.

NORTHERN PIKE & MUSKIE Early-season northerns are in the middle sectio of the east side of the lake. Toss a white spinnerbait with a white blade into th emerging weeds. The same locations produce in the summer, but stay on th weedline and the points. In the fall, the best area is the edge of the weeds on th north and east shoreline. On cloudy days, use a black spinnerbait with tander copper blades, and retrieve it slowly. On sunny days, try trolling slowly with large spoon. When water temperatures fall below 50 degrees, switch to a single blade spinnerbait (#5 or #6 Colorado). In late fall, start at the rock pile and tro down about half way to the narrows in 15 to 22 feet of water. In winter, work th points at the 16 to 18 foot depths. Look for muskies on the shallow edge of th weedline (less than 5 feet) anywhere on the lake in July and August.

CRAPPIE Look for early spring crappies on the sandy points suspended on th outside edge of last year's weed growth. As the water warms, move shallowe Use a small, silver, feather jig (1/64 or 1/32 oz.). Summer crappies are hard t find. The sandy points are the best bets. In the fall, the rock pile is a prim location. Winter crappies will be on the points but will move out if the northern move in.

SUNFISH Early spring sunfish are suspended on the gravel point in front of th boat launch; the point across the lake from it; and the point on the lower east sid of the lake. The inside turns of the points are prime locations. Start at the 15-fo depths, but work shallower if the weather is sunny and stable. Try worms or cor on a plain hook. In the summer, move to the deep weed edges on the tip of th points. In the fall, go back to the inside turns and fish the 8 to 12 foot breakline

Information about this lake was provided by John Dunlap and Denny Nesbitt.

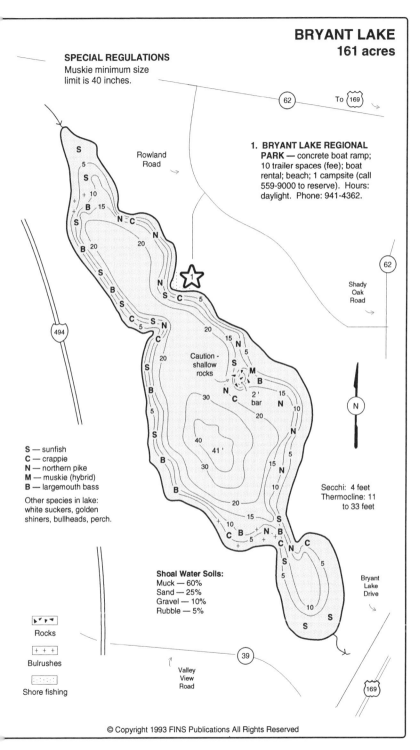

BRYANT LAKE
161 acres

To 169

SPECIAL REGULATIONS
Muskie minimum size
limit is 40 inches.

62

Rowland
Road

**1. BRYANT LAKE REGIONAL
PARK** — concrete boat ramp;
10 trailer spaces (fee); boat
rental; beach; 1 campsite (call
559-9000 to reserve). Hours:
daylight. Phone: 941-4362.

62

Shady
Oak
Road

494

N

Caution -
shallow
rocks

2'
bar

S — sunfish
C — crappie
N — northern pike
M — muskie (hybrid)
B — largemouth bass

Other species in lake:
white suckers, golden
shiners, bullheads, perch.

Secchi: 4 feet
Thermocline: 11
to 33 feet

Bryant
Lake
Drive

Shoal Water Soils:
Muck — 60%
Sand — 25%
Gravel — 10%
Rubble — 5%

Rocks

Bulrushes

Shore fishing

39

Valley
View
Road

169

Bush Lake, located in the city of Bloomington, is a small shallow lake that warms up fast in the spring and provides good early-season panfish action. It's ideal for small boats, and the long narrow shape allows even a canoe to hold its course on most windy days. A six-horsepower limit for outboard motors makes this lake the exclusive domain of swimmers and anglers. Because the water is clear, the best fishing hours are between dusk and dawn.

This lake has good populations of bass and northern pike as well as an unlimited supply of crappies and sunfish. Hybrid muskie fingerlings were stocked in 1984 and additional stocking takes place every 3 years. Some muskies are now over 20 pounds. The secret to success on this lake is light line and small lures.

SPECIES	POPULATION	AVERAGE SIZE
Bass	Good	Medium
Northern Pike	Good	Small
Muskie	Fair	Small to Large
Crappie	Good	Small to Medium
Sunfish	Excellent	Small

BASS   In June, cast a spinnerbait over the emerging lily pads and the edge of the weeds in 7 to 8 feet of water on the lower section of the lake. Use a slow retrieve. When the pads mature, work the edges with a plastic worm or a jig and pig. Don't pass up the fallen timber along the western shoreline of the middle section of the lake. In the summer, fish the weedy edges around Brown's Point with a jig and pig or plastic worm, or cast a spinnerbait over the weeds and into the pockets. Fish the same pattern on the shoreline south of the beach. On the north end of the lake, fish the shallow weed beds and lily pads with buzzbaits, or use a live-bait rig with a slip-bobber. In the fall look for the last of the green weeds in the lower section of the lake and the mid-west and southeast shorelines. Use a jig and worm or a slow-moving bait.

NORTHERN PIKE & MUSKIE   The lower section of the lake is productive from the season opener until late summer. Black, chartreuse, or yellow spinnerbaits are the choice of the experts. Also work the north end of the middle section between the points on the east and west sides. Stay here for summer action. Troll the weedy drop-offs with a flashy lure. In the fall, the east side of the middle section will hold most of the northerns. You'll find some in the shallow bass spots. Muskies are in the southern bay and on the northwest side of the lake. Use jerkbaits or surface lures.

CRAPPIE & SUNFISH   For early-spring crappies (right after ice-out), try the far upper section of the lake. When the water warms, move to the outside edge of the weeds, and look for small points or fingers that extend out toward deep water. Spring sunfish will be in the warmer shallow bays on both ends of the lake. Stay in the bass locations in the summer and fall.

Information about this lake was provided by Pat Buchanan.

BUSH LAKE
192 acres

SPECIAL REGULATIONS

No motors larger than 6 hp.

Largemouth bass minimum size limit is 16 inches.

Muskie minimum size limit is 40 inches.

To 494
West 86th St
West Bush Lake Road
ANDERSON LAKES
Amsden Road
To 18
Veness Road
To Bloomington Ferry Road
Wiencike's Point
Brown's Point
West Bush Lake Road
bar
East Bush Lake Road
28
96th St West
28
Bush Lake Road
N

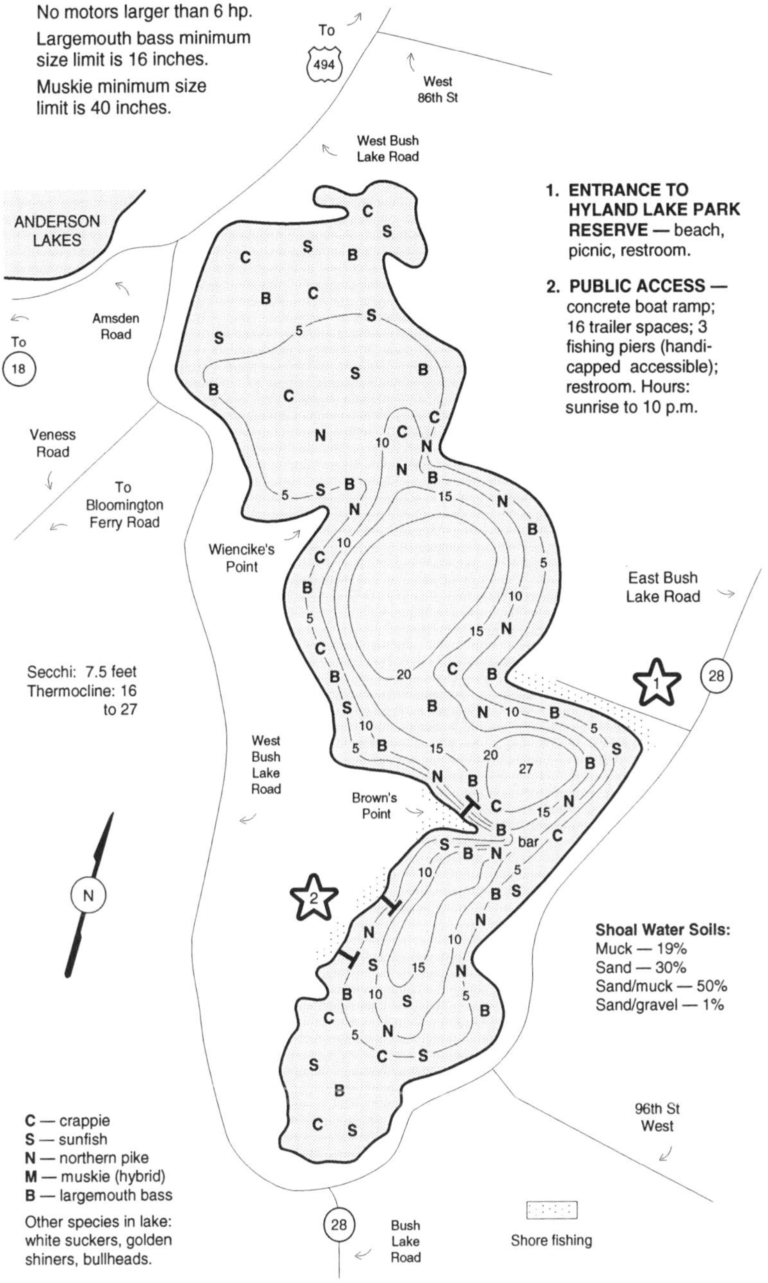

1. **ENTRANCE TO HYLAND LAKE PARK RESERVE** — beach, picnic, restroom.
2. **PUBLIC ACCESS** — concrete boat ramp; 16 trailer spaces; 3 fishing piers (handicapped accessible); restroom. Hours: sunrise to 10 p.m.

Secchi: 7.5 feet
Thermocline: 16 to 27

Shoal Water Soils:
Muck — 19%
Sand — 30%
Sand/muck — 50%
Sand/gravel — 1%

C — crappie
S — sunfish
N — northern pike
M — muskie (hybrid)
B — largemouth bass

Other species in lake: white suckers, golden shiners, bullheads.

Shore fishing

Lake Calhoun is the lake that yielded the 33-1/2 pound hybrid muskie that broke the state record in the summer of 1991, and it continues to offer mind-boggling catches for the ambitious angler. Big fish can be caught from shore, but for consistent success, you'll need a boat with an electric motor and depth finder to work the endless supply of weedy flats, humps, bars, underwater points, submerged islands, slots, troughs, and holes.

Slow to warm up in the spring, Lake Calhoun really shines in early summer. If weeds become scarce, the major fish-attracting structure will be the drop-offs. Walleye fingerlings have been stocked every three years since 1982, and hybrid muskies every three years since 1984.

SPECIES	POPULATION	AVERAGE SIZE
Bass	Good	Medium to Large
Northern Pike	Fair	Medium to Large
Muskie	Fair	Medium to Large
Walleye	Fair	Medium
Crappie	Excellent	Small to Medium
Sunfish	Excellent	Small

BASS In June, Cedar Lake and Lake of the Isles are best. When the water temperature reaches 68 degrees, move back to Lake Calhoun. The area just north of the beach on the northwest corner will warm up first. Fish the emerging weeds. As the water warms, or if the sun is high, move to the deeper weedlines. Some good summer and fall spots are the underwater point in front of Thomas Beach; the bars below Calhoun beach; above the boat dock and in front of the channel to Lake of the Isles; in front of the sailboat mooring on the upper east side; and the bar in front of 36th Street. A good multi-species technique is to snake-troll with a live-bait rig or a jig. Concentrate on the points, inside turns, and deep drop-offs in 11-1/2 to 22 feet of water.

NORTHERN PIKE & MUSKIE Work the weedy areas from Calhoun Beach down to Thomas Beach, especially in front of the air-conditioner inlet and around the fishing dock on the west side. The inside weedlines will be active until mid-July. Then the fish will move out to the deeper outside weedlines. Muskies bite best in the hottest weather. In the fall, look for the remaining patches of green weeds along the sharp drop-offs, underwater points, and shoreline flats. The north end of the lake by the channel is a favorite fall location. The west side is best.

WALLEYE In the spring and fall, try the channel to Lake of the Isles, especially at night. The flat in front of the gold dome on the east side of Lake Calhoun also produces in the spring before the weeds are up. In the summer, fish the weedy underwater points and bars in 12 to 15 feet of water. Work the deeper weedlines and sharper drop-offs in the fall.

CRAPPIE & SUNFISH In the spring, fish the channel to Lake of the Isles, the lagoon, and the docks. Spawning crappies are abundant on the west side from late May to early June. Summer sunfish are in the weedy bass locations. Crappies are suspended just outside the weedline or over deeper water.

Information about this lake was provided by Larry Bollig, Pat Buchanan, Steve Carney, Chet Meyers, and Chris Sager.

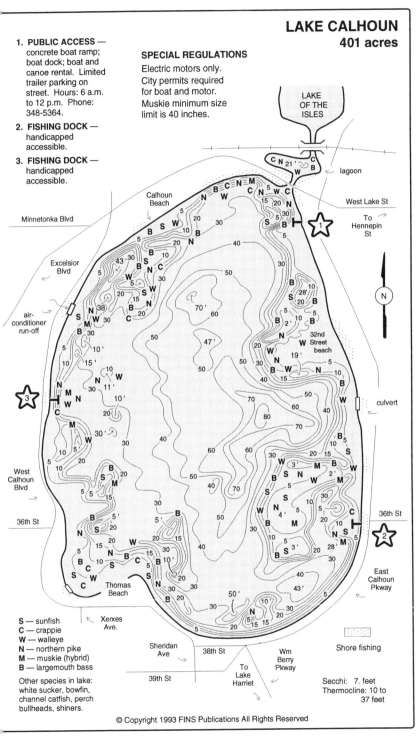

LAKE CALHOUN
401 acres

1. PUBLIC ACCESS — concrete boat ramp; boat dock; boat and canoe rental. Limited trailer parking on street. Hours: 6 a.m. to 12 p.m. Phone: 348-5364.

2. FISHING DOCK — handicapped accessible.

3. FISHING DOCK — handicapped accessible.

SPECIAL REGULATIONS

Electric motors only. City permits required for boat and motor. Muskie minimum size limit is 40 inches.

LAKE OF THE ISLES

lagoon

West Lake St

To Hennepin St

Minnetonka Blvd

Calhoun Beach

Excelsior Blvd

air-conditioner run-off

32nd Street beach

culvert

West Calhoun Blvd

36th St

East Calhoun Pkwy

36th St

Thomas Beach

Xerxes Ave.

S — sunfish
C — crappie
W — walleye
N — northern pike
M — muskie (hybrid)
B — largemouth bass

Other species in lake: white sucker, bowfin, channel catfish, perch bullheads, shiners.

Sheridan Ave

38th St

39th St

Wm Berry Pkwy

To Lake Harriet

Shore fishing

Secchi: 7. feet
Thermocline: 10 to 37 feet

This is a little gem of a lake that's blessed with a good supply of bass, northern pike, and tiny sunfish. Hybrid muskies have been stocked every 3 years since 1983, and some have reached the minimum keeping size (40 inches long). You may even find a few walleyes that have migrated in from Lake Calhoun.

Although there are many productive shore fishing areas, to catch fish consistently on Cedar Lake you'll need a boat to reach the bars, points, and sunken islands. The nearest boat launch is on Lake Calhoun, which is more than a half hour away with an electric motor and the passage can be difficult during low-water years.

Brownie Lake has suffered from oxygen depletion and the fishing dock has been removed. The west shoreline is the most accessible and holds a few bass, northerns, carp, crappies, and sunfish. The inlet on the north end can also be productive, especially when water is flowing in.

SPECIES	POPULATION	AVERAGE SIZE
Bass	Good	Medium
Northern Pike	Good	Medium
Muskie	Fair	Medium
Walleye	Poor to Fair	Large
Crappie	Poor	Medium
Sunfish	Good	Small

BASS For early-season shore fishing, try the northeast corner of Cedar Lake and the south shoreline from the swimming beach west to the lily pads. From a boat, look for the thick cabbage weeds on the long bar just below the channel to Lake of the Isles. In the summer, concentrate on the weedy edges of the points, bars, and sunken islands. The public fishing dock and the bars below and above the channel to Lake of the Isles are especially good in the summer. There are also some productive docks on the shoreline below the channel. The lily pads below the fishing dock and the shallow bay on the northeast corner of the lake are also summer producers. Try a rubber frog or Texas-rigged plastic worm dropped in the pocket of the pads or a shallow-running crankbait on the edges. A good fall location is the east shoreline from Hidden Beach down to the channel.

NORTHERN PIKE & MUSKIE In early season, use a crankbait, bucktail, or sucker minnow and spinner combination. Troll from the beach on the middle of the west side up to the north end of the lake. Before the weeds are up, stay in about 8 feet of water; after a weedline develops, move to the 12 to 14 foot depths. Also try the fishing dock. Make long casts. The shoreline just east of the channel to Brownie Lake is a good all-season shore fishing location. Try a bottom rig here with a large sucker minnow. In the fall, look for the remaining green weeds. Winter northerns can be found on the drop-off in front of the channel to Lake of the Isles or on the 7-foot sunken island (bar). Muskies are on the weedy points.

CRAPPIE & SUNFISH Sunfish are abundant in the bass locations and in the channel to Lake of the Isles. Crappies are harder to find. In the spring, look for them in the channel; the mouth of the channel into Brownie Lake; and the fishing dock. In the summer, they'll move deeper onto the points and sunken islands.

Information about this lake was provided by Larry Bollig, Jim Kirk, Chet Meyers, and Chris Sager.

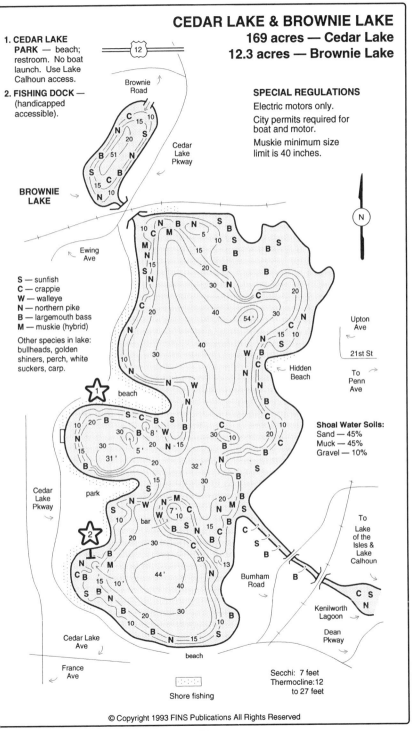

CEDAR LAKE & BROWNIE LAKE
169 acres — Cedar Lake
12.3 acres — Brownie Lake

1. **CEDAR LAKE PARK** — beach; restroom. No boat launch. Use Lake Calhoun access.

2. **FISHING DOCK** — (handicapped accessible).

BROWNIE LAKE

SPECIAL REGULATIONS

Electric motors only.

City permits required for boat and motor.

Muskie minimum size limit is 40 inches.

S — sunfish
C — crappie
W — walleye
N — northern pike
B — largemouth bass
M — muskie (hybrid)

Other species in lake: bullheads, golden shiners, perch, white suckers, carp.

Shoal Water Soils:
Sand — 45%
Muck — 45%
Gravel — 10%

Brownie Road

Cedar Lake Pkway

Ewing Ave

beach

park

Cedar Lake Pkway

Cedar Lake Ave

France Ave

Upton Ave

21st St

To Penn Ave

Hidden Beach

To Lake of the Isles & Lake Calhoun

Burnham Road

Kenilworth Lagoon

Dean Pkway

Secchi: 7 feet
Thermocline: 12 to 27 feet

Shore fishing

You'll be delighted with the size of the panfish and trout in this lake. When brood stock trout from the DNR hatchery are no longer good egg producers, they are released into Christmas Lake. The average size is 3 pounds with some as large as 8 pounds.

Christmas Lake, located just south of Hwy. 7 near Excelsior, is the second clearest lake in the metro area. It's not a popular early-season lake because it takes longer to warm up than shallower, murkier lakes. But it is one of the last lakes in the area to lose its heat in the fall. Use small-diameter lines with live bait; make long casts; and work slower and deeper than on other lakes. Low-light periods will be the most productive. This lake produces best in the winter but the ice is rarely safe until January. Use caution around the 80-foot hole on the upper east side where springs create treacherous winter ice conditions.

SPECIES	POPULATION	AVERAGE SIZE
Bass	Good	Medium
Northern Pike	Good	Small
Trout	Poor to Fair	Large
Crappie	Fair	Medium
Sunfish	Good	Medium to Large

BASS   The first bass of the season can be found at the far south end of the lake or in the two weedy bays on the northwest corner. Use chartreuse or white spinnerbaits or purple plastic worms, and make long casts into the weeds. In the summer, try the 10-foot sunken island. As the season progresses, move down to the weedy drop-offs. In the fall, go back to the spring areas.

NORTHERN PIKE   For early-season northerns, troll around the entire lake in 10 to 12 feet of water. Concentrate on areas where you see small panfish. In the summer and fall, move down to 22 feet, and use a sucker or shiner minnow. There's a good trolling run at the middle of the eastern shoreline. A slip-bobber rig works best in the fall. In the winter, try the 12 to 13 foot depths in front of the two bays on the northwest corner.

TROUT   In the early season, try the 8-foot depths in the same bay as the public access. As the water warms, take a few casts at 8 feet, and then move down to 30 feet until you find the fish. Christmas Lake Point is a good place to try next. Put a night crawler on a plain hook with a small sinker, and let it sink slowly. In the winter, try the two bays on the northwest corner. Use a very small crappie minnow.

CRAPPIE & SUNFISH   You'll find crappies and sunfish in the two bays on the northwest corner and in the marshy area on the upper east side of Christmas Lake Point. The best all-season location for sunfish is the bay in front of the public access. Stay in 10 feet of water in the spring, and move down to 18 feet in the summer. In the fall, try the 10 to 18 foot depths. You'll find summer and fall crappies in 20 to 24 feet of water around the 10-foot sunken island. At night they'll move up on the island to feed. Sunfish are here too. For winter sunfish and crappies, try the 3 to 5 foot depths at the far south end and the upper western bay. The best season for crappies will be just as the ice is melting.

Information about this lake was provided by Kurt Larson and Tiny Thomas.

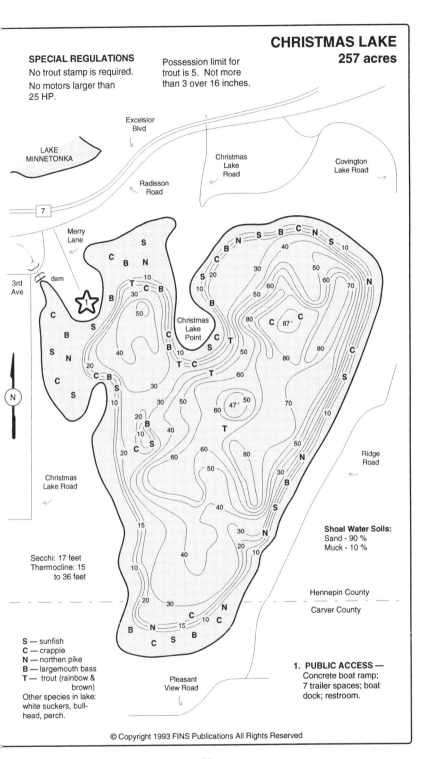

CHRISTMAS LAKE
257 acres

SPECIAL REGULATIONS

No trout stamp is required.

No motors larger than 25 HP.

Possession limit for trout is 5. Not more than 3 over 16 inches.

Excelsior Blvd

LAKE MINNETONKA

Christmas Lake Road

Covington Lake Road

Radisson Road

7

Merry Lane

3rd Ave

dam

Christmas Lake Point

Christmas Lake Road

Secchi: 17 feet
Thermocline: 15 to 36 feet

Shoal Water Soils:
Sand - 90 %
Muck - 10 %

Ridge Road

Hennepin County

Carver County

N

S — sunfish
C — crappie
N — northen pike
B — largemouth bass
T — trout (rainbow & brown)
Other species in lake: white suckers, bullhead, perch.

Pleasant View Road

1. PUBLIC ACCESS —
Concrete boat ramp; 7 trailer spaces; boat dock; restroom.

Eagle Lake, located in the southeast corner of Maple Grove, is very easy to fish. Walleye fry are stocked annually. Muskie stocking began in 1984, and will continue every three years. Eagle is one of the few lakes where the cattails grow in deeper water and are major fish-holding territory. It's also ranked as a good night-fishing lake because it has clear water and adequate cover near deep water.

Pike Lake can be good in the spring for northern pike, bass, sunfish, and crappie, but most of the fish will move out to Eagle Lake as the water warms and the oxygen diminishes.

SPECIES	POPULATION	AVERAGE SIZE
Bass	Good	Medium
Northern Pike	Poor	Medium
Muskie	Poor	Medium
Walleye	Fair	Medium
Crappie	Good	Small to Medium
Sunfish	Fair	Small

BASS   In the early season, cast to the edges and pockets of the cattails and lily pads in Pike Lake and along the shoreline on the north, west, and south sides of Eagle Lake. In the summer, work the floating cattail bog on the northwest side and the weedy slop in the spring areas. Cast a gold spoon to the holes and pockets of the heavy cover, and let it flutter down. The east side of the lake has the most productive docks. Don't pass up the excellent opportunity for summer night fishing on this lake. Use a black spinnerbait or a black spoon tipped with pork in the heavy weeds. In the fall, work the edge of the cattails in 2 feet of water, and then look for the last of the green healthy weeds in front of the cattails.

NORTHERN PIKE AND MUSKIE   You'll find the early-season northerns in the new weed growth in 2 to 15 feet of water around the entire lake and in Pike Lake. In the summer, cast to the weedlines or troll. Fall northerns will be found in the bass areas along the edges of the cattails and lily pads on the northwest, west, and southwest shoreline. Since the population of muskies is low, most will be caught while you fish for other species.

WALLEYE   In the early season, fish the 2-foot bar on the south end of the lake. Concentrate on the newly emergent weeds on the north and south sides of the bar in 7 to 8 feet of water. Summer walleyes will remain in the same areas at the same depth due to the oxygen deprivation in deeper water. After fall turnover, the walleyes will be scattered all over the lake at the 10 to 15 foot depths. As the water gets colder, slow down your presentation. Look for the last of the green weeds in 3 to 10 feet of water on the west side of the lake. For winter walleyes, go back to early-season locations, and work the 10 to 15 feet depths.

CRAPPIE & SUNFISH   Look for spring crappies and sunfish in Pike Lake and the boat canals and bays. Summer sunfish will stay in the same shallow areas. The crappies will be suspended 5 to 6 feet below the surface in about 20 feet of water. Fall crappies will be near the late remaining vegetation in 8 to 10 feet of water. Sunfish will be shallower. Look for winter crappies in 25 to 30 feet of water in the deepest part of the lake.

Information about this lake was provided by John Daily and Art Perry.

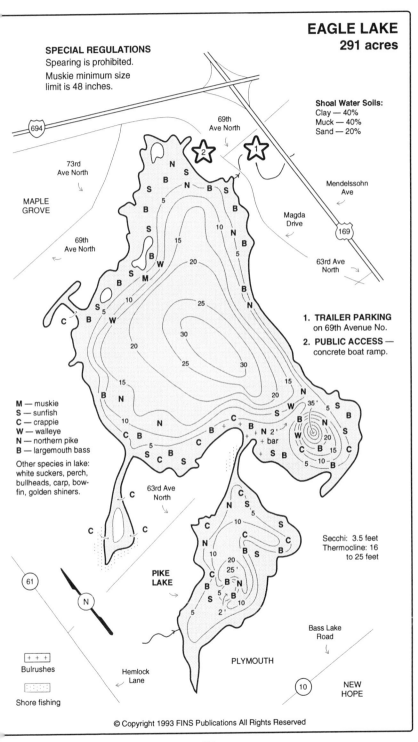

EAGLE LAKE
291 acres

SPECIAL REGULATIONS
Spearing is prohibited.
Muskie minimum size
limit is 48 inches.

Shoal Water Soils:
Clay — 40%
Muck — 40%
Sand — 20%

694

69th
Ave North

73rd
Ave North

MAPLE
GROVE

Mendelssohn
Ave

Magda
Drive

169

69th
Ave North

63rd Ave
North

1. **TRAILER PARKING**
on 69th Avenue No.

2. **PUBLIC ACCESS** —
concrete boat ramp.

M — muskie
S — sunfish
C — crappie
W — walleye
N — northern pike
B — largemouth bass

Other species in lake:
white suckers, perch,
bullheads, carp, bow-
fin, golden shiners.

Secchi: 3.5 feet
Thermocline: 16
to 25 feet

63rd Ave
North

61

N

**PIKE
LAKE**

Bass Lake
Road

+ + +
Bulrushes

Shore fishing

Hemlock
Lane

PLYMOUTH

10

NEW
HOPE

This scenic lake offers an abundance of good fish habitat: lots of points; inside turns; very steep breaks into deep water; pockets in the weedline; and an unlimited supply of weeds. It is also a very good trolling lake. DNR test nettings indicate that the northern pike population is 3 times the local average.

SPECIES	POPULATION	AVERAGE SIZE
Bass	Very Good	Medium
Northern Pike	Excellent	Medium
Crappie	Fair	Small to Medium
Sunfish	Excellent	Small to Medium

BASS During the first 3 weeks of the season, the bass will be in the small boat channels on the lower half of the lake and under the boat docks adjacent to these channels. Use a plastic worm or lizard with a single split shot, and let it drop slowly in 2 to 3 feet of water. In the early summer, concentrate on docks that are adjacent to deep-water points. Try a black jig with a black pork frog. Weeds will choke out these areas by the end of July. Then move to the deep points, and cast a deep-running crankbait in 5 to 8 feet of water. Also work the weedy slop and the deep lily pads. The pads grow deep in this lake (2 to 4 feet), especially on the south end near the boat launch. Toss a weedless silver spoon or rubber frog into the pockets of the pads. The best ones are at least 3 feet deep, and they produce best in the spring and in the fall until early October. In the fall, work the deep edges of the pads, or cast a spinnerbait with a large blade over the tops of the healthy green weeds on the points.

NORTHERN PIKE In the early season, work all the bass locations. A good technique is to cast to the deep breaks using a 1/4 ounce jig and the biggest fathead minnow you can find. Stay in the 8 to 15-foot depths. In the summer, troll or drift with a strip-on spinner, harness rig, or very flashy lure. Most of the fish will be slightly inside the weedline. Pay special attention to the rocky points on the west side of the lake. The two major points have rocks on the north side that attract the northerns. For fall northerns, cast a spinnerbait or bucktail across the tops of the deepest green weeds in 6 to 9 feet of water. The best selection is on the east side of the lake, especially the northeast area. You'll find a good supply of winter northerns in 8 to 12 feet of water at both ends of the lake and on the east side of the lower eastern lobe.

CRAPPIE & SUNFISH The boat channels will hold a good supply of crappies and sunfish in the spring. In the summer, the crappies will be suspended in 35 to 40 feet of water over the deep hole in the western lobe on the south end of the lake. In low-light periods, they will move back to the weedline areas. The summer sunfish will be around the swimming platform or concentrated on the edge of the weeds with the bass. In the evening, look for the dimpling on the surface of the water. Winter crappies will again be suspended over the deep hole. Early winter sunfish are on the shallow weed flats that are adjacent to the deepest weeds you can find. Later in the winter, they will mingle with the crappies on the southwest end of the lake in areas that have a mud bottom, from 10 feet down to 40 feet.

Information about this lake was provided by Steve Carney and Tom Zenanko.

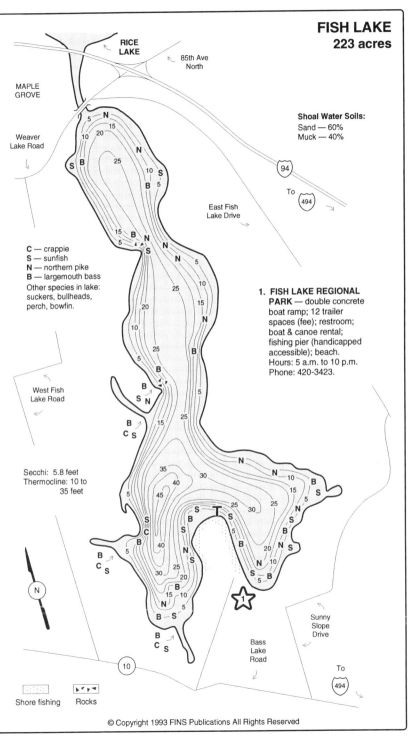

FISH LAKE
223 acres

RICE LAKE

← 85th Ave North

MAPLE GROVE

Weaver Lake Road

Shoal Water Soils:
Sand — 60%
Muck — 40%

94

To 494

East Fish Lake Drive

C — crappie
S — sunfish
N — northern pike
B — largemouth bass
Other species in lake: suckers, bullheads, perch, bowfin.

1. **FISH LAKE REGIONAL PARK** — double concrete boat ramp; 12 trailer spaces (fee); restroom; boat & canoe rental; fishing pier (handicapped accessible); beach. Hours: 5 a.m. to 10 p.m. Phone: 420-3423.

West Fish Lake Road

Secchi: 5.8 feet
Thermocline: 10 to 35 feet

N

Sunny Slope Drive

Bass Lake Road

To 494

10

Shore fishing   Rocks

Lake Harriet is gaining a reputation as a premier walleye and muskie lake. Both species have been stocked annually since 1974. Most of the northern pike were removed because they compete for food and consume the young walleyes before they're large enough to survive. Some muskies weigh over 40 pounds.

SPECIES	POPULATION	AVERAGE SIZE
Bass	Fair	Small to Medium
Walleye	Excellent	Medium
Muskie	Good	Medium to Large
Crappie	Good	Small to Medium
Sunfish	Excellent	Small

BASS   For shore fishing in June, look for bass in the sandy, weedy areas on the east side or on the west side from the drainpipe (44th Street) down to the tennis courts. Use waders or a boat to get to the deeper weeds. The early summer hotspot is the north side of the bar in front of 46th Street on the east side of the lake up to the new fishing pier. The inside turn of this bar is a bass attractor. Follow the weedline about a half block north. The weedy area on the northeast shoreline is a good summer producer. When muskies are in the shallows, bass move deeper.

WALLEYE   The bar in front of 46th Street on the east side is a good place to start the season. Give special attention to the inside turn on the north side of the bar. A light south wind blowing across it will increase the action. A south-southwest wind (8 m.p.h. or more) will attract larger fish. Then work the weedline from the 46th Street bar up to the drainpipe. Troll the 12-foot depths using a fluorescent red floating jig head with a leech and a 12-inch snell. Be alert for bites when your rig passes over the sparse patches of weeds. In the summer, try the bars on the west and north sides of the lake. Give special attention to the inside turns. In years when the weeds are very sparse, move down to the sandy sharp drop-offs in 20 to 28 feet of water, especially on the west and south sides of the lake. In the fall, fish the same areas with a medium-running crankbait. To conserve your battery and fish silently, drop 50 feet of anchor rope downwind from the spot. Fan cast the area as the boat swings back and forth. The area between the pavilion and the beach on the northwest corner is especially productive. The bar at 46th Street is a good winter location. Be sure to work the south side and the inside turn on the north side of the bar. Try a large shiner minnow at the 15 to 20 foot depths.

MUSKIE   A good all-season location is the bar on the west side, especially in front of the drainpipe. Muskies are most active after dark near drains when the water is flowing. Also work the weeds around the entire lake with a bucktail lure or tight-running, rattling crankbait. Sunset is best.

CRAPPIE & SUNFISH   For spring crappies, try the fishing piers, boat dock, and the area between the canoe rack and the street viaduct on the east side. There is a grassy point here with sharp drop-offs that attract summer crappies. Sunfish will be in the weedy bass areas. Try the west shoreline from the parking lot south to the sandbar on the middle of the west side. In the summer, work the weedline or around the docks.

Information about this lake was provided by Pat Buchanan, Steve Carney, Larry Hayes, Kevin MacDonald, and Chris Sager.

LAKE HARRIET
345 acres

1. **FISHING DOCK** — handicapped accessible.

2. **FISHING DOCK** — handicapped accessible.

3. **PUBLIC ACCESS** — concrete boat ramp; boat dock; 50 trailer spaces; food; beach; restroom. Hours: 6 a.m. to midnight.

SPECIAL REGULATIONS

Electric motors only.
City permits required for boat and motor.
Muskie minimum size limit is 40 inches.

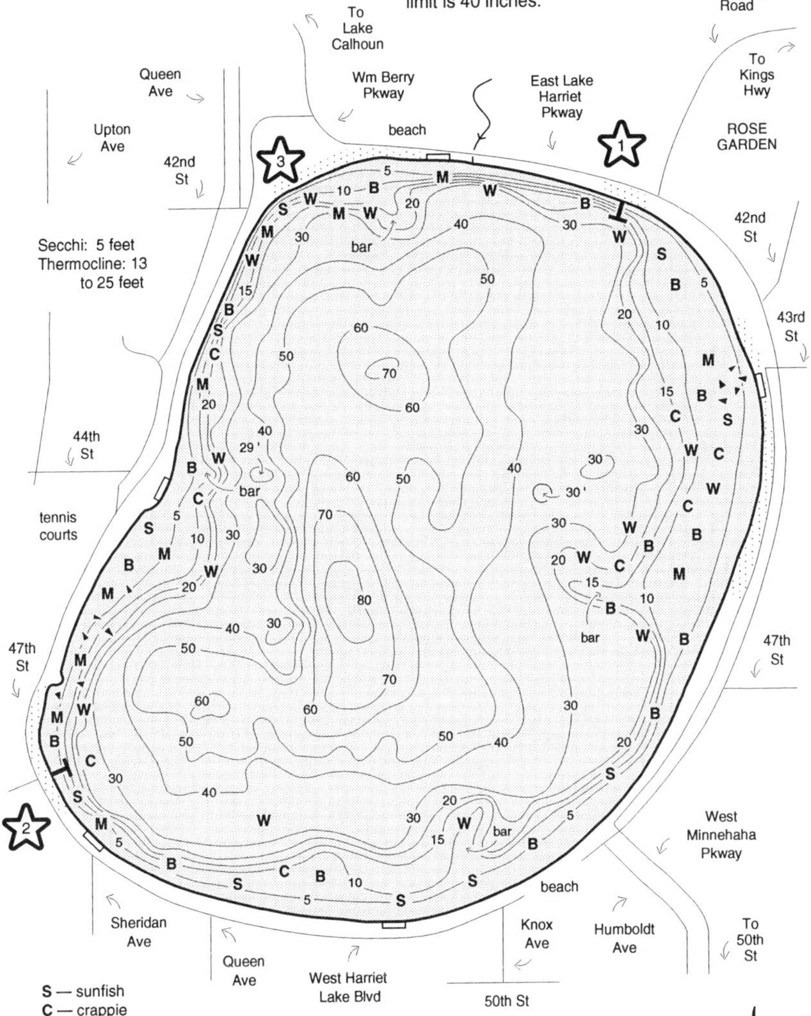

Secchi: 5 feet
Thermocline: 13 to 25 feet

Map labels: To Lake Calhoun, Queen Ave, Upton Ave, 42nd St, Wm Berry Pkway, beach, East Lake Harriet Pkway, Rose Way Road, To Kings Hwy, ROSE GARDEN, 42nd St, 43rd St, 44th St, tennis courts, 47th St, Sheridan Ave, Queen Ave, West Harriet Lake Blvd, 50th St, Knox Ave, Humboldt Ave, To 50th St, West Minnehaha Pkway, 47th St

Depth contours: 5, 10, 20, 30, 40, 50, 60, 70, 80, 29', 30', bar

S — sunfish
C — crappie
W — walleye
M — muskie
B — largemouth bass

Other species in lake: white suckers, carp, bullheads, perch, golden shiners.

Shoal Water Soils:
Sand — 95%
Gravel — 5%

Rocks

Shore fishing

N

Independence is touted as one of the best lakes in the metro area. It holds good populations of muskie, walleye, perch, bass, crappie, and sunfish. A seven and one half pound bass was caught out of this lake in 1991. There are so many places to fish that you can always find a productive location for at least one species. But you'll have to share the lake with an army of speedboaters and water skiers. Walleye fingerlings have been stocked annually since 1979, and muskies have been stocked since 1971.

SPECIES	POPULATION	AVERAGE SIZE
Bass	Very Good	Medium to Large
Northern Pike	Good	Medium to Large
Muskie	Fair to Good	Small to Medium
Walleye	Fair to Good	Medium to Large
Crappie	Very Good	Medium to Large
Sunfish	Fair to Good	Small to Medium

BASS In the early season, the bass will be in the stump area on the north end of the lake and the bulrush beds around the YWCA island. In the summer, fish the lily pads and bulrush beds around the island or move out to the edge of the weeds in 12 to 15 feet of water. In the fall, start at the south end of the island, and work down to the southwest bay. Concentrate on the deep-water drop-offs and points.

NORTHERN PIKE & MUSKIE For northerns, start trolling above the 42-foot hole at the north end and work down to the 14-foot bar in the middle of the east side of the lake. Use red and white spoons in 10 feet of water and keep the lure just above the new weed growth. In summer, move down to the 15-foot depths in the same areas. Concentrate on the sand points and holes in the fall. Stay in the 15 to 18 foot depths and use sucker minnows or deep-diving crankbaits. In the winter, fish the edges of the 42-foot hole on the north side of the YWCA island. The upper half of the lake is muskie territory throughout the season, especially around the island and the upper east side. The bulrush beds are productive in the spring. In summer, switch to larger bait such as a large jitterbug. Evening hours (5 to 8 p.m.) are best. In the fall, use dark colors and much larger lures.

WALLEYE Early-season walleyes will be on the sandy or rocky humps in 5 to 10 feet of water. Use a live-bait rig or a jig and fathead minnow with a slip bobber. Walleyes will continue to roam the humps in the summer. In the fall, fish the long sandy 14-foot bar in the middle of the east side. Stay here in the winter, but also check out the tip of the 18-foot bar at the south end of the lake. A jig and fathead minnow works best.

CRAPPIE & SUNFISH Spring crappies and sunfish are in the area east of the inlet at the north end of the lake. Work the stumps and old creek bed in 5 to 6 feet of water with a 1/64 ounce white or yellow feather jig and wax worm. In the summer, sunfish will stay in the same areas and crappies will be concentrated on the drop-offs in 12 to 15 feet of water, especially the inside turns of the points. You'll find fall crappies suspended 15 to 20 feet below the surface in about 30 feet of water at the edge of the two deep holes. Sunfish will be in the deep weedy areas around the entire lake. At the north end of the lake, the 42-foot hole is a good crappie producer in the fall and winter.

Information about this lake was provided by John Daily and Tim Sonnenstahl.

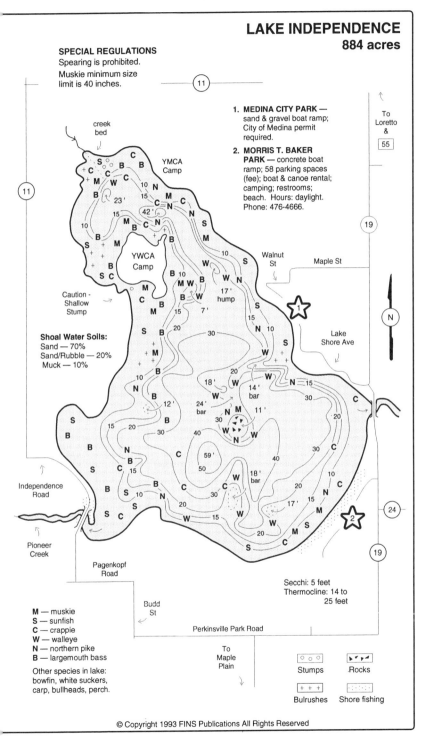

LAKE INDEPENDENCE
884 acres

SPECIAL REGULATIONS
Spearing is prohibited.
Muskie minimum size
limit is 40 inches.

1. **MEDINA CITY PARK** —
   sand & gravel boat ramp;
   City of Medina permit
   required.

2. **MORRIS T. BAKER
   PARK** — concrete boat
   ramp; 58 parking spaces
   (fee); boat & canoe rental;
   camping; restrooms;
   beach. Hours: daylight.
   Phone: 476-4666.

To Loretto & 55

creek bed

YMCA Camp

YWCA Camp

Caution - Shallow Stump

Walnut St

Maple St

Lake Shore Ave

Shoal Water Soils:
Sand — 70%
Sand/Rubble — 20%
Muck — 10%

17' hump

24' bar

14' bar

11'

18' bar

59'

17'

Independence Road

Pioneer Creek

Pagenkopf Road

Budd St

Secchi: 5 feet
Thermocline: 14 to 25 feet

Perkinsville Park Road

To Maple Plain

M — muskie
S — sunfish
C — crappie
W — walleye
N — northern pike
B — largemouth bass

Other species in lake:
bowfin, white suckers,
carp, bullheads, perch.

Stumps

Rocks

Bulrushes

Shore fishing

Lake of the Isles may not be ranked as high as nearby Calhoun or Cedar Lakes but you can't beat it for spring crappies, sunfish, and bass. Because it's a small, shallow, murky lake with plenty of shoreline runoff areas, it warms up first for some great early-season action. It's also a very popular shore fishing lake.

In midsummer when it's tough to get a boat through the weeds, try this technique for big fish. Use a long cane pole (18 or 24 feet) with heavy line (20-plus pound) and a jig and minnow or small plastic worm. Aim for the pockets or holes in the weeds, and try jigging with a pumping up and down motion. If you hook a big fish, lower your rod until the fish tires. This technique can also be used from shore.

Northern pike have been stocked every few years, and hybrid tiger muskies have been added every third year since 1985. Some are now legal size (40 inches). You may find an occasional walleye that has wandered in from the larger lakes.

SPECIES	POPULATION	AVERAGE SIZE
Bass	Very Good	Small to Medium
Northern Pike	Poor	Medium
Muskie	Fair	Medium
Crappie	Very Good	Small
Sunfish	Good	Small

BASS   The best June locations are the long arm on the north side of the lake; the southern shoreline; the shoreline in front of 28th Street; and the shoreline around the Game Refuge Islands. Try casting a small spinner or a silver and black crankbait over the tops of the weeds in 2 to 6 feet of water. You can hit most of these spots from shore. In the summer, use a small boat or canoe and a depth finder. Look for areas where deep water comes close to shore; or where flat weedy areas drop into 10 to 12 feet of water; or where there are small depressions on the bottom of the lake. A good example is the deep-dropping shoreline on the south side (west of the channel to Lake Calhoun). A black plastic worm is effective. This is not a good fall lake. Use live-bait rigs or jigs tipped with live bait, and concentrate on the troughs and depressions.

NORTHERN PIKE & MUSKIE   In the spring and fall, you'll find some northerns on the weedline in the long arm on the north side. In the summer, the water is too warm to keep a decent supply. Try working the long narrow troughs around the lake, or move to Cedar Lake or Lake Calhoun. In June, you'll find some muskies on the weedy points, especially where a clean bottom and weeds come together.

WALLEYE   In early season, a few walleyes will be concentrated on the points of the island. Try a black or white jig with a minnow or a minnow-pattern crankbait in 4 to 6 feet of water.

CRAPPIE & SUNFISH   You'll find sunfish and crappies everywhere in the spring, especially in the long arm on the north side. Also fish the west side of the small Game Refuge Island and the area above it. Try trolling here with a 1/64 ounce jig. For winter crappies, the best location is the 10-foot hole on the west side in front of the channel to Cedar Lake.

Information about this lake was provided by Pat Buchanan, Jim Kirk, Chet Meyers, and Chris Sager.

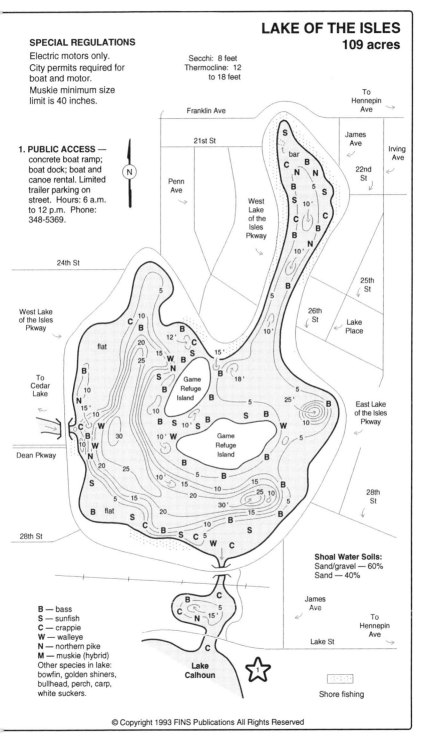

LAKE OF THE ISLES
109 acres

SPECIAL REGULATIONS

Electric motors only.
City permits required for
boat and motor.
Muskie minimum size
limit is 40 inches.

Secchi: 8 feet
Thermocline: 12
to 18 feet

1. PUBLIC ACCESS —
concrete boat ramp;
boat dock; boat and
canoe rental. Limited
trailer parking on
street. Hours: 6 a.m.
to 12 p.m. Phone:
348-5369.

B — bass
S — sunfish
C — crappie
W — walleye
N — northern pike
M — muskie (hybrid)
Other species in lake:
bowfin, golden shiners,
bullhead, perch, carp,
white suckers.

Shoal Water Soils:
Sand/gravel — 60%
Sand — 40%

Shore fishing

Little Long Lake, located just northeast of Whaletail Lake in southwestern Hennepin County, is a unique little lake with overhanging cliffs, underwater shelves, and sharp drop-offs into very deep water. It's spring fed with very clear water and cool temperatures even in mid-summer.

Rainbow trout have been stocked annually since 1987, and reports from local anglers indicate that the growth rate is good. But it's the northern pike that are really thriving, with some as large as 20 pounds. The larger northerns develop their rapid growth rate by eating the oily, nutrient-rich trout.

The lower lake is the favorite location for spring crappies and sunfish. It's smaller and shallower, and it will warm up first. It's also known for big winter sunfish and crappies. Heavy vegetation makes it almost impossible to get through the channel in the summer. Forget it in low water years.

For spring shore fishing, the best locations are the public access and the creek at the north end of the lake. You can also find bass, northerns, and sunfish from shore near the middle of the east side of the lake.

SPECIES	POPULATION	AVERAGE SIZE
Bass	Fair	Small to Medium
Northern Pike	Fair	Medium to Large
Trout	Good	Small to Medium
Crappie	Good	Small to Medium
Sunfish	Excellent	Small to Medium

BASS   In June, start at the southwest corner of the lake in 1 to 4 feet of water, and work up to the camp on the middle of the west side. There is good habitat here, including fallen trees. The rocky bulrush point on the middle of the east side can also be productive. Work both sides of the point — up to the public access and down about halfway between the point and the south end. In the summer, stay in the same area, but work the 2 to 8 foot depths.

NORTHERN PIKE   In the early season, you'll find northerns in 2 to 8 feet of water in the bass areas. Troll or drift with a bottom rig and sucker minnow, or cast a red and white spoon or a gold or silver crankbait. In the summer, troll the weedline in 20 to 30 feet of water with a red and white spoon or a crankbait. The big summer northerns will be chasing the trout, but they'll be hard to catch. You'll find them suspended 30 to 40 feet below the surface in 60 to 70 feet of water.

TROUT   Winter is the most productive time. Stay in 20 to 30 feet of water on the middle of the west side of the lake. Use a small jig (1/16 or 1/32 oz.) tipped with a Eurolarva or wax worm.

CRAPPIE & SUNFISH   Early-season sunfish can be caught from shore along the creek on the north end of the lake. The weeds, bulrushes, and submerged brush will attract both crappies and sunfish the rest of the season. The bass locations in both lakes are the best. The lower lake is a spring and winter hotspot.

Information about this lake was provided by Ted Welch.

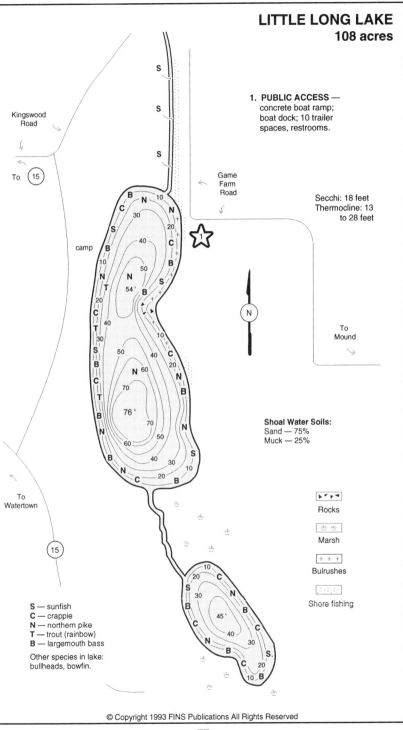

LITTLE LONG LAKE
108 acres

1. **PUBLIC ACCESS** — concrete boat ramp; boat dock; 10 trailer spaces, restrooms.

Kingswood Road

To (15)

Game Farm Road

Secchi: 18 feet
Thermocline: 13 to 28 feet

camp

N

To Mound

Shoal Water Soils:
Sand — 75%
Muck — 25%

To Watertown

(15)

▶ ◀ ▶ ◀
Rocks

Marsh

+ + +
Bulrushes

Shore fishing

S — sunfish
C — crappie
N — northern pike
T — trout (rainbow)
B — largemouth bass

Other species in lake:
bullheads, bowfin.

Crappies, northerns, carp, and bullheads are the major attraction on Long Lake. It's also a popular winter lake for big northerns. This lake is located in the community of Long Lake in western Hennepin County, and it receives little fishing pressure. Because it has an outlet into Lake Minnetonka, it always has a fresh supply of fish, including a few straggler walleyes. There is some shore fishing for crappies and northerns on the south side where Hwy. 12 runs parallel to the lake. Also try the east end around East Long Lake Road for bass, northerns, sunfish, and crappies.

SPECIES	POPULATION	AVERAGE SIZE
Bass	Fair	Medium to Large
Northern Pike	Very Good	Small to Medium
Crappie	Very Good	Medium
Sunfish	Fair	Small

BASS   In the morning, use a white spinnerbait or a jighead with a 4-inch plastic worm to work the shallow flat just west of the large land point on the north side of the lake. In the afternoon, switch to a brown plastic worm, and move out to the weedlines in front of the same flat and the large point. The weedline at the east end of the lake is also a productive early-season location. In the summer and fall, try the deep-water break off the round land point in front of East Long Lake Road on the southeast section of the lake. A jig and pig combination is a good fall technique.

NORTHERN PIKE   The shoreline that parallels Hwy. 12 is a prime early-season location. You can fish it effectively from a boat or from shore. Use a sucker minnow with a bobber, and work the edge of the weeds in 10 to 15 feet of water. Also try trolling the weedline here with a red and white spoon or crankbait, and work east to the second land point. In the summer, the same areas will be productive but go deeper to the 15 to 20 foot depths, especially if the water temperature is 75 degrees or higher. After fall turnover, try the 10 to 15 foot depths on the southeast side of the lake along East Long Lake Road. Use a large sucker minnow and bobber for the big fish. The south end of the 33-foot hole is also a good winter hotspot.

CRAPPIE   The two shallow bays on the north side of the lake will hold the majority of the spring crappies. The inlet on the northeast bay is especially good. Start the season with a 1/64 ounce feather jig and crappie minnow. In the summer, you'll find the fish suspended 10 to 15 feet below the surface on the points that extend out to deeper water. The prime areas are the two major points that face each other on the north and south sides. Fall crappies will be suspended in deep water. Watch your depth finder for the blips 10 to 15 feet below the surface. Winter crappies will be tightly schooled off the large point on the north side of the lake and in the deeper holes. Use small chartreuse ice flies or glo jigs. The evening hours from 5 to 8 p.m. will be best.

SUNFISH   Sunfish will be harder to find. Fish the weedy clumps in the northern bays all season. Also work the bass spots. Try small yellow or green ice jigs tipped with wax worms.

Information about this lake was provided by Brad Roehl and Tim Sonnenstahl.

LONG LAKE
261 acres

1. LONG LAKE CITY PARK — concrete boat ramp; restroom. Hours: 8 a.m. to 10 p.m.

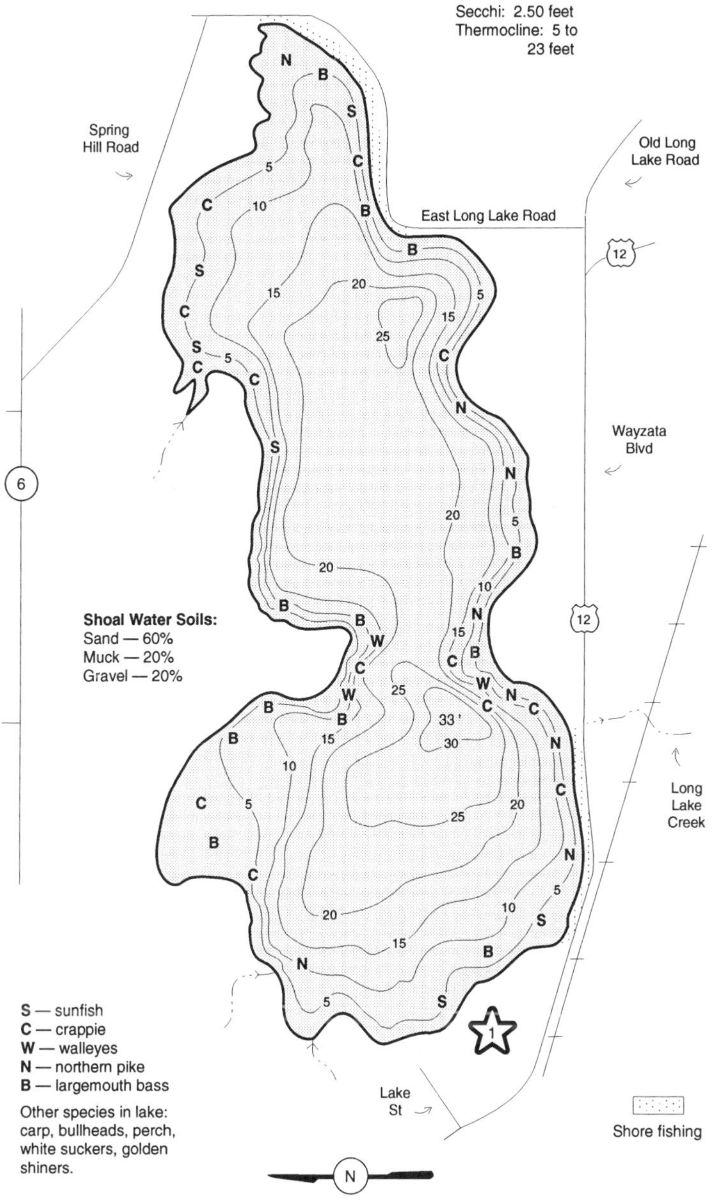

Secchi: 2.50 feet
Thermocline: 5 to 23 feet

Spring Hill Road

Old Long Lake Road

East Long Lake Road

12

Wayzata Blvd

6

12

Shoal Water Soils:
Sand — 60%
Muck — 20%
Gravel — 20%

Long Lake Creek

N

5
10
15
20
25
33'
30
20
15

1

S — sunfish
C — crappie
W — walleyes
N — northern pike
B — largemouth bass

Other species in lake: carp, bullheads, perch, white suckers, golden shiners.

Lake St

N

Shore fishing

Structure anglers will appreciate the assortment of bars, sunken islands, bays, deep-water docks, good weedlines, and a healthy supply of cabbage weeds. Although Medicine Lake is known as a premiere northern pike lake, it also produces good populations of bass, crappie, sunfish, perch, and bullheads. Walleye fry were stocked from 1984 to 1990, but few have survived.

Medicine Lake is located just east of I-494 in the city of Plymouth. The county park on the north end of the lake includes a fishing pier that is accessible to handicapped anglers. The canals at the north end offer good shore fishing areas for sunfish, crappies, and an occasional bass. There is also some productive shore fishing at the inlet on the west side in the West Medicine Lake Park. On weekends, you'll have to share the lake with an army of sailboats.

SPECIES	POPULATION	AVERAGE SIZE
Bass	Fair to Good	Medium
Northern Pike	Excellent	Small
Walleye	Poor	Small
Crappie	Excellent	Medium
Sunfish	Good	Small

BASS The north end of the lake and the upper west side hold early-season bass. Use a white skirted spinnerbait with copper blade tipped with a red pork frog. In summer, all the traditional bass lures work. The docks in the two bays on the southwest side are especially productive in the summer. Make certain you fish the shady side. A plastic worm or spinnerbait works here. Another good summer location is the deep edge of the bulrushes on the east side. In the fall, look for the last of the emergent green vegetation in 2 to 12 feet of water.

NORTHERN PIKE The outer edge of the lily pads are key northern locations in this lake. In the spring, concentrate on the north end of the lake and the southeast bay. Use a large shiner or sucker minnow. In the summer, fish the outer edge of the weeds in the entire northern arm and the southwest bays (on both sides of the peninsula). The same pattern will work in the fall, but be sure to stay with the green healthy vegetation. Winter northerns will be suspended in deep water about 2 to 3 feet off the bottom over the humps in the middle of the lake.

WALLEYE In the spring, look for a few walleyes on the bars and shoals that are exposed to wave action. Summer fish will be on the sharper breaklines on the sunken islands. Move back to the shallow breaklines in 5 to 8 feet of water in the fall and on the flats in 15 to 20 feet of water in the winter.

CRAPPIE & SUNFISH The prime early spring locations are the bays and canals in the Hennepin County Park on the northwest end of the lake. As the season progresses, the crappies will suspend 6 to 8 feet below the surface in 10 to 20 feet of water in the main lake. Try drifting, and use a slip bobber and a small crappie minnow on a plain hook. The sunfish can be found in any weedy area, especially in the bass locations. Fall crappies will be off the weeds in 8 to 12 feet of water. In the winter, check out the holes and sunken islands in the middle of the lake.

Information about this lake was provided by John Daily, Joe and Ann Harty, and Dick Kiefer.

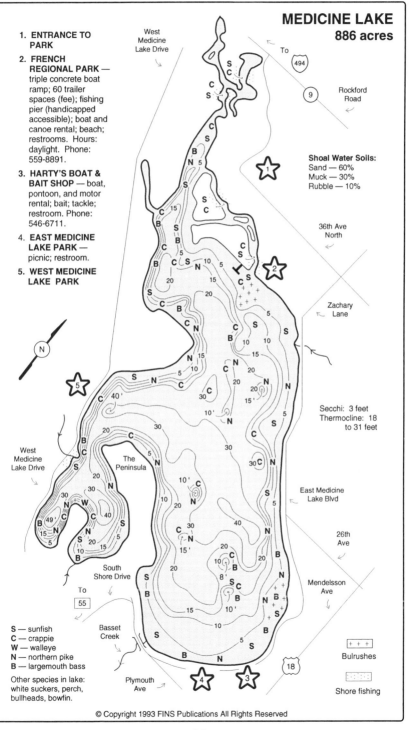

MEDICINE LAKE
886 acres

To 494

Rockford Road

9

Shoal Water Soils:
Sand — 60%
Muck — 30%
Rubble — 10%

36th Ave North

Zachary Lane

Secchi: 3 feet
Thermocline: 18 to 31 feet

East Medicine Lake Blvd

26th Ave

Mendelsson Ave

1. **ENTRANCE TO PARK**

2. **FRENCH REGIONAL PARK** — triple concrete boat ramp; 60 trailer spaces (fee); fishing pier (handicapped accessible); boat and canoe rental; beach; restrooms. Hours: daylight. Phone: 559-8891.

3. **HARTY'S BOAT & BAIT SHOP** — boat, pontoon, and motor rental; bait; tackle; restroom. Phone: 546-6711.

4. **EAST MEDICINE LAKE PARK** — picnic; restroom.

5. **WEST MEDICINE LAKE PARK**

West Medicine Lake Drive

N

The Peninsula

West Medicine Lake Drive

South Shore Drive

To 55

Basset Creek

Plymouth Ave

18

S — sunfish
C — crappie
W — walleye
N — northern pike
B — largemouth bass

Other species in lake: white suckers, perch, bullheads, bowfin.

+ + +
Bulrushes

Shore fishing

Lake Minnetonka is unquestionably the most popular and most productive fishing lake in the metro area. It contains 14,310 acres of water; has more than 100 miles of shoreline; and is surrounded by 15 separate communities. And the best part is that it's chock full of fish!

Minnetonka is one of the best bass lakes in the Upper Midwest. "The largemouth bass are increasing dramatically in size," claim guides and tournament anglers. The average size caught in tournaments is now 3 pounds, and 5 to 7 pounders are not unusual.

Some experts claim the explosion of the Eurasian Milfoil weed in Minnetonka is responsible. A virtual wall of weeds (about 3 feet thick) on the surface of the water and the sparse stems underneath provide more hiding places for the bass. Other experts believe that because milfoil is more difficult to fish, fewer bass are being caught, and the remaining ones are growing larger. For whatever reason, there is a small army of anglers who pound this lake regularly, convinced that the next state record will come out of these waters. The milfoil is also a haven for huge northern pike. See "Eurasian Water Milfoil" in the first section of this book.

Walleyes were first stocked in the mid-60's, and huge numbers of fingerlings are stocked annually. There is a good distribution of sizes, and with a lot of luck or hard work, you can find them up to 11 pounds. Expert angler Tom Zrust claims he saw a 20 pound plus walleye floating in Crystal Bay that had died of old age. (The state record is 17 pounds 8 ounces.)

Pure strain muskies have been stocked annually since 1975, and hybrids were added in 1988. Minnetonka is 1 of only 2 lakes in the metro area that contain smallmouth bass. There are also some monster northern pike (up to 15 pounds) caught regularly in this lake. The sunfish and crappie supply is limitless.

SPECIES	POPULATION	AVERAGE SIZE
Largemouth Bass	Excellent	Medium
Smallmouth Bass	Poor to Fair	Small to Medium
Northern Pike	Fair	Medium to Large
Muskie	Fair	Medium
Walleye	Good	Medium
Crappie	Excellent	Medium
Sunfish	Very Good	Small to Medium

Minnetonka is a massive, sprawling body of water composed of a series of about 40 virtually independent lakes and bays connected by bridges and channels. The biggest question for the angler is, "Where do I start?"

Lake Minnetonka contains a wide variety of habitat and natural structures (rock piles and reefs, sunken islands, saddles, holes, humps, weed beds, lily pads, etc.) that attract fish. Nevertheless, some of the best spots in the lake are man-made.

• Marker buoys indicate shallow rocky reefs, points, and bars that can be fish sanctuaries for most species.

• Some channels between lakes have metal sleeves (walls) along the sides. In many places the current has washed away the soil under these sleeves and created hollow areas that are resting spots for fish as they move from one section of the lake to another.

- Docks are notorious fish producers. The best ones are close to deeper water and healthy vegetation, and they have a minimum amount of space between the dock and the surface of the water. Also look for docks that have boats with high-powered motors. The turbulence from these motors creates depressions in the lake bottom that attract fish.

- Riprap areas where rocks have been piled up along embankment slopes to prevent erosion are natural fish magnets because the rocks provide hiding places for insects, minnows, crayfish, and other foods.

- Marinas can be a real gold mine. Usually, the area around the docks has been dredged to accommodate the big boats. Bass tournaments are frequently based at the marinas and, after weigh-in, hundreds of large fish are released back into the water. Because of the abundant food supply, good cover, and access to deep water, some people feel that many of these fish will stay in this vicinity.

The key to successful fishing on this lake is to understand that each bay has its own unique characteristics and should be fished as though it were a separate lake. Variations from bay to bay include basic factors such as water clarity, water color, maximum depth, bottom content, type and abundance of weeds, average weedline, and type of fish-holding structure. These factors dictate different fishing patterns, seasonal patterns, and fish population in each bay.

Be sure to check the Seasonal Fishing Patterns charts in this book to make certain you have selected the right location and technique for the type of fish you're after.

The murkiest water is on the west end of the lake where nutrient-rich fertilizer runoff from nearby farm fields causes an over-abundance of algae and reduces water clarity. In West Arm, Halsted Bay, Harrison Bay, and Stubb's Bay, the average weedline is at 2 to 4 feet, and these bays are ideal for early-season fishing, right after a cold front, or on sunny days. These bays also have the least amount of Eurasian Milfoil. Fish will be shallower here, more active throughout the day, and easier to catch. In Upper Lake, North Arm, Carmen's Bay, Spring Park Bay, Smithtown Bay, and Cook's Bay, the water is not as murky. There are expansive weedy areas, and the average weedline is at 6 to 8 feet. The clearest water is in Crystal Bay, Lower Lake, and almost everything east of the narrows including Excelsior Bay, Brown's Bay, Smith's Bay, and Wayzata Bay. You'll find deeper, clearer water here with rocky reefs and sandy bottom. The average weedline is at 8 to 10 feet. These areas offer the best fall fishing and can be very productive at night or when the sky is overcast.

Experts claim that this lake is so varied that when one lake or bay is turned off, another may be productive. All that variety, however, can be very confusing to the angler who isn't familiar with this lake. For the newcomer, the best solution is to select a bay that has the same characteristics as one of the lakes you fish most frequently. Look for similarities in water clarity, bottom content, weed growth, etc. The same lures and techniques that were successful on other lakes are likely to score for you here too. Or pick one bay and learn it well rather than jump from bay to bay. For the angler with only an electric motor, there's a surprising abundance of fish within a short distance of every boat launch. If you don't have a depth finder, fish the visible structure — docks, rocks, bridges, and lily pads.

There are dozens of productive shore fishing sites all around the lake, and some of the larger ones have picnic areas, restrooms, and parking facilities. Many of these areas have deep water fairly close to shore and hold bass, northerns, and walleyes as well as panfish. The channels are excellent shore fishing sites, and most of the backwater bays and canals are teeming with panfish. Anglers should be aware that shore fishing sites, parking regulations, and public accesses may be changed to meet the needs of the local communities.

LARGEMOUTH BASS Docks and other shoreline structures have always been popular bass spots on this lake. The best docks have deeper water and healthy weeds nearby. Try pitching, skipping, or flipping a jig and pig under the dock, or work a spinnerbait parallel to the dock. Some of the tournament anglers feel that the deeper structures such as sunken boats, humps, holes, rock piles, troughs, saddles, and underwater points are more productive because they are usually underfished. Smart anglers also use a depth finder to locate the lake-bottom breaklines where the bottom content changes from sand to mud, rock, weeds, etc. This strategy is especially effective in areas like the west side of the lake where there are few weeds or other objects to provide cover for the fish. All of the standard bass lures are productive. Plastic worms, jigs, and deep-running crank-baits work well for the deeper structures. The best early-season locations are the smaller, murkier bays, especially on the north side. The deeper structures produce best in the summer. In the fall, look for the remaining green, healthy vegetation on the deeper breaks.

SMALLMOUTH BASS This lake has a fair supply of smallmouths ranging up to five pounds. The most popular areas are Brown's Bay (Horseshoe Reef), Robinson's Bay, Wayzata Bay, the rocky reefs around Big Island, Spirit Island, Gibson's Point, and Lookout Point in Lower Lake. Look for submerged weeds on a rock or gravel bottom, particularly near deep water. Also check out the rocky points and reefs where crayfish are abundant. Many smallmouths are also caught under the boat docks that extend into deep water and have gravel or rubble under them. Walleye lures, small plastic worms, and crayfish-pattern crankbaits are most effective.

NORTHERN PIKE This lake is a spoonplugger's paradise with an abundance of large northerns and many good trolling runs. These fish can be caught along any weedline from Halsted's Bay to Gray's Bay. Deeper weedlines are best. Also check out the deeper structures such as holes, sunken boats, troughs, saddles, humps, and underwater points. Large sucker minnows, gaudy spinnerbaits, plastic worms, and jigs are very productive.

MUSKIE The largest concentrations are around Brown's Bay, Spring Park Bay, Wayzata Bay, Spray Island, Big Island, Crystal Bay, and Maxwell Bay. Look for them under docks or on weedlines where there are healthy cabbage weeds. The traditional muskie lures work best.

WALLEYE Bass anglers find a good supply of walleyes in the thickest weeds and under docks. Minnetonka walleye experts prefer the Lower Lake areas especially between Gibson's Point and Brackett's Point, Wayzata Bay, Diamond

Reef, Diamond Annex, Horseshoe Reef, and Ferguson's Point. Use a live-bait rig, a jig and minnow, or a floating crankbait, and backtroll along the steep drop-offs. The first 2 weeks in June are the best. Fall night fishing can be dynamite.

CRAPPIE This lake is paved with crappies, and tons of them are hauled out of Minnetonka every year. In the spring, the shallow, mud-filled bays with 3 to 6 feet of water produce first, especially on the north side. Black Lake, Seton Lake, Peavey Lake, and Grays Bay are the most popular. Canals and small lagoons are also terrific. Look for the warmest water. Bigger crappies will spawn in 8 to 10 feet of water, and smaller fish in 1 to 2 feet of water. In the summer, the fish are usually suspended 10 to 15 feet below the surface in 15 to 30 feet of water outside the deep weedline or over rocky humps and reefs, sunken islands, or sunken boats. Use a depth finder to locate the suspended fish. The most popular areas are the islands around Spring Park Bay, the rocky reefs in Brown's Bay, and Carmen's Bay. Use a small minnow on a white or pink jig or plain hook.

SUNFISH There is a good supply of sunfish along the shoreline in most of the dark-bottom, shallow bays, canals, and lagoons. In the summer, the larger fish will be in the walleye spots on the deeper weedlines and rock piles.

BULLHEAD Bullheads are plentiful all over the lake, especially in the small, shallow bays and canals. Some of the most popular spots are Black Lake, Seaton Lake, Forest Lake, Jennings Bay, and under the bridge at Tanager Lake.

Information about this lake was provided by Mark Allen, Randy Barkley, Larry Bollig, Bob Conkley, John Daily, Gary Lake, Tim Sonenstahl, Ted Welch, and Tom Zrust.

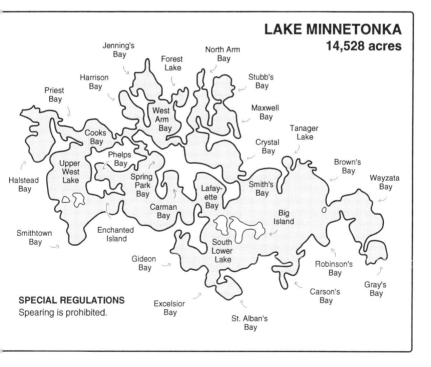

LAKE MINNETONKA
14,528 acres

Jenning's Bay
Forest Lake
North Arm Bay
Stubb's Bay
Harrison Bay
Priest Bay
Maxwell Bay
West Arm Bay
Tanager Lake
Cooks Bay
Crystal Bay
Phelps Bay
Brown's Bay
Upper West Lake
Spring Park Bay
Wayzata Bay
Halstead Bay
Lafay-ette Bay
Smith's Bay
Carman Bay
Big Island
Smithtown Bay
Enchanted Island
South Lower Lake
Gideon Bay
Robinson's Bay
Gray's Bay
Carson's Bay
SPECIAL REGULATIONS
Spearing is prohibited.
Excelsior Bay
St. Alban's Bay

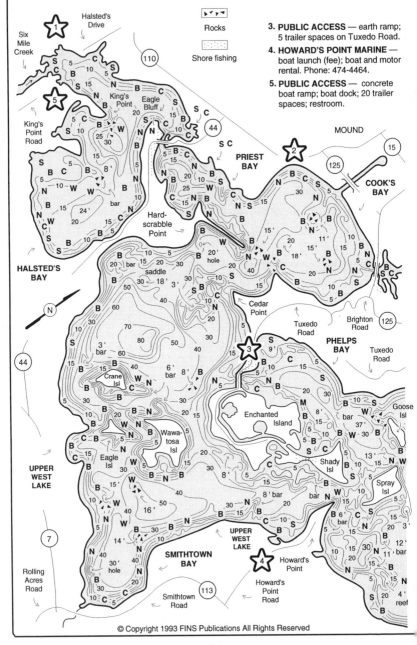

1. **MOUND'S BAY PARK** — concrete boat launch; 10 trailer spaces; beach. No parking on weekends and holidays except on west side of park.

2. **R & R BAIT & TACKLE** — 2630 Commerce Blvd. Phone: 472-1884.

LAKE MINNETONKA
Halsted, Priest, Cooks, Phelps, and Smithtown Bays.

Rocks

Shore fishing

3. **PUBLIC ACCESS** — earth ramp; 5 trailer spaces on Tuxedo Road.

4. **HOWARD'S POINT MARINE** — boat launch (fee); boat and motor rental. Phone: 474-4464.

5. **PUBLIC ACCESS** — concrete boat ramp; boat dock; 20 trailer spaces; restroom.

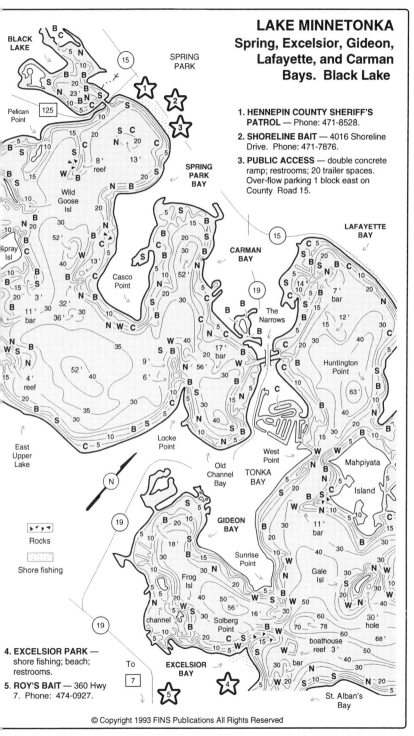

LAKE MINNETONKA
Spring, Excelsior, Gideon, Lafayette, and Carman Bays. Black Lake

BLACK LAKE

SPRING PARK

1. **HENNEPIN COUNTY SHERIFF'S PATROL** — Phone: 471-8528.

2. **SHORELINE BAIT** — 4016 Shoreline Drive. Phone: 471-7876.

3. **PUBLIC ACCESS** — double concrete ramp; restrooms; 20 trailer spaces. Over-flow parking 1 block east on County Road 15.

Pelican Point

125

SPRING PARK BAY

LAFAYETTE BAY

CARMAN BAY

Wild Goose Isl

Spray Isl

Casco Point

8' reef

13'

52'

40

13'

32'

36'

11' bar

4' reef

52'

The Narrows

7' bar

12'

Huntington Point

63'

East Upper Lake

Locke Point

17' bar

56'

9'

6'

35

Rocks

Shore fishing

Old Channel Bay

West Point

TONKA BAY

Mahpiyata

Island

11' bar

GIDEON BAY

Sunrise Point

Frog Isl

Gale Isl

30' hole

68'

channel

Solberg Point

16'

boathouse reef 3'

78

70

60

50

40

bar

4. **EXCELSIOR PARK** — shore fishing; beach; restrooms.

5. **ROY'S BAIT** — 360 Hwy 7. Phone: 474-0927.

To
7

EXCELSIOR BAY

St. Alban's Bay

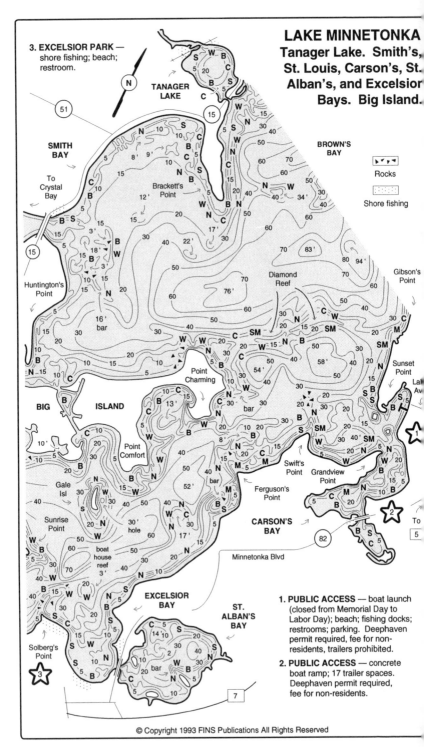

LAKE MINNETONKA
Tanager Lake. Smith's, St. Louis, Carson's, St. Alban's, and Excelsior Bays. Big Island.

3. EXCELSIOR PARK — shore fishing; beach; restroom.

Rocks

Shore fishing

1. **PUBLIC ACCESS** — boat launch (closed from Memorial Day to Labor Day); beach; fishing docks; restrooms; parking. Deephaven permit required, fee for non-residents, trailers prohibited.

2. **PUBLIC ACCESS** — concrete boat ramp; 17 trailer spaces. Deephaven permit required, fee for non-residents.

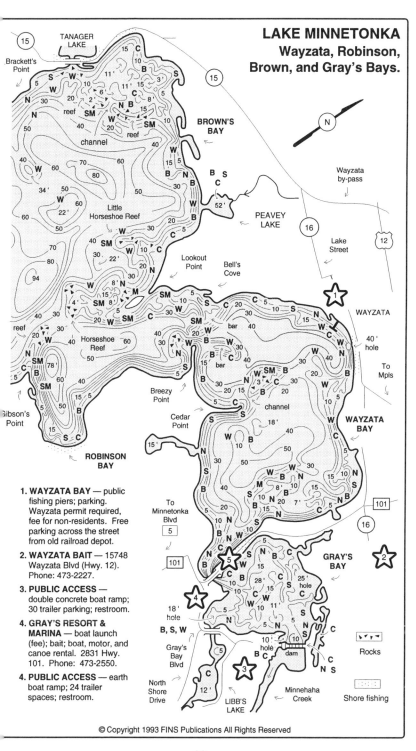

LAKE MINNETONKA
Wayzata, Robinson, Brown, and Gray's Bays.

TANAGER LAKE

15

Brackett's Point

BROWN'S BAY

15

Wayzata by-pass

16

12

Lake Street

PEAVEY LAKE

Little Horseshoe Reef

Lookout Point

Bell's Cove

To Mpls

WAYZATA

40' hole

1

Horseshoe Reef

Breezy Point

Cedar Point

Gibson's Point

channel

WAYZATA BAY

ROBINSON BAY

To Minnetonka Blvd

5

101

16

101

GRAY'S BAY

2

25' hole

18' hole

B, S, W

Gray's Bay Blvd

10' hole

dam

Rocks

North Shore Drive

12'

LIBB'S LAKE

Minnehaha Creek

Shore fishing

5

4

3

1. WAYZATA BAY — public fishing piers; parking. Wayzata permit required, fee for non-residents. Free parking across the street from old railroad depot.

2. WAYZATA BAIT — 15748 Wayzata Blvd (Hwy. 12). Phone: 473-2227.

3. PUBLIC ACCESS — double concrete boat ramp; 30 trailer parking; restroom.

4. GRAY'S RESORT & MARINA — boat launch (fee); bait; boat, motor, and canoe rental. 2831 Hwy. 101. Phone: 473-2550.

4. PUBLIC ACCESS — earth boat ramp; 24 trailer spaces; restroom.

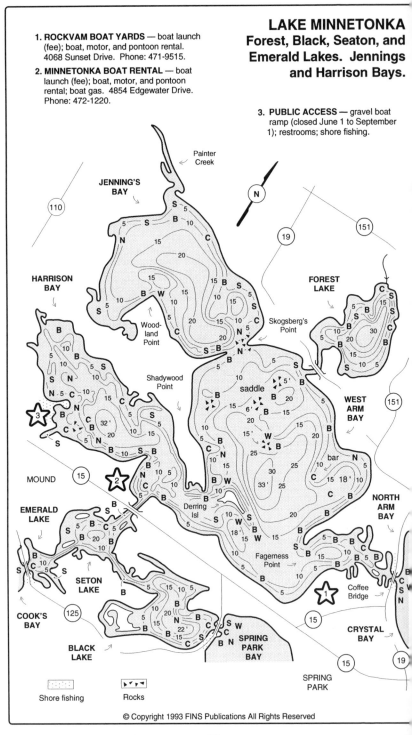

LAKE MINNETONKA
Forest, Black, Seaton, and Emerald Lakes. Jennings and Harrison Bays.

1. **ROCKVAM BOAT YARDS** — boat launch (fee); boat, motor, and pontoon rental. 4068 Sunset Drive. Phone: 471-9515.

2. **MINNETONKA BOAT RENTAL** — boat launch (fee); boat, motor, and pontoon rental; boat gas. 4854 Edgewater Drive. Phone: 472-1220.

3. **PUBLIC ACCESS** — gravel boat ramp (closed June 1 to September 1); restrooms; shore fishing.

Painter Creek

JENNING'S BAY

110

HARRISON BAY

FOREST LAKE

19

151

Skogsberg's Point

Woodland Point

Shadywood Point

saddle

WEST ARM BAY

151

MOUND

15

bar

NORTH ARM BAY

EMERALD LAKE

Derring Isl

Fagerness Point

SETON LAKE

Coffee Bridge

COOK'S BAY

125

CRYSTAL BAY

BLACK LAKE

SPRING PARK BAY

15

19

SPRING PARK

Shore fishing

Rocks

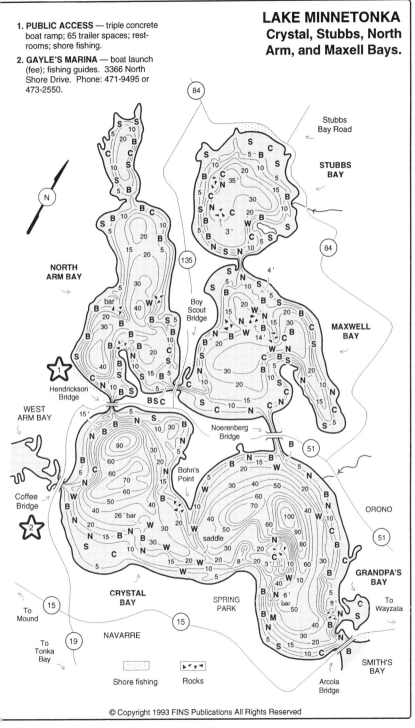

LAKE MINNETONKA
Crystal, Stubbs, North Arm, and Maxell Bays.

1. **PUBLIC ACCESS** — triple concrete boat ramp; 65 trailer spaces; restrooms; shore fishing.
2. **GAYLE'S MARINA** — boat launch (fee); fishing guides. 3366 North Shore Drive. Phone: 471-9495 or 473-2550.

Stubbs Bay Road

STUBBS BAY

NORTH ARM BAY

Boy Scout Bridge

MAXWELL BAY

bar

Hendrickson Bridge

WEST ARM BAY

Coffee Bridge

Noerenberg Bridge

Bohn's Point

26' bar

saddle

ORONO

CRYSTAL BAY

SPRING PARK

GRANDPA'S BAY

To Wayzata

To Mound

NAVARRE

To Tonka Bay

Shore fishing   Rocks

SMITH'S BAY

Arcola Bridge

Walleyes and muskies are getting most of the attention on these south Minneapolis lakes. Walleyes have been stocked in Nokomis every other year since 1979, and some are now over 9-1/2 pounds. Hybrid tiger muskies were added in 1984 and will be restocked every third year. They're growing larger: a 32-pound muskie was caught in 1991.

You can also find an occasional walleye in Hiawatha. Nokomis has the largest northerns, but Hiawatha has a better supply. There is no boat launch on Hiawatha. You can canoe up the Minnehaha Creek from Nokomis, but you must portage around the dam.

SPECIES	POPULATION	AVERAGE SIZE
Bass	Poor	Small to Medium
Northern Pike	Fair to Good	Small to Medium
Muskie	Fair	Medium
Walleye	Fair to Good	Small to Medium
Crappie	Good	Small to Medium
Sunfish	Good	Small to Medium

BASS   In the early season, your best bet is to cast a white spinnerbait around the shoreline of the lagoon on the far southwest corner. Also check out the south end of the bridge and the new weeds on the entire east side of Nokomis. On Hiawatha, look for the healthy weeds in front of the inlets and outlets.

NORTHERN PIKE & MUSKIE   For early-season northerns, fish both sides of the south end of the Cedar Avenue bridge. The drop-offs around the 29-foot hole are productive through mid-summer. The running water in front of the dam on the northwest corner attracts summer northerns. The north end is good in the summer and fall. In the winter, try the 12 to 18 foot depth on the bar on the southeast side of the lake. On Hiawatha, work from the inlet in front of the dam around to the outlet. Also fish the weedy areas on the north side of the lake. Look for muskies on the west side of Nokomis from the Cedar Avenue bridge up to the beach.

WALLEYE   A good early-season location is the bar on the southeast side of the lake. Stay in 15 to 29 feet. In the summer, start on the south side of the point (bar) between 53rd and 54th Streets and work down and around to the lagoon. The area under the Cedar Avenue Bridge is an all-season hotspot, especially on the east side of the bridge. The center pillars are best. Use a jig with a slip-bobber and leech. In the fall, work from the dock on the north end down to 51st Street on the east side. Cast a jointed injured-minnow lure over the top of the weeds. This is a good night spot. In the winter, work around the 30 and 29 foot holes.

CRAPPIE & SUNFISH   The lagoon and the north end of the bridge are the early-season crappie hotspots. In the summer and fall, the docks are the best locations. In the spring, the lagoon and the shoreline north of the bridge are good sunfish spots. Summer sunfish can be found scattered in weedy areas all over the lake. On Hiawatha, look for spring and fall crappies on the north end of the lake. Sunfish are scarce on Hiawatha; you'll find them in the weedy areas.

Information about these lakes was provided by Pat Buchanan, Kirk Larson, Chris Sager, and Jim Sivers, Jr.

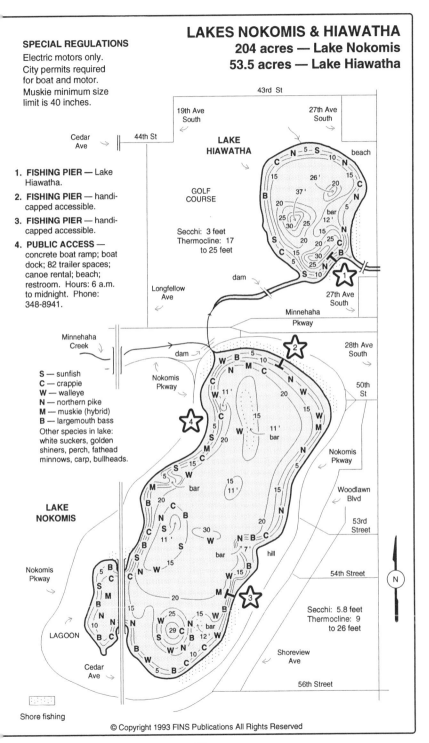

LAKES NOKOMIS & HIAWATHA
204 acres — Lake Nokomis
53.5 acres — Lake Hiawatha

SPECIAL REGULATIONS

Electric motors only.
City permits required
for boat and motor.
Muskie minimum size
limit is 40 inches.

43rd St

19th Ave South

27th Ave South

Cedar Ave

44th St

LAKE HIAWATHA

beach

GOLF COURSE

1. **FISHING PIER** — Lake Hiawatha.
2. **FISHING PIER** — handicapped accessible.
3. **FISHING PIER** — handicapped accessible.
4. **PUBLIC ACCESS** — concrete boat ramp; boat dock; 82 trailer spaces; canoe rental; beach; restroom. Hours: 6 a.m. to midnight. Phone: 348-8941.

Secchi: 3 feet
Thermocline: 17 to 25 feet

dam

Longfellow Ave

27th Ave South

Minnehaha Pkway

Minnehaha Creek

dam

28th Ave South

50th St

Nokomis Pkway

S — sunfish
C — crappie
W — walleye
N — northern pike
M — muskie (hybrid)
B — largemouth bass
Other species in lake: white suckers, golden shiners, perch, fathead minnows, carp, bullheads.

Nokomis Pkway

Woodlawn Blvd

LAKE NOKOMIS

53rd Street

54th Street

Nokomis Pkway

N

LAGOON

Secchi: 5.8 feet
Thermocline: 9 to 26 feet

Cedar Ave

Shoreview Ave

56th Street

Shore fishing

93

Lake Rebecca, located in the Hennepin County Park near Rockford, is a success story. A severe winterkill in 1979 wiped out the entire gamefish population. An aerator was installed, and the lake was restocked with bass, sunfish, and catfish. Today Lake Rebecca has some of the biggest bass, sunfish, and muskies in the metro area. Walleyes have been stocked intermittently since 1979, and muskies were added in 1982. Some are now over 25 pounds, and their eggs will provide future stock for other metro lakes.

SPECIES	POPULATION	AVERAGE SIZE
Bass	Excellent	Medium to Large
Walleye	Fair to Good	Medium
Muskie	Good	Small to Medium
Crappie	Excellent	Small to Medium
Sunfish	Excellent	Small to Medium
Catfish	Fair	Medium to Large

BASS   Look for June bass at the south end of the lake and the northeast corner. Use a small (1/32 or 1/16 oz.) purple beatle-spin type lure and cast to the weedy pockets in 5 to 6 feet of water. The lily pads on the south end can provide action from spring to early fall. Work the outside edges, pockets, and indentations with a brown or orange jig and black pig. In late spring, the lake gets extremely weedy with mats on the surface. Fish the weedline with a plastic worm or a jig and minnow. The sunken islands and humps are good summer locations.

WALLEYE   Early season walleyes will be on the mid-eastern side of the lake. Use a live-bait rig and backtroll slowly in 15 to 17 feet of water. In the summer and fall, stay in the same area and work deeper from 17 to 20 feet. When you find the fish, switch to a slip-bobber rig with a leech. Don't pass up the small underwater point in front of the inlet. Fish the point (bar) and the inside turns. Winter walleyes will be on the sunken islands in 12 feet of water.

MUSKIE   Look for muskies in the weedy areas on the sunken islands and around the lower half of the lake. Start at the middle of the west side and work around the south end of the lake and up the southeast shoreline. Use bucktail spinners, and jerkbaits.

CRAPPIE   The southeast corner of the lake and the eastern shoreline are the best spring locations. Fish the weedy pockets in 5 to 6 feet of water. From summer until fall turnover, move out to the deeper holes and use a slip-bobber rig with a crappie minnow or small leech. The crappies will be suspended 15 to 20 feet below the surface. The same areas will be productive in the winter. A glow-in-the-dark ice fly is a winner. The best time is from 4 to 8 p.m.

SUNFISH   The spring hotspots are the small pond; the channel; and the fishing piers on the northwest corner of the lake. In June and July, the sunfish move to the north and east sides of the lake to spawn. Concentrate on the inside edge of the weeds. In the summer, you'll find the larger sunfish in the weeds on the sunken islands, especially on the east side. In the winter, try the 5 to 8 foot depths on the northeast corner of the lake.

Information about this lake was provided by Dave Genz, Bob Gibson, Duane Shodeen, and Tim Sonnenstahl.

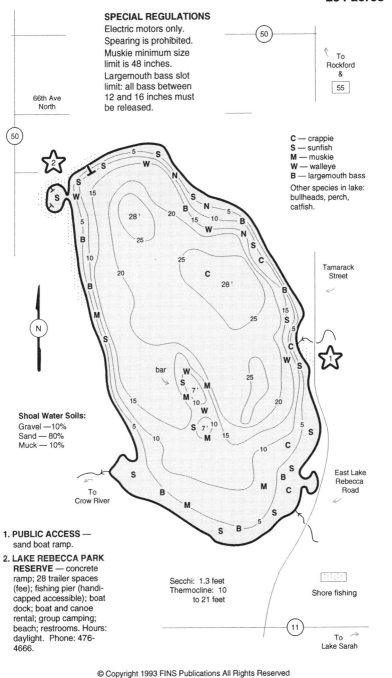

LAKE REBECCA
254 acres

SPECIAL REGULATIONS
Electric motors only.
Spearing is prohibited.
Muskie minimum size
limit is 48 inches.
Largemouth bass slot
limit: all bass between
12 and 16 inches must
be released.

50

↑ To
Rockford
&
55

66th Ave
North

50

C — crappie
S — sunfish
M — muskie
W — walleye
B — largemouth bass

Other species in lake:
bullheads, perch,
catfish.

2

S
S
W
N
S
15
W
B
5
28'
B
5
25
20
10
B
15
20
25
N
W
B
C
N
S
C
B
15
5
C

Tamarack
Street

C
28'
25

bar
W
S
M
7'
M
M
10
W
25
B
15
5
C
W
S

1

N

Shoal Water Soils:
Gravel —10%
Sand — 80%
Muck — 10%

15
5
S
10
W
7'
10
S
M
15
20

5
S

C
10
S

East Lake
Rebecca
Road

To
Crow River

S
B
M
M
B
5
S
S
B
5
M
C

1. **PUBLIC ACCESS —**
   sand boat ramp.

2. **LAKE REBECCA PARK
   RESERVE** — concrete
   ramp; 28 trailer spaces
   (fee); fishing pier (handicapped accessible); boat
   dock; boat and canoe
   rental; group camping;
   beach; restrooms. Hours:
   daylight. Phone: 476-
   4666.

Secchi: 1.3 feet
Thermocline: 10
to 21 feet

Shore fishing

11

To
Lake Sarah

Riley is one of those lakes with high recreational use. But if you can concentrate on the off hours, you'll be a happy angler. This lake has lots of big bass, plenty of northern pike, and an unlimited supply of sunfish and crappies. Riley is located on the Carver-Hennepin County line a half mile northwest of County Road 1 on Riley Lake Road.

The shape of this lake makes it ideal for trolling. There is little underwater structure; just follow the edge of the weeds around the lake and you're bound to find bass or northerns. A good supply of overhanging brush and trees provide shoreline cover in years when the water level is normal.

SPECIES	POPULATION	AVERAGE SIZE
Bass	Good	Medium
Northern	Good	Small to Medium
Crappie	Very Good	Medium
Sunfish	Good	Small to Medium

BASS   The shallow back bays are the key early-season locations. Look for overhanging brush or fallen trees. Use a 4-inch plastic worm or a white spinner-bait. You'll also find bass in the middle of the southern shoreline; on the south side of the southwestern bay; on the bar on the west side; and on the round, weedy, land point at the north side of the lake. This point is a good all-season location. The rocks, the docks, and the fallen trees on the west side of the round land point will produce in the summer. These are good flipping areas. Also try a jig and pig in the open areas outside the weed patches. Don't pass up the docks on the southeast corner of the lake or the sand point (bar) on the west side. Some anglers do well in mid-summer by trolling the weedline around the lake with bottom-bumping lures. In the fall, the docks may still produce. Also try the weedline near the fallen trees on the west side of the round land point.

NORTHERN PIKE   You'll find a supply of spring and summer northerns in front of the inlet on the northeast corner. Also try the south side from the old boat launch west about 1/4 mile to the first house. Start at the breaks (drop-offs) in 12 to 18 feet of water and work up to the shallows. Trollers do well here too. Stay on the weedline at the 10-foot depths. Use a chartreuse or orange shallow running crankbait, a white spinnerbait, or a sucker minnow. The round land point on the north side is a good all-season location. There is a fast drop-off here that also attracts northerns in the winter. Stay in 12 to 15 feet of water and use a sucker or shiner minnow.

CRAPPIE & SUNFISH   For spring crappies, fish the southwestern bay, especially the shady areas by the fallen trees and brush. This is a popular fly fishing location. Also try the northeast and southeast corners of the lake. In the summer you'll find the crappies suspended over deep water. For a good supply of spring and summer sunfish, work the bays, the area in front of the inlet on the northeast corner of the lake, the west side of the round land point, and the bar on the west side of the lake. Use ice flies or wax worms in 3 to 6 feet of water.

Information about this lake was provided by Randy Barkley, John Dunlap, Terry Hennor and Gary Lake.

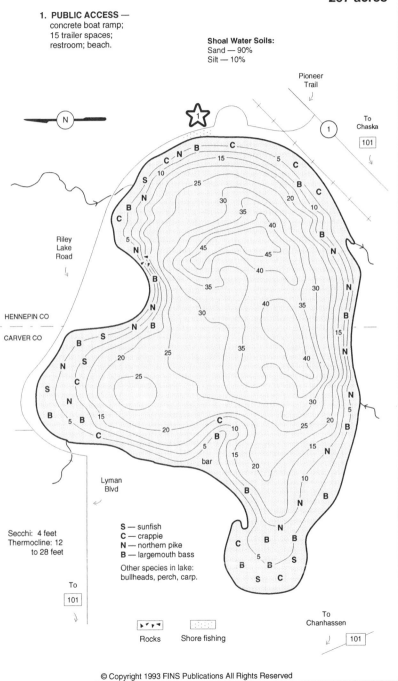

RILEY LAKE
297 acres

1. **PUBLIC ACCESS** — concrete boat ramp; 15 trailer spaces; restroom; beach.

Shoal Water Soils:
Sand — 90%
Silt — 10%

Pioneer Trail

To Chaska

101

N

Riley Lake Road

HENNEPIN CO

CARVER CO

Lyman Blvd

Secchi: 4 feet
Thermocline: 12 to 28 feet

To 101

S — sunfish
C — crappie
N — northern pike
B — largemouth bass

Other species in lake: bullheads, perch, carp.

bar

To Chanhassen

101

Rocks   Shore fishing

Lake Sarah, located near the western border of Hennepin County, is known as one of the better multi-species lakes in the Twin Cities. It has an above average supply of all species including perch and bullheads. Sarah is a long, narrow lake with a hard sand bottom and lots of structure — rocky reefs, sunken islands, steep drop-offs, and shoreline points.

SPECIES	POPULATION	AVERAGE SIZE
Bass	Good	Medium to Large
Northern Pike	Excellent	Medium to Large
Crappie	Excellent	Small
Sunfish	Excellent	Very Small

BASS Look for early-season bass in 2 to 4 feet of water in the emerging vegetation on both ends of the lake. Use a black, chartreuse, or white spinnerbait or a red and white stickbait. In the summer (about the first of July), the most productive time will be at night. Cast a black spinnerbait to the edge of the bulrushes in 2 to 4 feet of water. Start at Dance Hall Creek on the north side of the lake, and work west to Access Point. During the day, fish the weedline in the same area. Sunset Point is a good fall area. Start at the point, and work southeast around the inside turn. This area also produces in the fall. Seek out the remaining healthy weeds in 8 to 10 feet of water. Try a crankbait here. In late fall, cover the 3 to 10 foot depths with a spinnerbait or jig and pig.

NORTHERN PIKE You'll find early-season northerns on the large weedy flats in 2 to 8 feet of water on both ends of the lake. Try a fluorescent red floating-minnow lure on overcast days. In summer, troll the outside weedline at the 10-foot depths off Woodhill Point, Woodlawn Point, Deep Point, and the rock and sand bar off Stony Point. Use a red and white spoon. Deep Point and Beach Point are good fall locations. Stay in 10 to 15 feet. In winter, you'll find northerns in the same areas as the crappies.

CRAPPIE The boat canal above Sunset Point is a good ice-out location. Spring hotspots are the north side of the narrows and the 5 to 10 foot depths in front of the old boat launch off Hwy. 55. Summer crappies will be suspended above the thermocline (at 11 feet) in 15 to 40 feet of water. The best locations are the rocky bar southeast of Stony Point and the inside turn between Woodlawn Point and the boat canal. Troll with an electric motor and a small spinner or similar lure that runs 3 feet below the surface and you'll tic the top of the school. When you catch one, turn off the motor, toss out a marker, and fish the school. In early fall, move up to the 2 to 10 foot depths and then down to the 10 to 15 foot depths in late fall. The west side of the 62-foot hole in the east section of the lake is another good fall spot. It also shines in the winter. Work the 20 to 35 foot depths.

SUNFISH Spring sunfish will be in the heavy vegetation in 2 to 4 feet of water in the bass spots. The area in front of Dance Hall Creek is especially good. Work the same areas in the summer, but move out to the deeper weedline in 10 to 11 feet of water. In early fall, they'll be spread out in 2 to 10 feet of water in the same locations. Move to the 10 to 12 foot depths in late fall. In the winter, stay at the 10 to 15 foot depths in the same locations.

This information was provided by Steve Carney, John Daily, and Ted Welch.

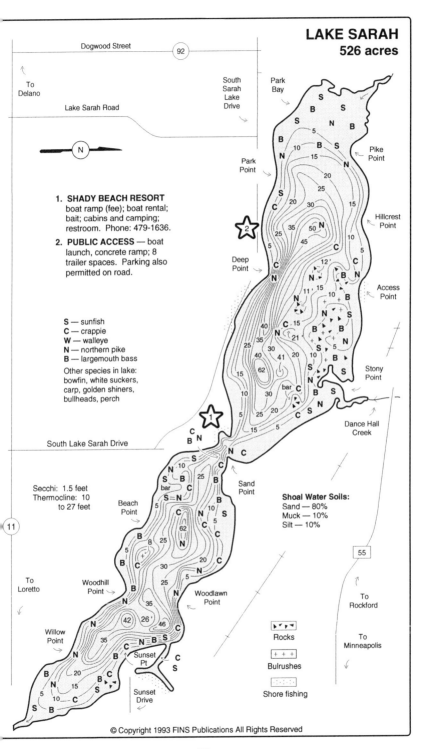

LAKE SARAH
526 acres

Dogwood Street — 92

To Delano

Lake Sarah Road

South Sarah Lake Drive

Park Bay

Park Point

Pike Point

Hillcrest Point

Deep Point

Access Point

Stony Point

Dance Hall Creek

1. **SHADY BEACH RESORT**
   boat ramp (fee); boat rental; bait; cabins and camping; restroom. Phone: 479-1636.

2. **PUBLIC ACCESS** — boat launch, concrete ramp; 8 trailer spaces. Parking also permitted on road.

S — sunfish
C — crappie
W — walleye
N — northern pike
B — largemouth bass

Other species in lake: bowfin, white suckers, carp, golden shiners, bullheads, perch

South Lake Sarah Drive

Secchi: 1.5 feet
Thermocline: 10 to 27 feet

11

To Loretto

Beach Point

Woodhill Point

Willow Point

Sunset Pt

Sunset Drive

Sand Point

Woodlawn Point

Shoal Water Soils:
Sand — 80%
Muck — 10%
Silt — 10%

55

To Rockford

To Minneapolis

Rocks

Bulrushes

Shore fishing

Twin Lakes is a series of three lakes spread over the communities of Robbins-dale, Brooklyn Center, and Crystal. DNR records indicate a high population of bass, northern pike, sunfish, bluegills, crappie, perch, carp, and bullheads. Many of the most productive locations are accessible from shore.

The upper and lower lakes are subject to frequent winterkill, and in the winter of 1988/89 both lakes sustained serious fish losses. The deeper middle lake eventually replenishes the other two lakes. The upper lake will take longer to recoup because only a long shallow channel connects it to the middle lake. The channel to the lower lake is dredged periodically. For a few years after a winterkill, you can expect the remaining panfish to double in size because there are fewer fish competing for the available food.

SPECIES	POPULATION	AVERAGE SIZE
Bass	Good	Medium
Northern Pike	Excellent	Small to Medium
Crappie	Good	Small to Medium
Sunfish	Good	Small to Medium

BASS   In early June, look for bass in the lily pads and weedy slop at the far north end of the upper lake. Toss a spinnerbait, buzzbait, or topwater lure in the pockets or edges. Also cast to the visible weeds on the long 7-foot flat on the west side of the upper lake. The middle lake holds the best supply and is considered to be a sleeper. The best action is on the north end in the shallow weeds. Also look for bass in the channel between the lower and middle lakes.

NORTHERN PIKE   Look for early-season northerns in the bass locations. The north end of the middle lake is a hotspot. A good all-season location is the middle of the western shoreline on the middle lake. Try trolling here with a small spoonplug on the edge of the weeds in 12 feet of water. There is a good inside turn off the bar on the northeast corner of the lower lake. You can cast to this spot from shore.

CRAPPIE & SUNFISH   The lily pads and weedy slop on the north end of the upper lake is the first area to produce a good supply of sunfish and crappies. It continues to produce throughout the year. This lake also yields the largest sunfish of the three lakes. On the lower lake, you'll find some good spring action in the long arm on the east side and the shallow south end. There are some sunfish spawning beds on the lower west side of the middle lake. As the water warms, move deeper. The inside turn of the bar on the lower lake (just east of the channel) holds a good summer population of sunfish and crappies. You can reach it from shore. Spring and winter anglers also do well on the north end of the middle lake. In the winter, you'll find the sunfish here in 5 to 12 feet of water off the break, and the crappies will be suspended 6 to 8 feet below the ice in 12 to 28 feet of water.

This information was provided by Dave Genz, Art Perry, and Tom Zenanko.

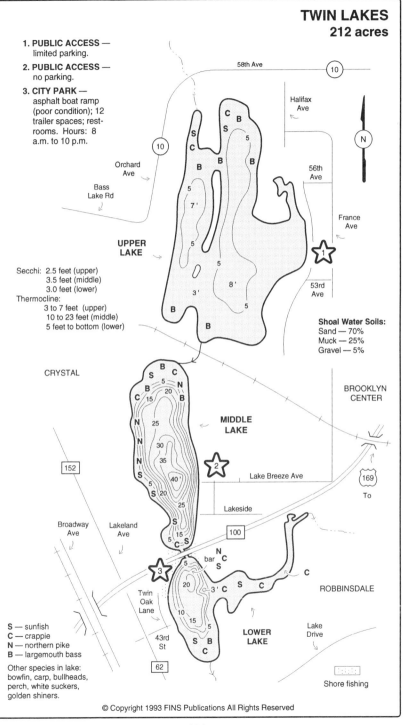

TWIN LAKES
212 acres

1. **PUBLIC ACCESS** — limited parking.
2. **PUBLIC ACCESS** — no parking.
3. **CITY PARK** — asphalt boat ramp (poor condition); 12 trailer spaces; restrooms. Hours: 8 a.m. to 10 p.m.

58th Ave
10

Halifax Ave

10

Orchard Ave

Bass Lake Rd

N

56th Ave

France Ave

UPPER LAKE

53rd Ave

1

Secchi: 2.5 feet (upper)
3.5 feet (middle)
3.0 feet (lower)
Thermocline:
3 to 7 feet (upper)
10 to 23 feet (middle)
5 feet to bottom (lower)

Shoal Water Soils:
Sand — 70%
Muck — 25%
Gravel — 5%

CRYSTAL

BROOKLYN CENTER

MIDDLE LAKE

152

Lake Breeze Ave

169
To

Lakeside

Broadway Ave

Lakeland Ave

100

bar

3

Twin Oak Lane

ROBBINSDALE

C

Lake Drive

LOWER LAKE

43rd St

62

S — sunfish
C — crappie
N — northern pike
B — largemouth bass

Other species in lake: bowfin, carp, bullheads, perch, white suckers, golden shiners.

Shore fishing

101

BALD EAGLE LAKE   Ramsey County

Bald Eagle is the best lake for trophy muskies in the metro area. Huge numbers of the fast growing Wisconsin strain have been stocked since 1981, and some are now over 50 inches. Bald Eagle is also a popular bass tournament lake, and walleyes have been stocked annually since 1977. The DNR calls this a sleeper lake for future supplies of walleyes.

SPECIES	POPULATION	AVERAGE SIZE
Bass	Good	Medium to Large
Northern Pike	Fair	Small
Muskie	Excellent	Medium to Large
Walleye	Fair	Medium
Crappie	Good	Medium
Sunfish	Good	Small to Medium

BASS In early June, work the emerging weeds in the upper third of the lake. In mid-June, move down to the thick beds of coontail weeds and bulrushes. The bulrush bed on Rocky Ridge is a good summer location. Flip a jig and pig to the inside (shallow) and outside edges. Also try the docks on the southeast, south, and southwest shorelines. Fish the thick weedy edges on the long curved sunken island (bar) at the south end of the lake from mid-summer until fall. About 2 weeks before fall turnover, look for bass on the inside turns of the points.

NORTHERN PIKE & MUSKIES Muskies will be on the far north end of the lake when the water warms up to 65 degrees, usually about July 4th. Work the edges of the alleys in the weeds, and the edges of the bulrushes on the east side of the lake. In the summer, fish the edges of the new weed growth in front of the bulrushes. Concentrate on the expansive weedy flats that break into a point. In August, try the docks from the public boat launch down to the southwest corner. During low-light periods, move out from the docks and work the weedy shallows. As the water cools in the fall, the muskies move back to the outside edge of the weeds. When the weeds die off, work the breaks, points, and rocks. On the southeast shoreline, the inside turn of the 3-foot bar is productive. Also try the deep breaks on the inside turns of the long curved sunken island (bar) below Cigar Island. As fall continues, work shallower as the vegetation permits. Look for northerns in the muskie and bass locations.

WALLEYE Look for spring walleyes around the land point above Otter Creek and on Rocky Ridge (Benson's Point). Summer walleyes will be on the hard-bottom areas in 10 to 14 feet of water below Cigar Island; in front of the regional park; and on Rocky Ridge. In the winter, go down to the 14 to 20 foot depths in the same areas. Be careful of weak ice around Rocky Ridge.

CRAPPIE & SUNFISH The northern tip of the lake is the best location for spring crappies and sunfish. You'll also find spring crappies on the southwest side of Cigar Island. In the summer, the crappies scatter and can be hard to find. Summer sunfish are in the bass locations. In fall, the big sunnies can be found in front of the swimming beach next to the boat launch. The upper third of the lake is a good early-ice location for sunfish and crappies. Look for winter crappies on the lower tip of Cigar Island and on the northwest and southwest shorelines.

This information was provided by Dale Glader, Bob Mehsikomer, and Brad Stanius.

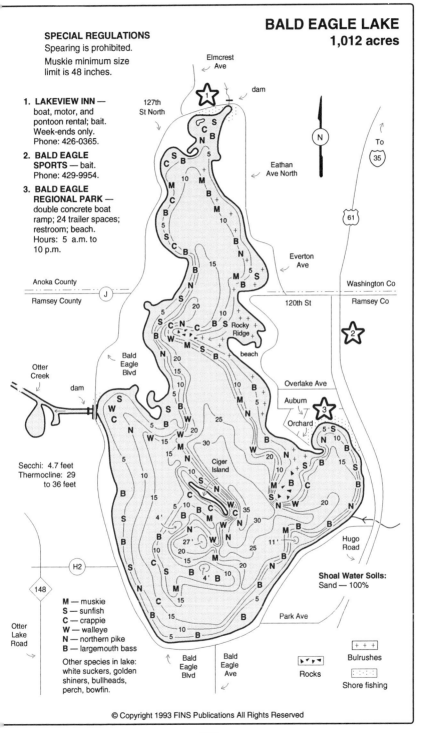

BALD EAGLE LAKE
1,012 acres

SPECIAL REGULATIONS
Spearing is prohibited.
Muskie minimum size
limit is 48 inches.

1. **LAKEVIEW INN** —
   boat, motor, and
   pontoon rental; bait.
   Week-ends only.
   Phone: 426-0365.
2. **BALD EAGLE
   SPORTS** — bait.
   Phone: 429-9954.
3. **BALD EAGLE
   REGIONAL PARK** —
   double concrete boat
   ramp; 24 trailer spaces;
   restroom; beach.
   Hours: 5 a.m. to
   10 p.m.

Anoka County

Ramsey County

Otter
Creek

Secchi: 4.7 feet
Thermocline: 29
to 36 feet

Elmcrest
Ave

dam

127th
St North

Eathan
Ave North

Everton
Ave

Washington Co

Ramsey Co

120th St

Rocky
Ridge

beach

Overlake Ave

Auburn

Orchard

Bald
Eagle
Blvd

dam

Ciger
Island

Hugo
Road

Shoal Water Soils:
Sand — 100%

Park Ave

H2

148

Otter
Lake
Road

M — muskie
S — sunfish
C — crappie
W — walleye
N — northern pike
B — largemouth bass

Other species in lake:
white suckers, golden
shiners, bullheads,
perch, bowfin.

Bald
Eagle
Blvd

Bald
Eagle
Ave

+ + +   Bulrushes

Rocks

Shore fishing

To 35

61

GERVAIS, KOHLMAN, & KELLER LAKES   Ramsey County

Gervais Lake in Little Canada is part of a chain that includes Phalen, Round, Keller, Spoon, and Kohlman Lakes. Keller, Gervais, and the channels between the lakes warm up very fast and provide some excellent early-season shore fishing.

Pure strain muskies were stocked in 1984, and hybrid tiger muskies have been added to Gervais Lake in most years since 1984. You'll also find a fair supply of walleyes that have migrated up from Phalen Lake. Look for them on the gravel patches or in the weeds with the bass.

Silt and nutrients from urban runoff have made the water very dark and murky, which can be an advantage to the angler because the fish spend more time in the shallows where they're easier to catch. Use lures that are brightly colored and noisy — something that vibrates, rattles, or churns up the water with lots of action.

SPECIES	POPULATION	AVERAGE SIZE
Bass	Very Good	Medium to Large
Northern Pike	Poor to Fair	Medium
Muskie	Fair to Good	Medium
Walleye	Poor to Fair	Small to Medium
Crappie	Good	Small to Medium
Sunfish	Excellent	Small to Medium

BASS   For early season bass, troll or cast to the weedy edges around Lake Gervais, especially on the lower eastern shoreline. Kohlman Lake provides action until mid-June. Look for the 9-foot hole near the northwest shoreline. On Keller, fish the fallen timber and overhanging willows along the shore. You'll find summer bass under the docks and around the bars and weedy areas on the east and west sides of Gervais. Docks should be fished slowly and with great finesse. Flip, pitch, or skip a slow-falling plastic worm or night crawler to the shadiest side. The lower east and lower west shorelines produce in the morning before the boat traffic gets heavy. In the fall, the best areas are the lower east shore and the south side of the large bar on the east side of the lake.

NORTHERN PIKE & MUSKIE   In the spring, look for northerns at the mouth of the creeks. For summer action, work the large bar, especially the inside turn on the north side of the bar. Also try trolling the weed edges in 8 to 10 feet of water on the lower west side of the lake above the swimming beach. In the fall, the lower eastern shoreline and the south side of the large bar are good locations. You'll find winter northerns on the lower eastern shoreline in 10 to 15 feet of water. Muskies will be on the bars on the north and east sides of the lake.

CRAPPIE & SUNFISH   Kohlman, Keller, and Spoon Lakes hold a nice supply of spring crappies and sunfish. At the northeast corner of Gervais by the channel to Kohlman Lake, try wading the shoreline and casting to the 4 to 6 foot depths. A reliable all-season crappie spot is the area on the east side of Gervais near the intersection of County Road C and Keller Parkway. When stable weather conditions prevail, look for crappies in 2 to 3 feet of water. Otherwise, work down to 10 feet. In the summer and fall, the sunfish will be in the weedy bass areas.

Information about this lake was provided by Dale Glader and Jim Hardman.

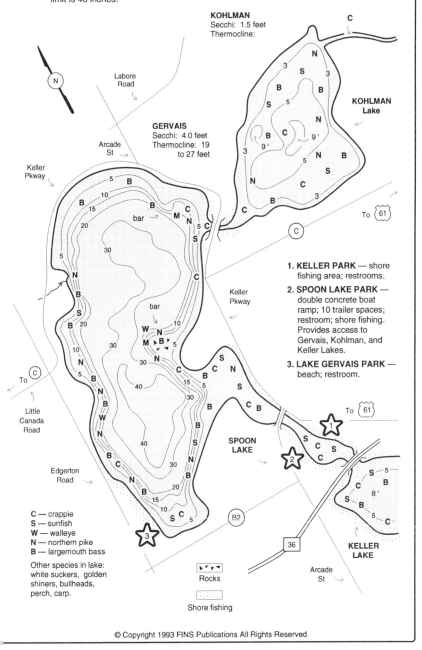

GERVAIS & KOHLMAN LAKES
234 acres — Gervais Lake
74 acres — Kohlman Lake

SPECIAL REGULATIONS
Muskie minimum size
limit is 40 inches.

KOHLMAN
Secchi: 1.5 feet
Thermocline:

KOHLMAN
Lake

Labore
Road

GERVAIS
Secchi: 4.0 feet
Thermocline: 19
to 27 feet

Arcade
St

Keller
Pkway

bar

To 61

Keller
Pkway

bar

To C

Little
Canada
Road

Edgerton
Road

1. **KELLER PARK** — shore
fishing area; restrooms.
2. **SPOON LAKE PARK** —
double concrete boat
ramp; 10 trailer spaces;
restroom; shore fishing.
Provides access to
Gervais, Kohlman, and
Keller Lakes.
3. **LAKE GERVAIS PARK** —
beach; restroom.

To 61

SPOON
LAKE

KELLER
LAKE

C — crappie
S — sunfish
W — walleye
N — northern pike
B — largemouth bass

Other species in lake:
white suckers, golden
shiners, bullheads,
perch, carp.

Rocks

Shore fishing

Arcade
St

36

B2

LAKE JOHANNA
Ramsey County

Lake Johanna, located on the southern edge of the community of Arden Hills, offers a variety of fishing cover and structure. Bass and panfish are the major attraction. The stocking of hybrid tiger muskies was started in 1984, and the lake is restocked every 3 years. Some of the muskies are now over 40 inches. A one-time stocking of walleyes occurred in 1986.

SPECIES	POPULATION	AVERAGE SIZE
Bass	Very Good	Small to Medium
Northern Pike	Fair	Medium
Muskie	Fair	Medium to Large
Walleye	Fair	Medium
Crappie	Very Good	Small to Medium
Sunfish	Excellent	Small

BASS   June bass will be in the 2 bays in the northeast corner of the lake. Use a spinnerbait with a white or yellow skirt, and cast it over the tops of the weeds. Try flipping the docks with a plastic worm or pig and jig in the early morning. In the summer, move out to the weedy breaklines. The weedy sunken island in the middle of the lake is a key summer and fall location. Cast a plastic worm to the weedy edges, especially the west side. Other good summer and early fall locations are the sunken island in the middle of the west side of the lake and the shoreline breaks on the lower east side. Also work the edges and pockets of the lily pads on the east side of the island. A weedless silver minnow, jig and pig, or white spinnerbait are effective here. After fall turnover, stay on the deep weedy edges. The rock pile east of the public boat access, the lily pads, and the steep breaks on the middle of the east side of the lake are good late fall producers.

NORTHERN PIKE & MUSKIE   You'll find northerns anywhere on the weedlines throughout the season. Use a white spinnerbait. The 3-foot sunken island and the edge of the lily pads around the land island are also good summer locations. The east side of the island produces larger fish. A 22-pound northern was caught here in 1990. Muskies are here too, but they're not active until July. After fall turnover, move to the weedy, steep, inside corners on the northeast and south-east corners of the lake and on the middle of the east side. Work the shoreline down to the weedline. An orange bucktail lure with an orange blade is a winner at this time of the year. In the winter, northerns will be around the 20 to 30 foot depths in front of the peninsula.

WALLEYE   The key location is the gravel area in front of the peninsula on the northeast corner of the lake. In the fall, work the rocky area east of the beach. In the winter, try the 32-foot hole in front of the peninsula.

CRAPPIE & SUNFISH   The shallow bays on the upper east side and the northeastern corner are popular early-season sunfish and crappie locations. As the water warms, crappies can be found in 4 to 5 feet of water on the west side of the lake. They'll move out to the weedline during the summer months. The 32-foot hole in front of the peninsula is a winter hotspot. Sunfish can be found in the weedy bass locations.

This information was provided by Dave Genz, Dale Glader, Ken Matheson, and Greg Thorne.

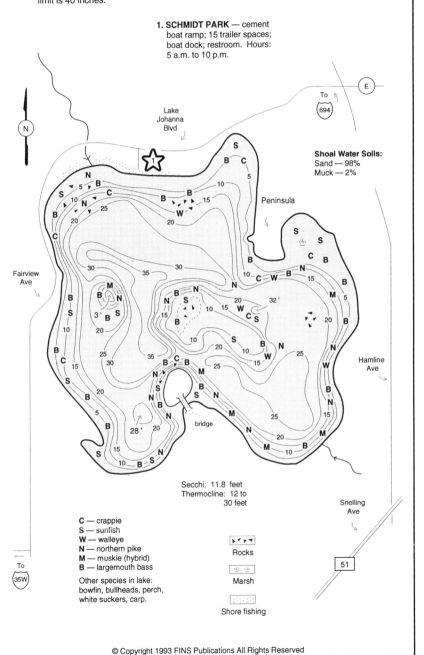

LAKE JOHANNA
200 acres

SPECIAL REGULATIONS
Muskie minimum size
limit is 40 inches.

1. SCHMIDT PARK — cement
boat ramp; 15 trailer spaces;
boat dock; restroom. Hours:
5 a.m. to 10 p.m.

To
694

N

Lake
Johanna
Blvd

Shoal Water Soils:
Sand — 98%
Muck — 2%

Peninsula

Fairview
Ave

Hamline
Ave

bridge

Snelling
Ave

51

To
35W

Secchi: 11.8 feet
Thermocline: 12 to
30 feet

C — crappie
S — sunfish
W — walleye
N — northern pike
M — muskie (hybrid)
B — largemouth bass

Other species in lake:
bowfin, bullheads, perch,
white suckers, carp.

Rocks

Marsh

Shore fishing

LONG LAKE   Ramsey County

This is the lake that produced a 29-pound northern pike a few years ago, and according to local gossip, at least one 20-pounder is hauled in every season. Walleye fry are stocked annually, and hybrid tiger muskies have been added every 3 years since 1984. Huge numbers of carp in this lake have rooted up most of the vegetation, so you will have to concentrate on the visual structure and breaks. A new boat launch and a new regional park are added attractions.

SPECIES	POPULATION	AVERAGE SIZE
Bass	Poor to Fair	Small to Large
Northern Pike	Good	Small to Large
Muskie	Fair	Small
Walleye	Fair to Good	Medium to Large
Crappie	Fair to Good	Small to Medium
Sunfish	Poor	Large

BASS   The west side of the main lake will produce an occasional bass. Work the docks, boats, and drop-offs.

NORTHERN PIKE & MUSKIE   Early-season northerns will be on the south end of the lake, especially around the inlet on the southeast corner. Also try Rice Creek up to the railroad bridge. In early summer before the thermocline forms, try trolling the 15 to 25 foot depths of both lake basins with bottom-bumping lures or a live-bait rig with a fathead minnow. The same method with a live-bait rig also works from mid-September to first ice. In the fall, try the flats and the inlet on the south end of the lake. Cast a medium-sized sucker minnow to the shallows, and work down to the 10-foot depths. In the winter, go back to the inlet on the southeast corner. Be cautious here — the moving water weakens the ice. Also try the bar (underwater point) on the lower west side of the lake. For larger fish, use smelt on a quick-strike rig.

WALLEYE   Look for early-season walleyes around the railroad bridge in Rice Creek or the first land point below the Rice Creek inlet on the east side of the upper lake. A jig and minnow is a good technique in the spring and summer. In early summer and after the fall turnover, troll the 15 to 25 foot depths in both basins with a live-bait rig and fathead minnow. The south end of the lower lake is also prime territory in the fall. Give special attention to the "mud line" here where the sand and mud converge. Also work the area around the inlet on the southeast corner. Use a jig and a medium-sized sucker minnow, or try trolling with floating crankbaits. The fast break on the long point on the lower east side is also a good late fall or early-ice location. For winter fishing, try the point below Rice Creek and the south end of the lower lake.

CRAPPIE & SUNFISH   You'll find spring crappies in the warmer water in front of the Pike Creek inlet and throughout the channel in Rice Creek. In the summer, they'll be suspended on the points, and you'll find them adjacent to the points in the fall. For winter crappies, fish the 26-foot hole below the Pike Lake Creek inlet in the middle of the west side of the lake. A few sunfish may be found near the docks and pontoons on the west side of the lower lake.

Information about this lake was provided by Ken Matheson and Greg Thorne.

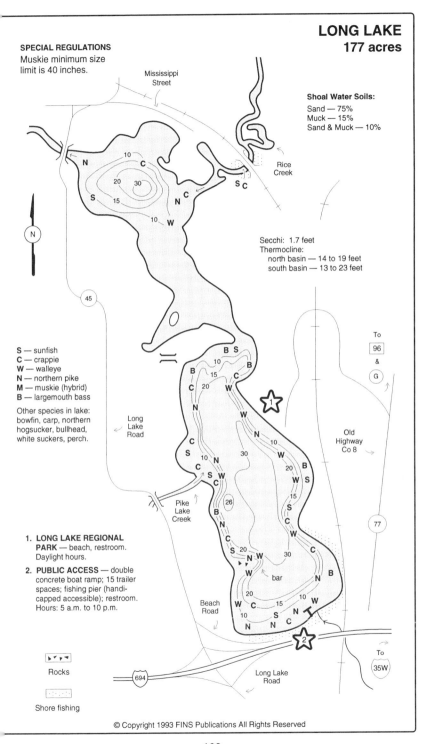

LONG LAKE
177 acres

SPECIAL REGULATIONS
Muskie minimum size
limit is 40 inches.

Mississippi
Street

Shoal Water Soils:
Sand — 75%
Muck — 15%
Sand & Muck — 10%

Rice
Creek

N

Secchi: 1.7 feet
Thermocline:
   north basin — 14 to 19 feet
   south basin — 13 to 23 feet

45

S — sunfish
C — crappie
W — walleye
N — northern pike
M — muskie (hybrid)
B — largemouth bass

Other species in lake:
bowfin, carp, northern
hogsucker, bullhead,
white suckers, perch.

Long
Lake
Road

Old
Highway
Co 8

To
96
&
G

77

Pike
Lake
Creek

1. **LONG LAKE REGIONAL
   PARK** — beach, restroom.
   Daylight hours.

2. **PUBLIC ACCESS** — double
   concrete boat ramp; 15 trailer
   spaces; fishing pier (handicapped accessible); restroom.
   Hours: 5 a.m. to 10 p.m.

bar

Beach
Road

Rocks

Shore fishing

Long Lake
Road

694

To
35W

LAKES OWASSO & WABASSO   Ramsey County

Lake Owasso is stocked with pure strain muskies, and the eggs from these muskies are being used to develop stock to supply other metro lakes. In addition, walleyes have been stocked annually since 1984.

When the water-skiers are driving you daft, move over to Lake Wabasso. This is a small, deep lake with very sharp breaks and clearer water than Lake Owasso, but it has a history of partial winterkill. Wabasso contains small bass, northerns, and panfish. Find the openings in the weeds and dangle live bait from a bobber, or use a slow-falling plastic worm or weedless lure.

SPECIES	POPULATION	AVERAGE SIZE
Bass	Good	Medium
Muskie	Good	Small to Large
Northern Pike	Fair	Small to Medium
Walleye	Poor to Fair	Small
Crappie	Excellent	Small
Sunfish	Excellent	Small

BASS   In June, try the lily pads and cabbage weeds from the railroad bridge on the southeast side down (west) to the first small bay. Also work the west side of the 5-foot hole across from the marina. Stickbaits and spinnerbaits are a first choice here. In summer, fish a plastic worm on the sharp break in front of the land point just southwest of the ski jump. In early morning, work the flat around the land point with a buzzbait or surface lure. In fall, try a jig and pig on the sharp break here. Also fish the land point west of the swimming beach and the northeast and northwest corners on the west side of the lake.

NORTHERN PIKE & MUSKIE   For early-season muskies and northerns, work around the mouth of the bay in front of the railroad trestle, or try drifting the large expansive weed flat in the center of the lake. Another good spot is the 3 to 5 foot depths on the west side of the 20-foot hole in front of the marina. Try a sucker minnow here. In the summer, work around the ski jump (especially good for summer muskies) and the west side of the large weed flat that separates the east and west sections of the lake. Fall northerns can be found on the upper western shoreline and the inside turns in the northwest bay in about 15 feet of water. Try a jig with a reaper tail. Look for winter northerns in front of the round land point west of the beach.

WALLEYE   Work the sharp breaks in front of the first land point southwest of the ski jump. You may also find some winter walleyes on the breaks on the west side of the large flat in the center of the lake.

CRAPPIE & SUNFISH   Both sides of the railroad trestle produce a good supply of early season crappies and sunfish. Summer crappies will be suspended in the deep basins. There's an unlimited supply of summer sunfish on the weedlines, but you'll find the largest ones on the inside corners, especially on the north end of the western section. Try a small black jig and small leech here. In the early morning during mid-summer, work the top of the large, expansive flat. Winter sunfish and crappies will be in 10 to 15 feet of water in front of the beach and the inside corners of the north end of the western section.

This information was provided by Dick McCarthy, Greg Thorne, and Joe Unger.

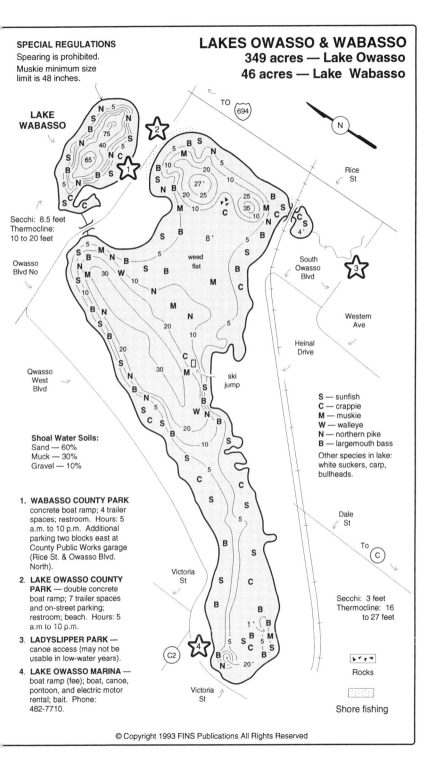

LAKES OWASSO & WABASSO
349 acres — Lake Owasso
46 acres — Lake Wabasso

LAKE WABASSO

N

TO 694

Rice St

Secchi: 8.5 feet
Thermocline:
10 to 20 feet

Owasso Blvd No

South Owasso Blvd

weed flat

Western Ave

Heinal Drive

Qwasso West Blvd

ski jump

Shoal Water Soils:
Sand — 60%
Muck — 30%
Gravel — 10%

S — sunfish
C — crappie
M — muskie
W — walleye
N — northern pike
B — largemouth bass

Other species in lake:
white suckers, carp,
bullheads.

Dale St

To C

1. **WABASSO COUNTY PARK**
concrete boat ramp; 4 trailer
spaces; restroom. Hours: 5
a.m. to 10 p.m. Additional
parking two blocks east at
County Public Works garage
(Rice St. & Owasso Blvd.
North).

2. **LAKE OWASSO COUNTY
PARK** — double concrete
boat ramp; 7 trailer spaces
and on-street parking;
restroom; beach. Hours: 5
a.m to 10 p.m.

3. **LADYSLIPPER PARK** —
canoe access (may not be
usable in low-water years).

4. **LAKE OWASSO MARINA** —
boat ramp (fee); boat, canoe,
pontoon, and electric motor
rental; bait. Phone:
482-7710.

Victoria St

Victoria St

Secchi: 3 feet
Thermocline: 16
to 27 feet

Rocks

Shore fishing

Phalen Lake is one of the best shore fishing lakes in the Twin Cities: good fish-holding structure within easy casting distance. Parkland surrounds the entire lake, and there are many storm drains that bring in food to attract the bait fish that lure other species. This lake is loaded with good structure and cover. Walleyes have been stocked annually since 1978. Stocking of hybrid tiger muskies started in 1983 and will be continued every 3 years. Use caution on the north side of this lake in the winter; it's the last area to freeze.

SPECIES	POPULATION	AVERAGE SIZE
Bass	Excellent	Small to Medium
Northern Pike	Good	Medium to Large
Walleye	Good	Medium
Muskie	Poor	Medium
Crappie	Good	Small
Sunfish	Good	Medium

BASS Start the season at the southeast side of Round Lake; the Lagoon; around the fishing pier; and down to the retaining wall in front of the boathouse. In late June, check out the lily pads at the south end of the lake. On summer days, work the weedline from the fishing pier down and around and up to Sandy Point on the east side of the lake. Don't pass up the storm drain on the lower east side. The edges of the cabbage weeds in front of the retaining wall are productive until fall.

NORTHERN PIKE & MUSKIE The shoreline from the fishing pier down to the retaining wall in front of the boat house is an all-season location. In summer and fall, troll the 6 to 15 foot depths from the 53-foot hole, across the dike, and up to the swimming beach. For winter northerns, fish Sandy Point; the beach area; and the boat house. Muskies are around the rock pile in front of the beach.

WALLEYE In early season, fish the southeast side of Round Lake, the 15 to 18 foot depths around the fishing pier, the beach area, and Sandy Point. In the summer, start on the northeast corner and work down to the Larpenteur Avenue storm drain on the lower east side of the lake. Also try the rock pile in front of the beach early or late in the day. The 6 to 30 foot depths on the east side of the 53-foot hole is a good location. Then move down and west across the dike area to the west side of the lake and up to the beach. Sandy Point will produce in the fall. In the winter, work the west side of the 42-foot hole; the north side of the saddle in the middle of the lake; and the area between the dike and the 53-foot hole.

CRAPPIE & SUNFISH Key locations for sunfish and crappies are the lagoon; Round Lake; the channels; and Spoon Creek. Concentrate on last year's weed growth. The sandy flats at the north end of Phalen Lake start producing in early June. After mid-June, sunfish are in all the bass locations. In low water years, waders can stand on the dike and cast to productive spots. For crappies, try the east side from Ripley Avenue down to the storm drain (Larpenteur Avenue); the deep drop-off in front of the fishing pier; and Sandy Point. For fall crappies, work the drop-off in front of the fishing pier; the rocks in the beach area; and the storm drain near Arlington Avenue. Winter crappies are suspended over the deep holes (42 feet and 53 feet) and on the north end of the lake. Winter sunfish are in the remaining green weeds on the north and south ends of the lake.

Information about this lake was provided by Dick Grzywinski and Skip Virchow.

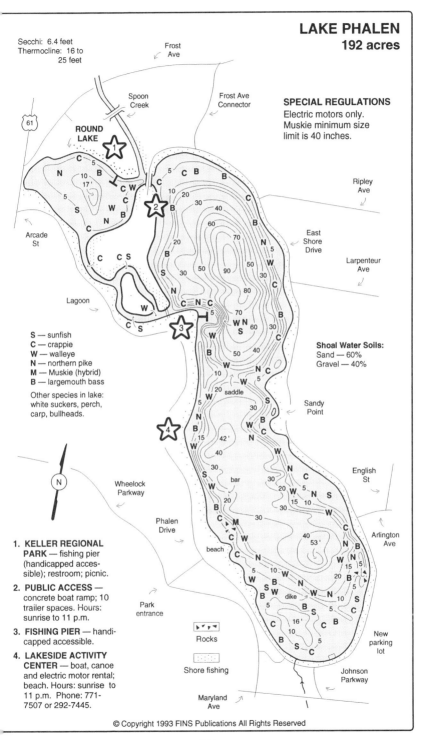

LAKE PHALEN
192 acres

Secchi: 6.4 feet
Thermocline: 16 to 25 feet

Frost Ave

Spoon Creek

Frost Ave Connector

SPECIAL REGULATIONS
Electric motors only.
Muskie minimum size limit is 40 inches.

61

ROUND LAKE

Ripley Ave

East Shore Drive

Larpenteur Ave

Arcade St

Lagoon

S — sunfish
C — crappie
W — walleye
N — northern pike
M — Muskie (hybrid)
B — largemouth bass

Other species in lake:
white suckers, perch, carp, bullheads.

Shoal Water Soils:
Sand — 60%
Gravel — 40%

Sandy Point

N

saddle

bar

English St

Wheelock Parkway

Phalen Drive

beach

Arlington Ave

1. **KELLER REGIONAL PARK** — fishing pier (handicapped accessible); restroom; picnic.

2. **PUBLIC ACCESS** — concrete boat ramp; 10 trailer spaces. Hours: sunrise to 11 p.m.

3. **FISHING PIER** — handicapped accessible.

4. **LAKESIDE ACTIVITY CENTER** — boat, canoe and electric motor rental; beach. Hours: sunrise to 11 p.m. Phone: 771-7507 or 292-7445.

Park entrance

dike

New parking lot

Rocks

Shore fishing

Johnson Parkway

Maryland Ave

A new public access and an excellent supply of largemouth bass are the major attractions on Turtle Lake, located in Shoreview off Hodgson Road (County Road 49). In the past, few anglers could navigate the very shallow boat launch, and the super bass supply remained intact. Strict Catch and Release practices will preserve the supply for everybody. Use caution; there are scattered rocks in the shallows in front of the new boat launch and north up to the old boat launch. These rocks took a healthy chunk out of my prop.

SPECIES	POPULATION	AVERAGE SIZE
Bass	Excellent	Medium
Northern Pike	Fair	Medium
Crappie	Good	Medium
Sunfish	Fair	Medium to Large

BASS In early June, you can find a supply of small bass on the weedy flat on the upper west side of the lake. Drift across the 8 to 12 foot depths in any direction, and toss a buzzbait or spinnerbait. The little bump on the 10-foot contour line in front of this area is especially active from June until late July. Use a live-bait rig or jig. Also try Center Bar and Shifsky's Bar. Look for the sharpest breaks. The southwest section of the lake is a good all-season location. There is a slight break between the two humps. In the summer, try speedtrolling on the east side from the pump house at the old boat launch up to the bar (underwater point) on the upper east side of the lake. The same areas are productive in the spring and fall, but use a slower technique. The northeast corner is especially good. In September, move down to the 15-foot depths and down to 25 feet in October.

NORTHERN PIKE Early-season northerns roam the north side of the center bar and the bump on the 10-foot contour line on the upper west side. Concentrate on the weedline and then work down to 25 feet. Troll with a red and white spoon or chrome or shad-colored crankbaits. Also fish the weedy points on the humps in the southwest corner. Toss a white spinnerbait on the weedline, or use a chrome crankbait that resembles a shiner minnow. Sucker or shiner minnows are also a prime choice. After Labor Day, especially in late September, look for northerns on Shifsky's Bar. All of these areas should be active until the ice season. In the winter, check out the 30-foot hole on the north side.

CRAPPIE & SUNFISH Any area with green weeds will attract spring crappies and sunfish. On the upper west side of the lake, the weedy flats and the bump on the 10-foot contour line are productive. On the lower west side, the weeds on the humps are prime spring territory. Beginning in early June when water temperature reaches 65 degrees, drift or backtroll on the west side in about 10 feet of water. Use a small jig (1/8 oz.) with a 3 to 4 inch white plastic worm or twister. You'll find sunfish under the old diving platforms on the middle of the east side. For summer crappies, seek out the cabbage weeds on the drop-offs at the south end and on the northeast and northwest corners. From July through September, the 15 to 25 foot depths on the south end are productive in the evening. The north end produces big crappies in the winter.

Information about this lake was provided by Dick Daly, Ken Matheson, and Greg Thorne and Joe Unger.

TURTLE LAKE
447 acres

1. **TURTLE LAKE COUNTY PARK** — double concrete boat ramp; 22 trailer spaces; boat dock; picnic area; restroom. Hours: 5 p.m. to 10 p.m.

Secchi: 10 feet
Thermocline: None

Shoal Water Soils:
Sand — 100%

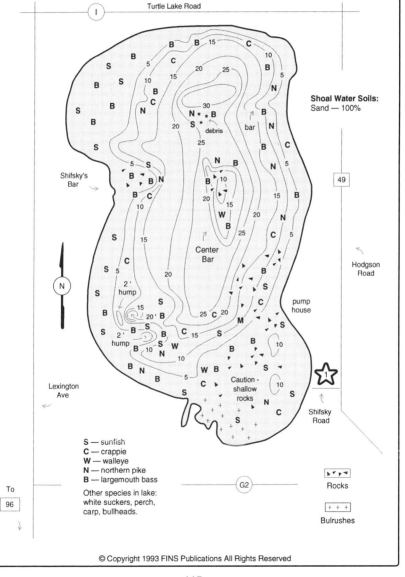

S — sunfish
C — crappie
W — walleye
N — northern pike
B — largemouth bass

Other species in lake: white suckers, perch, carp, bullheads.

Rocks

Bulrushes

Cedar Lake is a very fertile fish factory. Once the victim of frequent winterkills, this lake now has an aeration system financed by the New Prague Sportsmans Club and has been restocked with largemouth bass, sunfish, northern pike, and walleyes. Yellow perch were added to provide a forage base for the walleyes. The growth rate increased dramatically, and walleyes are now stocked annually.

Fast-growing hybrid tiger muskies were added in 1984, and stocking will continue every 3 years. Cedar Lake is designated as a non-spearing lake to increase the odds of trophy-sized fish. This restriction also protects the northern pike population. A 26-pound monster was caught here in the winter of 1988/89.

Use caution in the winter. The aerator weakens the ice and opens a large amount of water.

SPECIES	POPULATION	AVERAGE SIZE
Bass	Poor to Fair	Small to Medium
Northern Pike	Fair	Medium to Large
Walleye	Good	Small to Medium
Muskie	Good	Medium
Crappie	Excellent	Medium
Sunfish	Excellent	Medium to Large

BASS   Look for early-season bass in Church Bay, in the small bay above the rocky point on the lower west side of the lake, and on the east side from the tip of "The Point" southeast and down along the eastern shoreline. In the summer, they'll be concentrated on the points and the edge of the deep weeds.

NORTHERN PIKE & MUSKIE   For northerns and muskies in the spring, summer, and fall, troll the weedy edges around the entire lake, especially the lower half of the east side. Muskies are especially attracted to the rock piles. Red and white spoons or perch-pattern crankbaits are good for northerns. For muskies use a black jerkbait or crawfish-pattern crankbait. Bobber fishing with a sucker or golden shiner minnow is a good fall and winter technique.

WALLEYE   You'll find early-season walleyes by the dam at the north end of the lake, around the rocky bar, and in any weeds you can find along the shoreline on the west side and the middle of the east side. A shallow-diving blue and silver crankbait or a white jig and leech can be effective. Stay in the weedy areas in the summer. Nighttime is best. In the fall, work the rocky bar with a jig and minnow.

CRAPPIE & SUNFISH   The small bays, the dam area, and the south end of the lake will warm up fast and produce abundant spring crappies and sunfish. Summer crappies are along the shoreline at the north and south ends of the lake and on the long rocky bar in front of "The Point." Summer sunfish will be on the inside of the weedy edges in 6 to 8 feet of water. Use a wax worm or angleworm on a plain hook or ice fly. In the fall and winter, the west and south sides of the 11-foot hole in the center of the lake are prime crappie spots. Winter sunfish will be on the south end of the lake.

Information about this lake was provided by John Daily, Terry Hennon, Jim Picka, and Terry Tuma.

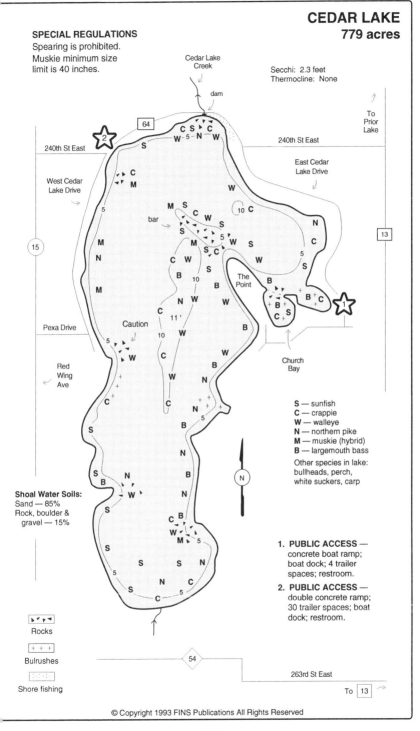

CEDAR LAKE
779 acres

SPECIAL REGULATIONS
Spearing is prohibited.
Muskie minimum size
limit is 40 inches.

Cedar Lake Creek

dam

Secchi: 2.3 feet
Thermocline: None

To Prior Lake

240th St East

East Cedar Lake Drive

West Cedar Lake Drive

bar

The Point

Pexa Drive

Caution

Red Wing Ave

Church Bay

S — sunfish
C — crappie
W — walleye
N — northern pike
M — muskie (hybrid)
B — largemouth bass

Other species in lake:
bullheads, perch,
white suckers, carp

Shoal Water Soils:
Sand — 85%
Rock, boulder &
gravel — 15%

1. **PUBLIC ACCESS** —
   concrete boat ramp;
   boat dock; 4 trailer
   spaces; restroom.
2. **PUBLIC ACCESS** —
   double concrete ramp;
   30 trailer spaces; boat
   dock; restroom.

Rocks

Bulrushes

Shore fishing

263rd St East

To 13

117

FISH LAKE Scott County

This lake was once known as "Carp City", but seining and a carp barrier built on the lake's outlet have dramatically reduced the supply and enhanced the habitat for other species. Fish Lake is now teeming with bass and panfish, including perch, and the size of the crappies is improving. Walleyes were stocked annually from 1979 to 1985, and stocking resumed in 1990.

SPECIES	POPULATION	AVERAGE SIZE
Bass	Very Good	Medium
Northern Pike	Very Poor	Medium to Large
Walleye	Fair to Good	Medium to Large
Crappie	Excellent	Small to Medium
Sunfish	Good	Medium to Large

BASS   For early-season bass, toss a white spinnerbait or slow-dropping plastic worm in holes and pockets of the lily pads on the south and west sides of the lake. The sandbar in the center of the lake is a good summer location, especially the small rocks and scattered weeds on the southeast corner. Try a black plastic worm here. Summer fish are on the sides and over the top of the bar on the west side of the lake. In the fall, go back to the lily pads. Cast a weedless lure over the top and outside edges.

NORTHERN PIKE   In early season, try trolling with a red and white spoon at the 4 to 6 foot depths on the east side of the lake. Also fish the outside edge of the weeds on the bar on the west side. A slip-bobber rig with a sucker minnow works well here. After July 4th, work the rock pile on the southeast corner of the Center Bar, or try trolling in 13 to 14 feet of water on the west side of the bar. Use bottom-bumping lures that kick up the muck. In the winter, drop a sucker minnow in 8 to 10 feet of water on the west side of the Center Bar.

WALLEYE   For early-season walleyes, the prime locations are Kaiser's Point at the north end of the lake and the bar on the west side. The weeds here are up by now, so work the edges with a slip bobber and minnow or leech set about 1 foot off the bottom in 6 feet of water. Summer walleyes will be harder to find, especially on days with heavy boat traffic. Drift or troll over the Center Bar with a live-bait rig in about 11 feet of water. The Center Bar is also a good winter spot, especially at night. Use a shiner minnow on a plain hook in about 11 feet of water. This lake produces best when fishing traffic is minimal.

CRAPPIE   The northwest corner by the outlet is a spring crappie producer. Summer crappies can be found on the south side of the lake and on the bars, especially the Center Bar. In the fall, the crappies will stay on the bars. In the winter, you'll find the crappies about 15 feet below the surface in 22 feet of water by the Center Bar. Use a slip bobber with a green ice fly and crappie minnow.

SUNFISH   Look for spring sunfish on the south, east, and west sides of the lake, especially the lily pads. Summer sunnies are on the south side and on the bars, particularly on the Center Bar. In the fall, the sunfish will go to the shallow lily pads. Kaiser's Point is a good winter location. Try an orange or green ice fly tipped with a wax worm and work it off the bottom in about 6 feet of water.

Information about this lake was provided by Shawn O'Hern.

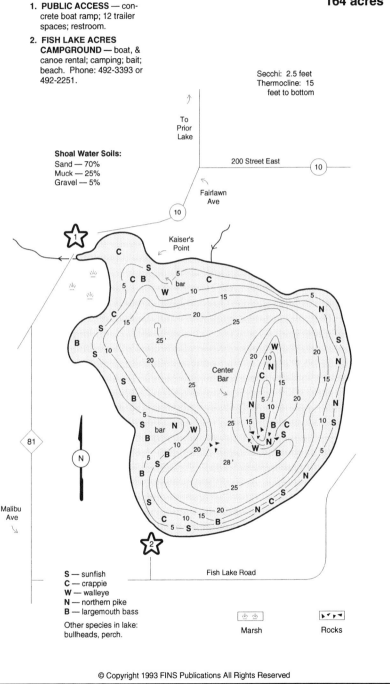

FISH LAKE
164 acres

1. **PUBLIC ACCESS** — concrete boat ramp; 12 trailer spaces; restroom.
2. **FISH LAKE ACRES CAMPGROUND** — boat, & canoe rental; camping; bait; beach. Phone: 492-3393 or 492-2251.

Secchi: 2.5 feet
Thermocline: 15 feet to bottom

To Prior Lake

Shoal Water Soils:
Sand — 70%
Muck — 25%
Gravel — 5%

200 Street East

Fairlawn Ave

Kaiser's Point

Center Bar

Malibu Ave

S — sunfish
C — crappie
W — walleye
N — northern pike
B — largemouth bass

Other species in lake: bullheads, perch.

Fish Lake Road

Marsh

Rocks

Located 3-1/2 miles south of Shakopee on County Road 79, O'Dowd is a shore fishing paradise with plenty of shoreline structure and lots of fish. This fertile lake has populations of crappies, northern pike, and sunfish that are far above local and state median levels. Walleye fry were stocked from 1984 to 1991, but few have survived. Catfish yearlings were added in 1987. This is a quiet sprawling lake with many islands, bays, rocks, and weedbeds. Due to the lake's small size, shallow depths, and very stained water, it warms up fast in the spring. An aeration device was installed in 1982 to prevent winterkill. Use caution around these areas while ice fishing.

Don't pass up Thole Lake across the road from O'Dowd. It is also a good early-season lake with about the same mix of fish, and it has an aeration system and fishing pier. Walleyes are stocked annually. Very shallow Schneider Lake (south of Thole) suffers frequent winterkill and may contain stunted sunfish.

SPECIES	POPULATION	AVERAGE SIZE
Bass	Fair to Good	Small to Medium
Northern Pike	Very Good	Medium
Walleye	Poor	Small
Crappie	Very Good	Small
Sunfish	Excellent	Small

BASS The best early-season spot is in the weedy area below the big island in the middle of the lake. The small bays on the upper section of the lake are also good early-season producers, especially the small bay just above the long finger point. The fallen trees here attract hordes of small bass. In the summer, the hotspots are the weedy areas below the big island and below the long land point on the upper west side. In Thole Lake, you'll find most of the bass in the cabbage and coontail weeds in the western bays off the main lake and on the western side of the main lake. Look for the fallen trees, brush, and rocky areas.

NORTHERN PIKE The best all-season location is the southwest corner of the big island where it almost connects to shore. Try still fishing here with a bobber and a golden shiner minnow. Also work the western shoreline from the fishing pier up and around the long finger point and into the first small bay. Shore anglers do well here. Winter northerns can be found below the big island in about 12 feet of water. In Thole Lake, the best location is along the eastern shoreline. Try trolling the 5 to 8 foot depths. There's also some good shore fishing here.

WALLEYE The points on the north and east sides of the big island are the best spots in all seasons, including winter. Look for the gravel on the tip of the points.

CRAPPIE & SUNFISH Spring sunfish and crappies will be in the shallow bays. The fishing pier and the western shoreline are also productive. The long land point on the upper west side is a super shore fishing location. Look for the fallen trees. Winter sunfish will be below the big island and on the northeast and northwest sides of it. Crappies will be around the 22-foot hole. In Thole Lake, the best spring locations are the west side of the lake and the far southern and western bays.

Information about this lake was provided by Steve Culhane and Terry Hannon.

O'DOWD & THOLE LAKES
258 acres — O'Dowd Lake
141 acres — Thole Lake

1. **FISHING PIER** — handicapped accessible.
2. **PUBLIC ACCESS** — concrete boat ramp; boat dock; 12 trailer spaces; restroom.
3. **PUBLIC ACCESS** — concrete boat ramp; 15 trailer spaces; fishing pier (handicapped accessible); boat dock; restroom.

Shoal Water Soils:
Sand — 40%
Muck — 30%
Gravel — 15%
Boulders — 5%

Shoal Water Soils:
Mud — 100%
Scattered boulders

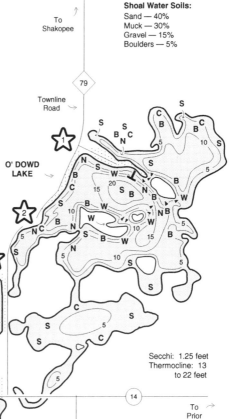

To Shakopee

79

Townline Road

O' DOWD LAKE

THOLE LAKE

15

150th St West

Secchi: 1.25 feet
Thermocline: 13 to 22 feet

14

To Prior Lake

To 169

Baseline Road

SCHNEIDER LAKE

N

79

Rocks

Shore fishing

Secchi: 1.10 feet
Thermocline: None

S — sunfish
C — crappie
W — walleye
N — northern pike
B — largemouth bass

Other species in lake: white suckers, golden shiner, channel catfish, bullheads.

Prior Lake is touted as one of the best multi-species lakes in the metro area. Bas
in the 5 to 6 pound range are caught regularly. Walleyes have been stocke
annually since 1978. The population is twice the state average and getting bette
You may even haul in a 10 to 11 pound wallhanger if you put in your time.

Since the watershed flow is from the southwest to the northeast, the southwester
section of the lake is referred to as Upper Lake and the northeastern section i
referred to as Lower Lake. Lower Lake holds the best supply of fish and ha
clearer water and more prominent big-fish structure such as deep weedlines, roc
piles, islands, points, bays, deep-water breaks, and sunken islands.

SPECIES	POPULATION	AVERAGE SIZE
Bass	Excellent	Medium
Northern Pike	Good	Medium
Walleye	Good	Medium to Large
Crappie	Good	Small to Medium
Sunfish	Good	Small to Medium

BASS In June, work the 2 to 10 foot depths in the weedy bays. The bay wes
of Martinson Island is productive when other bays are dry. Also look for an
niche, point, or irregularity on the drop-off or weedline. In the summer, work th
points, outside weedlines, sunken islands, and docks next to deep structure. O
Lower Lake, the best areas are the large body of water between Candy Cone Ba
and the main lake; the first bay east of Sand Point Beach; Frost Point; around th
islands; and the sunken islands marked with buoys. In the fall, go back to th
inside weedlines and shallow points. Try the round point and inside turn jus
above Kneafsey Cove or the west side of Twin Island. Points near entrances t
bays are often good transition areas from the main lake in the fall.

NORTHERN PIKE In the early-season, troll the weedlines with sharp break
(drop-offs). Most of the weedy bass locations also hold northerns. In th
summer, work the second break at about 15 feet. Koep's Bay is a good al
season location. For winter northerns, try the 8 to 14 foot depths around Martinso
Island and Sand Point Beach.

WALLEYE The rocky areas attract walleyes most of the year. Frost Point an
the point off the northeast side of Martinson Island are also all-season hotspo
and are known to produce big fish. Troll the entire shoreline between Sand Poi
Beach and Martinson Island with live-bait rigs, crankbaits, or jigs tipped wit
leeches. Give special attention to the weedline in front of the boat launch and th
rocky humps in front of Sand Point. In spring and fall, fish the 5 to 15 foot depth
in summer and winter, the 10 to 20 foot depths are best.

CRAPPIE & SUNFISH Spring sunfish and crappies will be in the shallo
muddy bays; otherwise, look for the warmest water. Martinson Island chann
and the channel between Upper and Lower Lakes are good spring crapp
producers. Summer sunfish are on the weedlines in the bass areas, and crappie
are suspended over the rock piles in deeper water. For winter sunfish an
crappies, try the 8 to 12 foot depths in the summer areas and also the deep
holes and flats on the upper portion of the Lower Lake.

This information was provided by John Craig, Gary Lake, and Bud Miller.

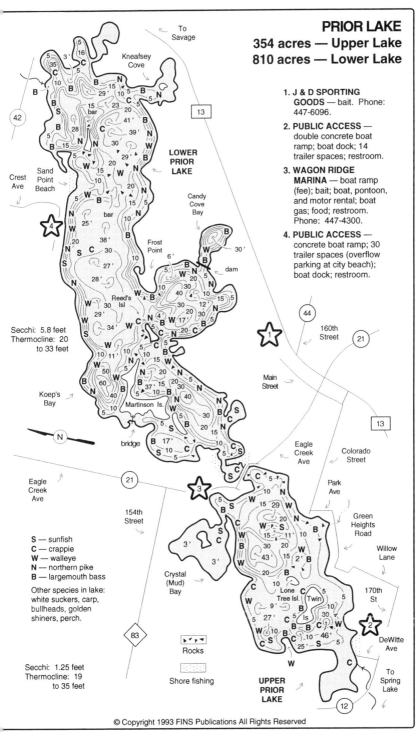

PRIOR LAKE
354 acres — Upper Lake
810 acres — Lower Lake

To Savage

Kneafsey Cove

LOWER PRIOR LAKE

Crest Ave

Sand Point Beach

Candy Cove Bay

Frost Point

dam

Reed's Isl

Secchi: 5.8 feet
Thermocline: 20 to 33 feet

Koep's Bay

Martinson Is.

bridge

N

Eagle Creek Ave

154th Street

Crystal (Mud) Bay

S — sunfish
C — crappie
W — walleye
N — northern pike
B — largemouth bass

Other species in lake: white suckers, carp, bullheads, golden shiners, perch.

Secchi: 1.25 feet
Thermocline: 19 to 35 feet

Rocks

Shore fishing

Main Street

Eagle Creek Ave

Colorado Street

Park Ave

Green Heights Road

Willow Lane

170th St

DeWitte Ave

To Spring Lake

Lone Tree Isl.
Twin Isl

UPPER PRIOR LAKE

160th Street

1. J & D SPORTING GOODS — bait. Phone: 447-6096.

2. PUBLIC ACCESS — double concrete boat ramp; boat dock; 14 trailer spaces; restroom.

3. WAGON RIDGE MARINA — boat ramp (fee); bait; boat, pontoon, and motor rental; boat gas; food; restroom. Phone: 447-4300.

4. PUBLIC ACCESS — concrete boat ramp; 30 trailer spaces (overflow parking at city beach); boat dock; restroom.

DNR records indicate above-average populations of northern pike, walleyes, crappies, and bullheads in Spring Lake. Annual walleye stocking was started in 1975, and the average size is 2 to 3 pounds. Spring Lake is a good early-season producer, unlike Prior Lake across the road, which has clearer, deeper water and takes longer to warm up in the spring.

SPECIES	POPULATION	AVERAGE SIZE
Bass	Good	Medium
Northern Pike	Very Good	Medium
Walleye	Good to Excellent	Medium
Crappie	Very Good	Medium to Large
Sunfish	Poor to Fair	Medium

BASS In the early season, work the 3 to 6 foot depth from the middle of the south side and up the east side of the lake. The inlets are also prime areas. As the water warms, move down to the 6 to 15 foot depths in these same areas. Also try the rock pile on the west side and the underwater points (bars). The east side of the rocky point in front of the resort is a popular spot. The docks are also prime summer locations. Don't pass up the bulrush island between Thorton's Point and Hunters Point, especially the north side. The same areas will produce in the fall.

NORTHERN PIKE To find northerns in the spring, summer, and fall, troll in front of both inlets. Speed-trolling is the preferred summer technique. Vary the depth from 8 to 20 feet. Also work the rock pile on the west side as well as the underwater points (bars) and areas with fast-dropping breaks on the south and east sides of the lake. In the winter, stay in 6 to 15 feet of water on the rock pile on the west side and the underwater points.

WALLEYE In early season, the action is on or between the two rocky points and the area in front of the outlet (bar) on the northeastern side of the lake. Use small minnow lures or a chartreuse or orange jig tipped with a leech. Vertical jigging is best. In the summer and fall, stay adjacent to the points in 15 to 22 feet of water. Work the top of the rocky structures in low light periods. Also fish the rock pile on the west side of the lake. Try trolling in 15 feet of water with a live-bait rig and leech. Look for a good supply of winter walleyes on the east side of the lake in 8 to 20 feet of water. A minnow on a butterfly ice jig is a popular technique.

CRAPPIE Spring crappies will be in 3 to 6 feet of water between Hunter's Point and Thorton's Point. Also start at the outlet on the northeast side of the lake, and work west for about 1/4 mile. Vary your depth until you find them. For summer crappies, the points and the rock piles are prime locations. You'll also find suspended crappies in the eastern half of the lake in 15 to 18 feet of water. Fall crappies will be hanging off the points and the rock piles in 4 to 15 feet of water. In the winter, try the 10 to 30 foot depth in front of the resort. You'll find the biggest fish for about an hour during sunrise and sunset.

SUNFISH Spring sunfish are in the shallow areas next to docks and bulrushes. Summer sunnies will suspend over isolated clumps of weeds, especially near docks. They will be easily spooked, so a quiet presentation is essential.

This information was provided by John Craig, Steve Culhane, and Bud Miller.

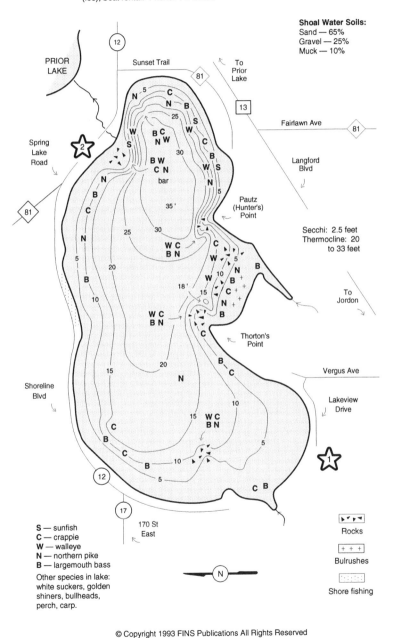

SPRING LAKE
579 acres

1. **PUBLIC ACCESS** — concrete boat ramp; 24 trailer spaces; boat dock; restroom.

2. **CRAIG'S RESORT** — boat ramp (fee); boat rental. Phone: 447-2338.

Shoal Water Soils:
Sand — 65%
Gravel — 25%
Muck — 10%

PRIOR LAKE

Sunset Trail

To Prior Lake

Fairlawn Ave

Spring Lake Road

Langford Blvd

bar

35'

Pautz (Hunter's) Point

Secchi: 2.5 feet
Thermocline: 20 to 33 feet

To Jordon

18'

Thorton's Point

Vergus Ave

Shoreline Blvd

Lakeview Drive

170 St East

S — sunfish
C — crappie
W — walleye
N — northern pike
B — largemouth bass

Other species in lake: white suckers, golden shiners, bullheads, perch, carp.

Rocks

Bulrushes

Shore fishing

125

Big Carnelian, located 6 miles north of Stillwater in Washington County, is hailed as a superb multi-species lake and is considered one of the better bass lakes in the metro area. Recent DNR tests rank the bass population here as 5 times the regional average. There are also very good populations of northern pike, crappies, perch, and bullheads. The average size of the crappies is a half pound. A few walleyes may have migrated in from Big Marine Lake. Walleyes are not stocked because this species would not have much chance for survival with such a large population of northern pike.

This lake suffered severe flooding in the early 80's, but the water level has now returned to normal. In some cases, the fish locations and patterns have changed.

SPECIES	POPULATION	AVERAGE SIZE
Bass	Very Good	Medium
Northern Pike	Very Good	Medium
Crappie	Good	Medium to Large
Sunfish	Excellent	Small

BASS In June, try the 4-foot sunken island in the southeast section of the lake. Cast to the bulrushes with a purple plastic worm, let it sink, and slowly pump it back to the boat. The weedlines on the middle and lower sections of the western shoreline are the prime summer spots. There are some good cabbage weeds and fast drop-offs here. Cast a black jig and pig (pork frog) into the pockets and edges of the weeds, or try a medium or deep diving crankbait. The weedline on the east side of the small island in front of the boat launch and the large land point on the upper east side of the lake are especially good in the summer and fall. The entire area from the point down to the middle of the east side is another good fall producer.

NORTHERN PIKE Look for spring northerns in the weeds in front of the stumps in Stump Bay. Spinnerbaits and sucker minnows are the preferred method. In the summer, troll the weedline in the middle of the west side of the lake, or work the sharp weedy drop-offs at the northern end of the lake. Also check out the grass and bulrushes on the 4-foot sunken island. Use spoons, crankbaits, and sucker minnows. In the fall, try all of the summer spots, and then work the area from the public access down to the south end of the lake. In the winter, the most popular area is the 10-foot depth around the very small island in front of the public boat access.

CRAPPIE & SUNFISH For early-season crappies and sunfish, the most popular spots are the area in front of the boat launch; the small bay above the boat launch and the area around the small island. This island is a good all-season sunfish location. In the summer and fall, you'll also find sunfish in the weeds along the eastern shoreline of Stump Bay. Summer crappies will be suspended about 15 feet off the bottom in the 54-foot hole at the north end of the lake and on the drop-off on the east side of Stump Bay. For winter fishing, the 54-foot hole is the hotspot. The crappies will be suspended from 10 to 35 feet below the ice. Sunfish will be around the small island.

This information was provided by Joey Rauscher, Roger Rucci, and Bill Tomberlin.

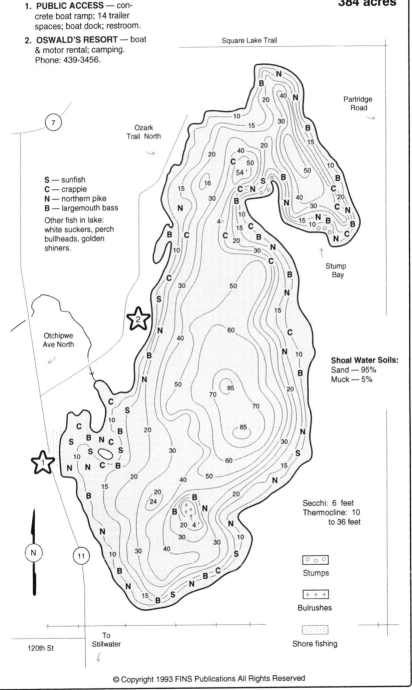

BIG CARNELIAN LAKE
384 acres

1. **PUBLIC ACCESS** — concrete boat ramp; 14 trailer spaces; boat dock; restroom.

2. **OSWALD'S RESORT** — boat & motor rental; camping. Phone: 439-3456.

Square Lake Trail

Partridge Road

Ozark Trail North

S — sunfish
C — crappie
N — northern pike
B — largemouth bass

Other fish in lake: white suckers, perch bullheads, golden shiners.

Otchipwe Ave North

Stump Bay

Shoal Water Soils:
Sand — 95%
Muck — 5%

Secchi: 6 feet
Thermocline: 10 to 36 feet

Stumps

Bulrushes

Shore fishing

To Stillwater

120th St

© Copyright 1993 FINS Publications All Rights Reserved

127

Big Marine Lake, located 4 miles west of the St. Croix River in northern Washington County, is known as one of the top producers of lunker bass in the metro area. Walleyes have been stocked in most years since 1982, and the population is almost twice the metro average.

SPECIES	POPULATION	AVERAGE SIZE
Bass	Excellent	Medium
Northern Pike	Excellent	Small to Medium
Walleye	Fair to Good	Small to Medium
Crappie	Good	Medium
Sunfish	Fair to Good	Small to Medium

BASS   Early-season bass are on the bulrush point on the eastern arm of the lake. The east side is best. Cast a purple plastic worm to the edge of the bulrushes, let it drop to the bottom, pause, and then retrieve. Also work the point on the west side of the northern arm and the large bay above Shady Birch Resort. In the summer, the deep-water cabbage weeds are prime producers. Try the upper east side of the main lake just before you enter the northern arm. The underwater point (bar) on the lower west side of the northern arm is a good all-season location. The weed patch below the island is good in summer and fall. Toss a brown jig dressed with crayfish-colored pork to the pockets in the weeds.

NORTHERN PIKE   The northwest side of the main lake and the east end of the eastern arm are good early-season locations. Stay in the 10 to 15 depths. The trough on the lower east side of the eastern arm stays productive throughout the summer. In the summer, troll the edge of the weeds with red and white spoons in about 15 feet of water. For fall northerns, work the weedy edges in the small bay at the south end of the main lake. During early ice, fish the area just northwest of the tip of the long bulrush bar on the eastern arm.

WALLEYE   Look for early-season walleyes in the big rocks on the west side of the island. This is also a good night-fishing spot in the summer. Other good summer spots are the weedy drop-offs outside the 34-foot hole at the lower end of the northern arm and the sand and gravel bar that connects the island to the eastern shoreline. The north side of the bar is the most productive. This is another good night-fishing area. Also try the rocky 19-foot hump northwest of the island. Vertical fishing with jigs or spoons is the preferred technique. Use chartreuse color during the day and black or orange at night. Work the top of the hump first, and then sit on the hump and work the edges of the rocks.

CRAPPIE & SUNFISH   The stumps and weedy areas on the north end of the northern arm provide the best action for spring crappies. There's a good supply of all-season sunfish in the bulrushes in front of the little finger-shaped bay on the northeast corner of the east arm. In the main lake, the area below the island is a good all-season location for sunfish and crappies. The bar on the west side where the main lake joins the northern arm is a hotspot for winter crappies. They'll be suspended about 3 feet off the bottom in 12 to 15 feet of water. You'll also find winter crappies and sunfish in front of the bulrushes on the north end of the north arm.

This information was provided by Roger Rucci, Bill Tomberlin, and Joe Unger.

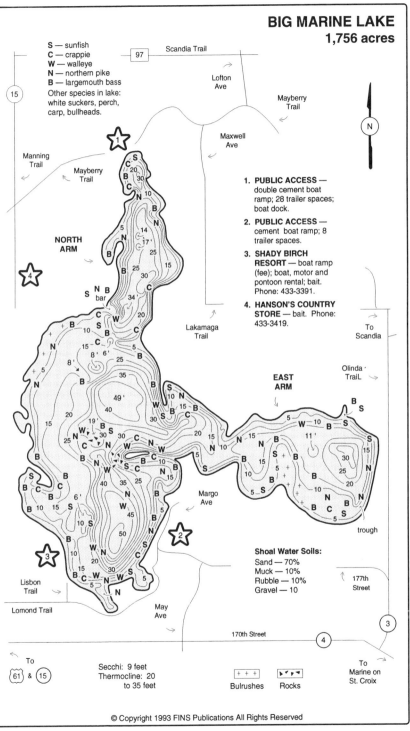

BIG MARINE LAKE
1,756 acres

S — sunfish
C — crappie
W — walleye
N — northern pike
B — largemouth bass
Other species in lake:
white suckers, perch,
carp, bullheads.

NORTH ARM

EAST ARM

1. **PUBLIC ACCESS** — double cement boat ramp; 28 trailer spaces; boat dock.

2. **PUBLIC ACCESS** — cement boat ramp; 8 trailer spaces.

3. **SHADY BIRCH RESORT** — boat ramp (fee); boat, motor and pontoon rental; bait. Phone: 433-3391.

4. **HANSON'S COUNTRY STORE** — bait. Phone: 433-3419.

Shoal Water Soils:
Sand — 70%
Muck — 10%
Rubble — 10%
Gravel — 10

Secchi: 9 feet
Thermocline: 20 to 35 feet

+ + + Bulrushes

▶▼▶◀ Rocks

Bone Lake, located 5 miles east of Forest Lake on the border of Washington and Chisago Counties, has gained an enviable reputation as a decent walleye lake. Walleye fingerlings are stocked annually, and huge numbers of northern pike fingerlings were stocked in 1985 to boost the sagging population. Trollers will appreciate the well defined weedline.

SPECIES	POPULATION	AVERAGE SIZE
Bass	Fair	Medium
Northern Pike	Fair	Medium
Walleye	Fair to Good	Medium
Crappie	Good	Medium
Sunfish	Very Good	Medium

BASS   Look for June bass on the south end of the lake. Toss a spinnerbait or plastic worm to the pockets and edges of the weeds. Also check out the lily pads on the north end of the lake. The south side is the best summer location. Put your boat in 15 feet of water, and cast a spinnerbait to the openings in the weeds. Drop it in the pockets, bring it back across the top of the weeds, and let it drop on the outside edge of the weeds. In late summer and fall, stay on the south end, but also check out any weedy points and the healthy weed patch on the northeast corner. Try casting to the weed edge with a medium-diving crankbait, and crank it down the slope of the drop-off.

NORTHERN PIKE   For early-season northerns, troll with a red and white spoon along the weed edges on the upper west and south sides of the lake. A sucker minnow and bobber is also a popular method. In the summer, stay in the same areas. The weed edges will hold most of the fish. Winter northerns can be found in the weeds on the south end of the lake in 8 to 15 feet of water.

WALLEYE   For early-season walleyes, troll the 8 to 10 foot depths from the northwest corner of the lake down to the middle of the west side. Also work the underwater point (or bar) near the middle of the east side of the lake, particularly the inside curve on the north side of the point. Try a slip-bobber technique here in 10 feet of water. In the summer, work the same areas but move down to 15 feet. Also try the upper half of the 25-foot flat in the center of the lake. Begin at the 12-foot depths and work down to 25 feet with a live-bait rig. In the fall, work from the shallows to deeper water at the 5 to 20 foot depths on the upper two-thirds of the lake.

CRAPPIE   Spring crappies will be on the south end of the lake and the point near the middle of the east side. Also try the sparse weed patch in the middle of the west side. During the spawn, use a plain hook and crappie minnow or a black jig head and minnow. Before and after the spawn, a pink jig head with yellow or white hair works well. Summer crappies will be suspended in the deeper areas and will be tough to find. Look for the blips on your flasher. In the fall and winter, the upper half of the 25-foot flat is a good location. Try a glow-in-the-dark jig.

SUNFISH   The weedy areas on both ends of the lake are the prime all-season sunfish locations. Concentrate on the edge of the weeds and the weedy pockets in the bass locations.

Information about this lake was provided by Bill Tomberlin.

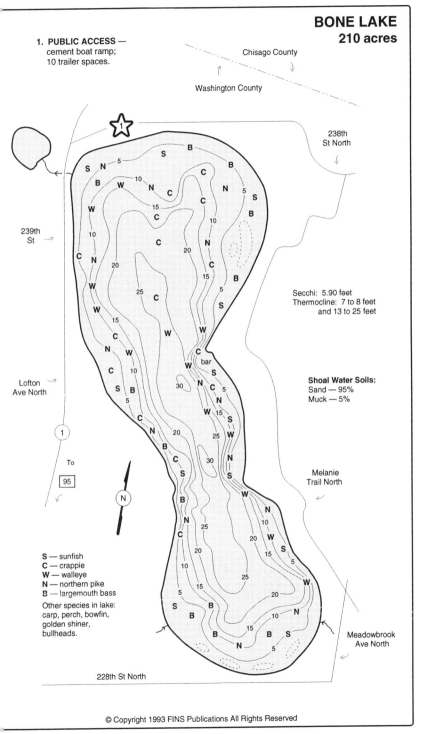

BONE LAKE
210 acres

1. **PUBLIC ACCESS** —
   cement boat ramp;
   10 trailer spaces.

Chisago County

Washington County

238th
St North

239th
St

Secchi: 5.90 feet
Thermocline: 7 to 8 feet
and 13 to 25 feet

Shoal Water Soils:
Sand — 95%
Muck — 5%

Lofton
Ave North

bar

Melanie
Trail North

To
95

N

Meadowbrook
Ave North

S — sunfish
C — crappie
W — walleye
N — northern pike
B — largemouth bass
Other species in lake:
carp, perch, bowfin,
golden shiner,
bullheads.

228th St North

Clear Lake is located just east of I-35 in northeastern Washington County. Walleyes are stocked annually, and some are as large as 12 pounds. The high population of perch in this lake provides a good food supply for steady growth. In 1985, 425 tiger muskie fingerlings were stocked. The survival rate will determine whether stocking will continue.

For early-winter anglers, caution is advised. Springs can weaken the ice, especially on the west side of the lake near the outlet.

SPECIES	POPULATION	AVERAGE SIZE
Bass	Poor to Fair	Medium
Northern Pike	Poor	Medium to Large
Muskie	Poor	Small to Medium
Walleye	Good	Medium
Crappie	Very Good	Small to Medium
Sunfish	Very Good	Small to Medium

BASS From early season to early summer, the area below Ashbach Point is productive. Toss a weedless silver spoon in the lily pads.

NORTHERN PIKE AND MUSKIE In the early season, troll the edge of the weeds on the eastern shoreline. Use a red and white spoon or floating minnow lure in the 6 to 7 foot depths. As the water warms, move deeper to 15 to 17 feet. The 18-foot hole on the west side of the lake and the trough and sunken island just east of the hole are good summer locations. Also work the edge of the weeds and lily pads on the western shoreline. Continue up the shoreline here in 8 to 10 feet of water, and concentrate on the weeds.

WALLEYE For early-season walleyes, fish the 4-foot sunken island in the middle of the lake and the scattered rocky areas along the northwest shoreline. Start at the 15-foot depth, and work up to 3 or 4 feet. Troll or cast with a live-bait rig or a floating minnow lure with a split-shot sinker 12 to 18 inches from the lure. In the summer, stay in the same area, but start at the 15-foot depth work deeper Give special attention to the bottom of the drop-offs. A jig and minnow is the best method. In the fall, fish the inside turn on the northeast corner of the lake. Use a jig and minnow at the 18 to 25 foot depths. For winter success, try the 18-foot hole on the west side. This spot can be a good all-season producer.

CRAPPIE For spring crappies, start on the edge of the lily pads in the mucky bay at the southwest end of the lake near Hwy. I-35. Work up the shoreline until you run out of cover. Include the floating raft north of the public access. Also try the bay below Ashbach Point. Toss your bait to the edge of the timber. Look for summer crappies on the fast drop-offs around the 5-foot sunken island in the center of the lake. The fish will be 8 to 12 feet below the surface in about 20 feet of water. In the fall, the crappies will move down to 1 or 2 feet off the bottom in the same area. Winter crappies are around the 4-foot sunken island and the 18-foot hole.

SUNFISH In the spring, the sunnies will be in the same areas as the crappies. Summer sunfish will be around the docks and near the weed edges.

Information about this lake was provided by Ken Schak and Brad Stanius.

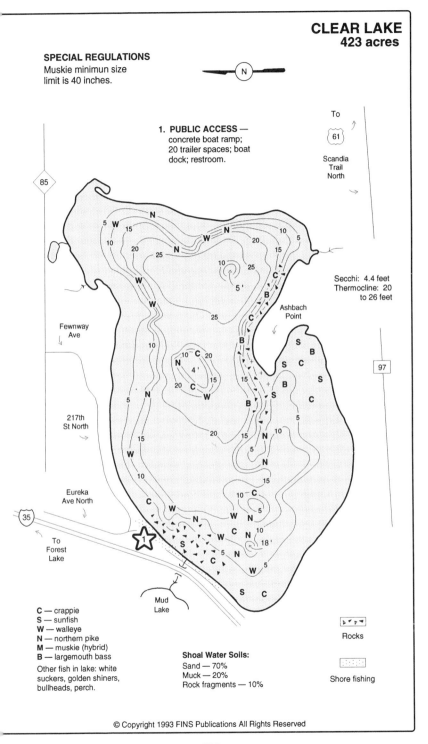

CLEAR LAKE
423 acres

SPECIAL REGULATIONS
Muskie minimun size
limit is 40 inches.

N

1. **PUBLIC ACCESS** —
concrete boat ramp;
20 trailer spaces; boat
dock; restroom.

To
61

Scandia
Trail
North

85

Secchi: 4.4 feet
Thermocline: 20
to 26 feet

Ashbach
Point

Fewnway
Ave

97

217th
St North

Eureka
Ave North

35

To
Forest
Lake

Mud
Lake

C — crappie
S — sunfish
W — walleye
N — northern pike
M — muskie (hybrid)
B — largemouth bass

Other fish in lake: white
suckers, golden shiners,
bullheads, perch.

Shoal Water Soils:
Sand — 70%
Muck — 20%
Rock fragments — 10%

Rocks

Shore fishing

DeMontreville and Olson Lakes, located in western Washington County, are small lakes that have good water quality and are crammed full of fish. According to Mike Bonn, owner of Blue Ribbon Bait who grew up on these lakes, they offer one of the nicest supplies of good-sized bass in the area. The boat launch is on DeMontreville, but you can get through the channel to Olson Lake in most years.

SPECIES	POPULATION	AVERAGE SIZE
Bass	Good	Medium to Large
Northern Pike	Good	Medium
Crappie	Good	Medium
Sunfish	Excellent	Small to Medium

BASS   In June, you'll find the bass in Demontreville in brushy areas on the north and west sides of the upper section. Other good locations are the upper east side of the middle section; below the long land point on the lower east side; the point on the west side separating the upper and middle sections; and the small point and docks on the lower west side. The lower side of this point is better. The bay in the far southeastern portion of the lower section is a good June and fall location. In the summer months, work the same areas but move deeper to the weedy edges. The points are also good fall locations.

NORTHERN PIKE   In the spring and fall, work a sucker minnow in front of the inlet from Olson Lake. The deeper weedy flat (10 to 12 feet) in the upper section is also productive. In the summer, try trolling crankbaits from the point on the lower east side up to the Retreat House. The long point on the upper west side separating the upper and middle sections is also a good summer producer. The lower east side of the 25-foot hole in the middle section is a productive summer and winter location. The west side of this hole is also good in the winter.

CRAPPIE & SUNFISH   Look for early spring crappies and sunfish on the west side of the upper section. Start at the boat launch and work down to the lower end of this bay. Sunfish are also abundant in the southeast corner of the lower section. In late spring and early summer, you'll find crappies in the brushy areas on the upper east side of the middle section of the lake. The long point separating the upper and middle sections produces sunnies and crappies in the summer. You'll also find summer crappies around the 25-foot hole.

OLSON LAKE

Olson Lake shines in the spring and early summer. For June bass, check out the brush on the lower west side of this lake; the stumps and lily pads in the southern bay; and the thick weeds on the north end of the lake. The curved underwater point on the east side is the best all-season location for all species. Concentrate on the 2 to 7 foot depths at the inside turns on both sides of this point. The upper west side of the lake attracts bass, northerns, crappies, and sunfish in the summer. There's a good supply of spring crappies around the shoreline in the lower two-thirds of the lake. In the summer, they will stay in the deeper water during the day and move up to the weedlines and the last break to feed during low-light periods. The weeds, brush, and fallen trees in the southern bay hold crappies and sunfish throughout the season. Go back to Demontreville Lake for the best winter success.

This information was provided by Mike Bonn, Dave Brandeman, Tina Outlaw, and Joe Unger.

DEMONTREVILLE & OLSON LAKES
143 acres — Demontreville
79 acres — Olson

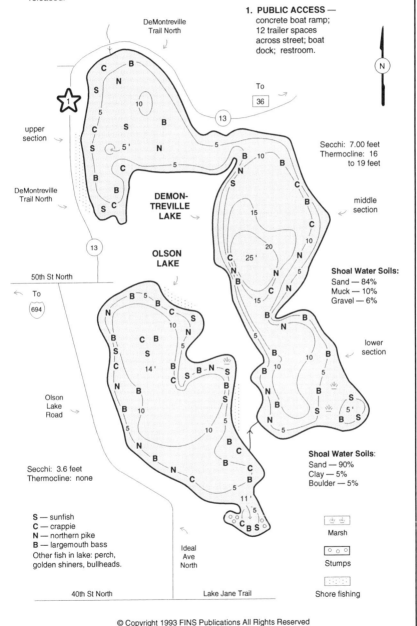

SPECIAL REGULATIONS
Largemouth bass slot limit:
all bass between 12 and
16 inches must be
released.

DeMontreville
Trail North

1. PUBLIC ACCESS —
concrete boat ramp;
12 trailer spaces
across street; boat
dock; restroom.

N

To
36

13

C   B
N
S
5
10
B
S
5'
C
S
C
S
B
S
B
C

upper
section

DeMontreville
Trail North

**DEMON-
TREVILLE
LAKE**

13

**OLSON
LAKE**

50th St North

To
694

Secchi: 7.00 feet
Thermocline: 16
to 19 feet

B   10   B
N
S   C
15   B
20   C
25'   N
C   10
N   B   B
15   N
B   B
N

middle
section

lower
section

Shoal Water Soils:
Sand — 84%
Muck — 10%
Gravel — 6%

B   5   B
N   C   S
10   N
B   5
S   C   S
S   14'
C   B
N   B-N-S
B   10
S   B
N   10
B
N
B
N   C
5
B   C
C   B
5
11'
5
C   B   S

B
S   B
5
10   B
5
B   B
N
S   5'   S
S

Shoal Water Soils:
Sand — 90%
Clay — 5%
Boulder — 5%

Olson
Lake
Road

Secchi: 3.6 feet
Thermocline: none

S — sunfish
C — crappie
N — northern pike
B — largemouth bass
Other fish in lake: perch,
golden shiners, bullheads.

Ideal
Ave
North

Marsh

Stumps

Shore fishing

40th St North

Lake Jane Trail

Lake Elmo, located about 2-1/2 miles east of I-694 in southern Washington County, is the deepest lake in the metro area. It has a history of yielding 20-pound northerns, and every year at least two bass over 8 pounds are caught here. But you'll have to work for them. Even the sunfish are spooky at times. Local experts consider Elmo a tough lake to fish because it has cold, clear water and very deep drop-offs which one frustrated angler claims, "fall into eternity". The action starts in late June and early July, and the trophies aren't usually caught until late summer or fall. Walleyes are stocked annually. Hybrid muskie fingerlings were added in 1983, and stocking will continue every 3 years.

SPECIES	POPULATION	AVERAGE SIZE
Bass	Good	Medium to Large
Northern Pike	Excellent	Small to Large
Muskie	Poor	Medium
Walleye	Poor to Fair	Small
Crappie	Fair	Medium
Sunfish	Good	Medium

BASS Early-season bass are in the weeds and trees in 1 to 5 feet of water on the south end of the lake. In the summer, most of the bass are in the shallow brush rather than schooled on the weedy edges and breaks as they are in other lakes. The best supply is on the west side with some on the north and south ends of the lake. The bass bonanza starts in mid-September and continues into October if the weather stays warm. Both the shallow brush areas and the deeper water (10 to 20 foot depths) produce at this time of the year. Look for the little bends or inverted points in the contours at the 12 to 18 foot depths where deep water runs closer to shore. If this doesn't produce, move up to the 6 to 8 foot depths.

NORTHERN PIKE & MUSKIE The creek beds (inlets) and the bay at the south end of the lake attract northerns all season. The upper west side in front of the small bay is also productive. Work a deep-diving crankbait or a big spinnerbait with a drop retrieve outside the weedy edge. In the summer, try speedtrolling on the east side. Start at 15 feet, and work down to 35 feet. Be sure to use the right sized bottom-bumping lures for the different depths. In the fall, fish the submerged trees, weeds, and brush in 4 to 6 feet of water around the land point on the upper west side. The 7 to 12 foot depths in front of the southern bay are winter hotspots. You'll find a few muskies in the same locations as the northerns.

WALLEYE The sharp drop-offs on the lower east side offers the best chance for walleyes. Slowly work a jig and leech in the 10 to 25 foot depths. Winter walleyes have been caught above the flooded boat house on the lower east side.

CRAPPIE & SUNFISH Panfish are in the bays at both ends of the lake throughout the season. Also check out the brushy areas on the lower half of the east side. The cabbage-weed flat just above 20th Street is especially good. Summer sunfish can also be found on the deeper points and weedlines in the bass areas. Look for winter crappies in front of the flooded boat house on the lower east side and sunfish in front of the long point on the upper west side.

This information was provided by Dave Brandeman, Mike Bonn, and Chuck Hammer.

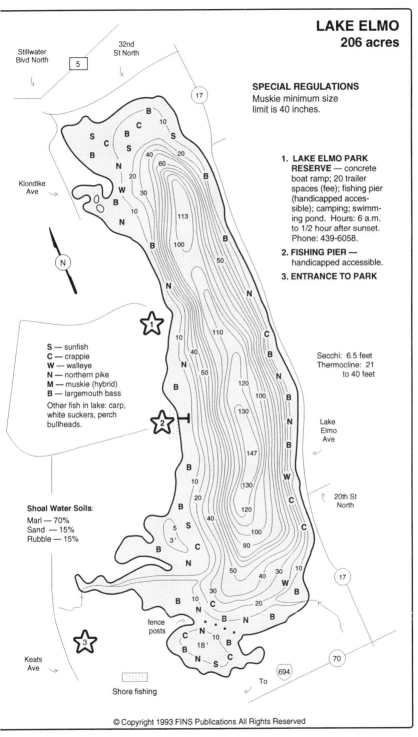

LAKE ELMO
206 acres

SPECIAL REGULATIONS
Muskie minimum size
limit is 40 inches.

1. **LAKE ELMO PARK RESERVE** — concrete boat ramp; 20 trailer spaces (fee); fishing pier (handicapped accessible); camping; swimming pond. Hours: 6 a.m. to 1/2 hour after sunset. Phone: 439-6058.

2. **FISHING PIER** — handicapped accessible.

3. **ENTRANCE TO PARK**

Secchi: 6.5 feet
Thermocline: 21
to 40 feet

S — sunfish
C — crappie
W — walleye
N — northern pike
M — muskie (hybrid)
B — largemouth bass

Other fish in lake: carp, white suckers, perch bullheads.

Shoal Water Soils:
Marl — 70%
Sand — 15%
Rubble — 15%

Shore fishing

Stillwater Blvd North
32nd St North
Klondike Ave
Lake Elmo Ave
20th St North
Keats Ave
fence posts
To

FOREST LAKE   Washington County

Forest Lake is touted as one of the best bass lakes in the state. Six-pound trophy bass are not unusual, and every year someone pulls out a 10 to 20 pound northern pike. Walleyes are stocked annually. Muskies were first stocked in 1985 and 1986, and hybrid tiger muskies were added in 1988.

Watch for very shallow rocky areas in the channel between Lake One and Lake Two. Lakes One and Three are considered the most productive for bass and walleyes. Lakes Two and Three are the best crappie locations. Big northerns are attracted to Lake Three, especially in August and September. Anglers participating in the big January ice-fishing contest do well by staying on the north and west sides of the outer edges of the ring.

SPECIES	POPULATION	AVERAGE SIZE
Bass	Excellent	Medium
Northern Pike	Excellent	Small to Large
Muskie	Poor	Small to Medium
Walleye	Good	Medium
Crappie	Excellent	Small to Medium
Sunfish	Excellent	Small

BASS The north side of the lakes will warm up first. Look for clumps of weeds, bulrushes, docks, and dark-bottom areas. In the summer, start the day on the weedy flats in the same areas. As the morning progresses, check out the docks, and then move to the weedline and points. A crankbait cast into the weedy edges can help locate the bass and cover a lot of water quickly. Follow up with a plastic worm. Lake One contains the most bass-attracting weedy points. A good all-season technique is to use a slip-bobber rig with a leech or small shiner minnow. Toss it into the clumps of weeds, and let it float just over the top. Move to the lily pads and shallow weedy areas (3 to 4 feet) in early fall. When the water gets colder, concentrate on the deep weedy edges.

NORTHERN PIKE & MUSKIE The east side of King's Point is a good early-season location. In August and September, try large spinnerbaits or spoons in 12 to 15 feet of water in Lake Three. Early winter is the best time for big fish. Try the 6 to 14 foot depths in front of Willow Point, then work eastward.

WALLEYE Look for humps, bars, and elongated points that drop into deep water. Fish the sharp drop-offs. Use a slip bobber with live bait on the edge of the weeds. Also try the sharp drop-offs in Lake Three halfway between Simon's Point and the marina. The weedy area in front of the outlet on the west side of Lake One is another walleye producer. Winter is the best season. Work the channels connecting the lakes. Use dead smelt, and keep it on the bottom.

CRAPPIE & SUNFISH Look for spring panfish in the back bays and channels and along the edge of the cattails and bulrushes. The area in front of the outlet at the west side of Lake One is a favorite crappie location. In spring and summer, crappies and sunfish can be found in front of the marina on Lake Three. Work west to about halfway to Simon's Point. Crappies will be at 12 feet or deeper. For winter crappies, fish the 22-foot hole on the upper east side of Lake One.

Information about this lake was provided by Dave Brandeman, Dick Grzywinski, Roger Rucci, Ken Schak, Brian Shaw, and Tim Walsh.

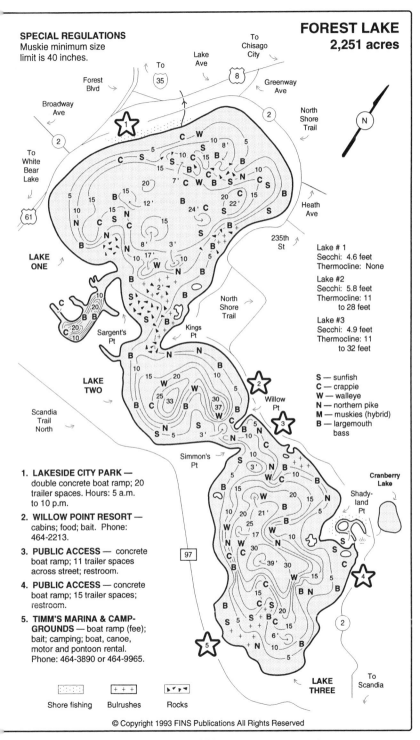

SPECIAL REGULATIONS
Muskie minimum size
limit is 40 inches.

FOREST LAKE
2,251 acres

To Chisago City

Lake Ave

Forest Blvd

To 35

Greenway Ave

Broadway Ave

North Shore Trail

To White Bear Lake

Heath Ave

LAKE ONE

235th St

Sargent's Pt

North Shore Trail

Kings Pt

LAKE TWO

Scandia Trail North

Willow Pt

Simmon's Pt

Cranberry Lake

Shadyland Pt

Lake # 1
Secchi: 4.6 feet
Thermocline: None

Lake #2
Secchi: 5.8 feet
Thermocline: 11 to 28 feet

Lake #3
Secchi: 4.9 feet
Thermocline: 11 to 32 feet

S — sunfish
C — crappie
W — walleye
N — northern pike
M — muskies (hybrid)
B — largemouth bass

1. **LAKESIDE CITY PARK** —
   double concrete boat ramp; 20
   trailer spaces. Hours: 5 a.m.
   to 10 p.m.

2. **WILLOW POINT RESORT** —
   cabins; food; bait. Phone:
   464-2213.

3. **PUBLIC ACCESS** — concrete
   boat ramp; 11 trailer spaces
   across street; restroom.

4. **PUBLIC ACCESS** — concrete
   boat ramp; 15 trailer spaces;
   restroom.

5. **TIMM'S MARINA & CAMP-
   GROUNDS** — boat ramp (fee);
   bait; camping; boat, canoe,
   motor and pontoon rental.
   Phone: 464-3890 or 464-9965.

97

LAKE THREE

To Scandia

Shore fishing   Bulrushes   Rocks

139

Square Lake, located 7 miles north of Stillwater, is the metro area's prime trout lake. Rainbow trout have been stocked annually since 1981, and atlantic salmon since 1988. The northern pike population continues to be good despite the DNR's efforts to remove them and curtail their spawning activity so small trout and salmon would have a better chance to grow. The high oil content of the trout provides an exceptional nutritional boost for the northern pike, and trophy northerns up to 23 pounds are caught every year. This is a deep, cold, spring-fed lake with few weeds, lots of sharp drop-offs, and very clear water.

SPECIES	POPULATION	AVERAGE SIZE
Bass	Fair	Small to Medium
Northern Pike	Good	Small to Large
Trout & Salmon	Good	Small to Medium
Crappie	Poor	Medium to Large
Sunfish	Fair to Good	Medium

BASS Work the overhanging trees from the barn on the north side to the middle of the west side of the lake.

NORTHERN PIKE Fish the trout areas on the north side of the lake with a medium sized sucker minnow. Or try trolling in 3 to 12 feet of water with a large stickbait or spinnerbait.

TROUT & SALMON The best all-season locations are the north, northeast, and northwest sides of the lake. Give special attention to the sunken platform on the northeastern side of the lake in about 22 feet of water; the 2-foot shelf at the 32 to 34 foot depths in front of the barn; and the area from the barn west to the first buoy. Keep your bait on the bottom, start at 32 feet, and work down to 45 feet. Summer and fall are the most productive times; the hotter the better. The trout will either be off the bottom in 32 to 40 feet of water or suspended in 20 to 40 feet of water in the same locations. For suspended fish, use a slip bobber with a light line (6-pound test or lighter) and a #10 or #12 hook dressed with a corn and crawler. Also try trolling for suspended fish (best in June and July). Keep your lure 20 to 30 feet below the surface. Use a medium to large (#8 to #13) floating lure with 2 to 4 small splitshot sinkers about 3 feet from the lure, or try a corn and crawler combination rigged with a cowbell.

You'll find the bigger trout on the bottom. Use a corn and crawler combination without the slip bobber, and add two 1/4 ounce splitshot sinkers about 18 inches from the hook. It's best to be anchored (you'll need about 100 feet of anchor rope) because the fish don't respond to trolling when they're on the bottom. In the winter, start in front of the barn and work the 10 to 12 foot depths west to the second dock. Use a small hook and a crappie minnow on a light line (4-pound test).

CRAPPIE & SUNFISH Spring sunfish and crappies are on the inside edge of the weeds on the north and northwest sides of the lake. Summer sunfish are in the 5 to 12 foot depths, and crappies are on the deepest weedlines. The area in front of the cattails holds sunnies all season. For fly fishing, work both sides of the cattails at the boat launch and the shoreline down to the beach.

This information was provided by Randy Barkley, Mike Bonn, and Patty Holman.

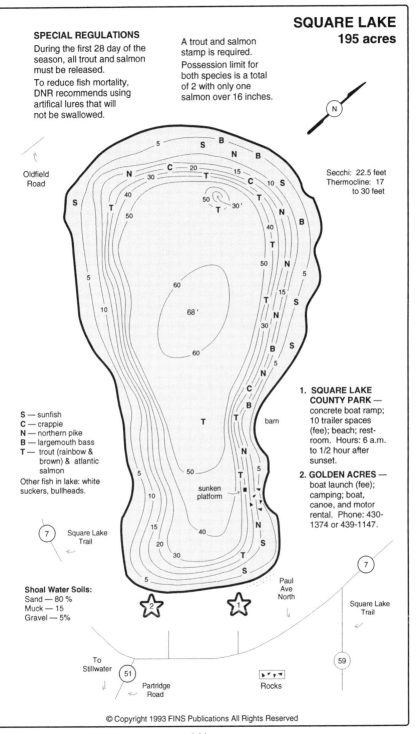

SQUARE LAKE
195 acres

SPECIAL REGULATIONS

During the first 28 day of the season, all trout and salmon must be released.

To reduce fish mortality, DNR recommends using artifical lures that will not be swallowed.

A trout and salmon stamp is required. Possession limit for both species is a total of 2 with only one salmon over 16 inches.

Oldfield Road

Secchi: 22.5 feet
Thermocline: 17 to 30 feet

S — sunfish
C — crappie
N — northern pike
B — largemouth bass
T — trout (rainbow & brown) & atlantic salmon
Other fish in lake: white suckers, bullheads.

barn

1. **SQUARE LAKE COUNTY PARK** — concrete boat ramp; 10 trailer spaces (fee); beach; restroom. Hours: 6 a.m. to 1/2 hour after sunset.

2. **GOLDEN ACRES** — boat launch (fee); camping; boat, canoe, and motor rental. Phone: 430-1374 or 439-1147.

sunken platform

7 Square Lake Trail

Shoal Water Soils:
Sand — 80 %
Muck — 15
Gravel — 5%

Paul Ave North

7 Square Lake Trail

To Stillwater 51
Partridge Road

59

Rocks

White Bear Lake is one of the better walleye lakes in the metro area. Huge numbers of walleye fingerlings have been stocked annually since 1977. Large-mouth bass tournament anglers claim that White Bear Lake is as good as Lake Minnetonka in June and July, and sometimes it's better. Smallmouth bass are harder to find. Muskie yearlings, donated by Muskies Inc., were added in 1991 and 1992. There are also a few muskies here from an earlier stocking effort.

The secret to success on this very clear lake is to move deeper when you're not catching fish, particularly on sunny days. The best times will be during low-light periods, especially the hours from dusk to dawn. Perch and crayfish are the major food source for the larger gamefish, and the wise angler takes that into consideration when selecting lures and locations.

White Bear Lake is loaded with more structure per acre than any other lake in the metro area. It offers an abundance of rocky reefs, deep weedlines, and weedy bars and flats. The south and east ends of the lake have solid rock or sand and gravel bottom and are the best areas for smallmouth bass and walleyes.

In the spring and fall, the best shore fishing for bass and panfish is at Matoska Park and both sides of the Manitou Island bridge.

Use caution on this lake in the winter. White Bear has a history of dumping cars through the ice, especially when the water level is low. According to the White Bear Lake Conservation District, the poor ice conditions are caused by the warmer water entering the lake through springs. This water is not sufficiently cooled before it reaches the surface and creates weak areas in the ice.

SPECIES	POPULATION	AVERAGE SIZE
Bass	Good	Small to Medium
Smallmouth	Fair	Medium to Large
Northern Pike	Excellent	Small to Medium
Walleye	Good	Small to Medium
Crappie	Fair	Medium
Sunfish	Excellent	Small to Medium

BASS In June, a good place to start is Gardenette Bar, a bulrush and sand structure in front of Lions Park on the western section of the lake. Also work the little boggy bay east of "The Peninsula" where Mahtomedi Avenue touches the shoreline. The area in front of the Ramsey County beach near the pumphouse is also productive. Try a topwater bait, white spinnerbait, or rattling lure.

After the weeds here get too thick, from mid-June to the end of July, fish the points, inside turns, and shoreline breaks. A good example is the north side of "The Peninsula". Look for small points and inside turns on this shoreline structure. It's much more irregular than it appears on the map. Just above this area, there's a long sunken island that tops at 11 feet on one end and 14 feet on the other end. It holds smallmouth bass, largemouth bass, and walleyes. The shoreline breaks and small underwater points from the southwestern tip of Manitou Island to the northwest side of Ordway's Bar are also productive. You'll find some good docks that hold summer fish from the southeastern end of the lake west to about half a block below East County Line Road (Century Avenue). They are the most productive on sunny days in August. The best ones are adjacent to deep water and healthy vegetation. Also fish both the inside weedline and deeper breaks around these docks. In the fall, look for structure with tight, fast drop-offs such as the west side of Ordway's Bar and the southeast point on Manitou Island.

NORTHERN PIKE & MUSKIES You'll find northerns in the cabbage weed patches around Manitou Island. Also work the far southern bay; the weedy areas on the west side of "The Peninsula"; and the south side of Ordway's Bar. Cast your lure over the tops of the weeds. Try a white or yellow spinnerbait on clear days, and switch to a black one on cloudy days. The 18-foot gravel and rock bar in front of Birchwood Village is a popular location for summer and fall muskies.

WALLEYE In the early season, work a jig and minnow at the 18-foot depths on the classic walleye structures. Look for hard bottom areas, especially bars, humps, and sunken islands with a sand, gravel, or rock bottom. By the first of June, these areas are so hammered by anglers that the walleyes move into the weeds until the end of August. Look for the cabbage weeds at least 18 feet deep. There is no preferred location. Try vertical jigging or use a live-bait rig on the weedline, especially on the inside turns. Minnows work better than leeches. This clear water dictates a subtle presentation; flashy, noisy or vibrating lures are not effective.

In the fall, move back to the classic walleye structures (sand, gravel, or rocky bars) in 15 to 25 feet of water. A live-bait rig with a minnow is still preferred. In the winter, try the 15-foot depths on the rocky Ordway's Bar and the Bellaire Bar.

SMALLMOUTH BASS In the early season, use the same techniques as for walleyes. You'll find the smallmouth bass scattered in 5 to 7 feet of water in the hard-bottom areas in front of Bellaire Beach and Birchwood Village. Also try the rocky weedy area on the west side of Ordway's Bar. In the summer, work the deeper edges of the bars in these same areas. Fall smallmouth bass will be in 12 to 15 feet of water along the top of the drop-offs around the rocky bars. The small 2-foot rocky hump above the Peninsula is a good early and late season location.

CRAPPIE The rocky area in front of Matoska Park and around the Ramsey County Park beach are good spring locations. The entire Ordway's Bar is the best crappie spot on the lake in all seasons. In addition, you'll probably pick up walleyes, largemouth bass, smallmouth bass, and northern pike here too. For spring crappies, start with a plain hook or with a 1/32 or 1/16 ounce jig with a tube or twister tail, and tip it with a crappie minnow. As the water warms, use a larger jig. Summer crappies will be near the weedline (18 feet) during low-light periods and suspended over deeper areas during the day. Look for irregularities (indentations, fingers, etc.) on the bars. The 11-foot hump in front of Bellaire Beach and the north side of Ordway's Bar are good winter locations.

SUNFISH Most of the shallow weedy bays will hold spring sunfish. The bulrushes, cattails, and weeds on the northwest side of Manitou Island are prime spawning areas. Also work around the Manitou Island bridge and up into the bay in front of Matoska Park. There's a good supply of summer sunfish here too. Concentrate on the weedy points in the bay or the inside curves of the island. Most of the bass haunts in the lake are also productive.

Information about this lake was provided by Mark Allen, Durk Berrisford, Bob Mehsikomer, Tina Outlaw, Brad Stanius, and Joe Unger.

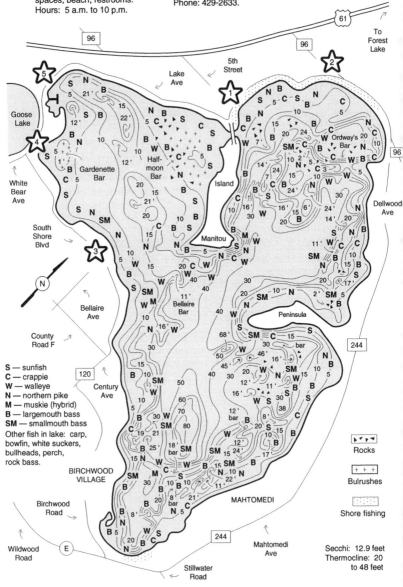

WHITE BEAR LAKE
2,368 acres

1. **MATOSKA PARK** — concrete boat ramp; 15 trailer spaces. White Bear Lake permit required by non-residents.

2. **RAMSEY COUNTY PARK** — double concrete boat ramp (very shallow in low-water years); 37 trailer spaces; beach; restrooms. Hours: 5 a.m. to 10 p.m.

3. **BELLAIRE PARK** — beach; picnic.

4. **LIONS PARK** — fishing dock (dry in low-water years).

5. **TALLY'S** — boat launch (fee); boat, motor and pontoon rental; bait. Phone: 429-2633.

SPECIAL REGULATIONS
Muskie minimum size limit is 40 inches.

61
To Forest Lake

96
96
96

5th Street
Lake Ave

Goose Lake

White Bear Ave

South Shore Blvd

Bellaire Ave

County Road F

120

Century Ave

BIRCHWOOD VILLAGE

Birchwood Road

Wildwood Road

Stillwater Road

Mahtomedi Ave

MAHTOMEDI

244

244

Dellwood Ave

Ordway's Bar

Island

Manitou

Peninsula

Gardenette Bar

Half-moon Bar

Bellaire Bar

S — sunfish
C — crappie
W — walleye
N — northern pike
M — muskie (hybrid)
B — largemouth bass
SM — smallmouth bass
Other fish in lake: carp, bowfin, white suckers, bullheads, perch, rock bass.

Rocks

+ + +
Bulrushes

Shore fishing

Secchi: 12.9 feet
Thermocline: 20 to 48 feet

144

Additional Lakes

Since DNR studies have concluded that the majority of Twin Cities anglers fish for panfish, we have included some smaller lakes that are known to have good supplies of sunfish, crappies, and perch.

Not much has been written about these lakes, but many of them have decent public boat accesses, attractive parks or beaches, good shorefishing opportunities — including handicapped accessible fishing piers. Some of them even offer camping facilities. Most important, all of them contain a decent supply of fish.

Here are some of the differences between these small lakes and larger bodies of water.

- Small, shallow lakes will warm up faster and provide the earliest spring fishing.

- They are not usually considered good fall lakes because they cool down faster and lose their green weeds earlier than larger lakes.

- Small lakes are more prone to winterkill in harsh winters. Many of them have aeration devices to reduce the impact of winterkill and to provide a continuous supply of fish.

  The good news is that crappies and sunfish benefit from a partial winterkill because it reduces the population. The survivors grow larger because there is less competition for the available food.

- Smaller lakes are also prone to summerkill due to oxygen depletion. In large lakes, the oxygen supply is continuously renewed throughout the summer by wind action and healthy green weeds. Because smaller lakes have less surface area, they receive less wind action and produce less oxygen. On very fertile lakes, a heavy summer algae bloom on the surface can block out the sunlight and kill the oxygen-producing weeds.

The practice of Catch & Release for the larger game fish is critical for future fishing in these lakes. Small lakes don't have an unlimited supply of big fish, and indiscriminate harvesting by a few anglers could wipe them out.

Crooked Lake is a sunfish and crappie factory with populations well above the state and local averages, but most are very small. There are also some bass and northern pike here, and you may even find a few walleyes from an earlier stocking. This lake has a history of winterkills, but the installation of an aerator in 1988 will result in stable populations. A handicapped-accessible fishing pier was added in 1992 in Crooked Lake Beach Park on the east side of the lake.

SPECIES	POPULATION	AVERAGE SIZE
Bass	Fair	Medium
Northern Pike	Fair	Medium to Large
Crappie	Very Good	Small
Sunfish	Very Good	Small

BASS For all-season bass, the south, southwest, and west sides of the lake are the best locations. For a consistent supply, stay in the cabbage weeds. The heavy boat traffic spooks the fish and forces them to retreat from the edges of the weeds. A flashing vibrating lure like a spinnerbait with a large blade works best in the murky water. The lily pads in the shallow bay at the south end of the lake also produce bass all season. Try a black or purple plastic worm here.

NORTHERN PIKE Toss a yellow or white spinnerbait to the cabbage weeds on the south and southwest part of the lake.

CRAPPIE & SUNFISH The northern bay warms up first and attracts the early-season panfish. A little later, the southern bay will be productive too. This area holds sunfish all season. Stay near the bulrushes in 4 to 5 feet of water. Use a small white jig tipped with a worm. In the summer, the crappies will be suspended off the edge of the weeds, and the sunfish will be in all the bass areas. Winter is the most popular crappie season on this lake. The 26-foot hole in the lower section of the lake is the winter hotspot for both sunfish and crappies.

Information about this lake was provided by Lee Schoneman and Bob McLean.

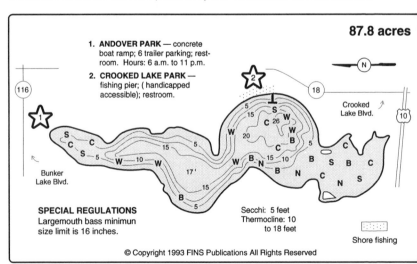

87.8 acres

1. **ANDOVER PARK** — concrete boat ramp; 6 trailer parking; restroom. Hours: 6 a.m. to 11 p.m.

2. **CROOKED LAKE PARK** — fishing pier; (handicapped accessible); restroom.

Crooked Lake Blvd.

Bunker Lake Blvd.

SPECIAL REGULATIONS
Largemouth bass minimun size limit is 16 inches.

Secchi: 5 feet
Thermocline: 10 to 18 feet

Shore fishing

Golden is a little gem of a lake that is part of the Rice Creek chain of lakes in Circle Pines. It was chemically rehabilitated in 1984 and huge numbers of bluegills, sunfish, channel catfish, largemouth bass, and walleyes were stocked in 1985. Northern pike and crappies have migrated in from the Loch Ness Children's Pond up at the headwaters near Blaine. An aerator has been installed to prevent winterkill.

The average size of the catfish is 2 to 4 pounds. There's a 16-inch size limit for largemouth bass. That means that you must release all bass that are less than 16 inches long. That's the size that is the most prolific and consumes the most small bluegills and sunfish. This keeps the lake from becoming overpopulated with stunted panfish.

SPECIES	POPULATION	AVERAGE SIZE
Bass	Good	Medium
Northern Pike	Good	Medium
Walleye	Poor	Medium
Crappie	Good	Medium
Sunfish	Excellent	Medium
Catfish	Good	Medium

There are some good shore fishing areas here. The shallow delta in front of the inlet on the northwest side of the lake has been removed so you can cast to deeper water from shore for sunnies, crappies, and bass. The land point on the lower west side of the lake in front of the county park holds walleyes, bass, sunfish, and crappies. The beach area attracts summer walleyes when the swimmers aren't present.

Information about this lake was provided by Dave Genz.

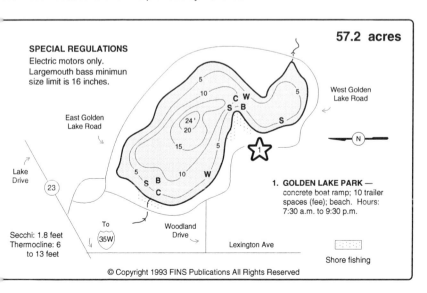

57.2 acres

SPECIAL REGULATIONS
Electric motors only.
Largemouth bass minimun
size limit is 16 inches.

West Golden
Lake Road

East Golden
Lake Road

Lake
Drive
23

Secchi: 1.8 feet
Thermocline: 6
to 13 feet

To
35W

Woodland
Drive

Lexington Ave

1. GOLDEN LAKE PARK —
concrete boat ramp; 10 trailer
spaces (fee); beach. Hours:
7:30 a.m. to 9:30 p.m.

Shore fishing

Ham Lake, located 1/8 mile east of Hwy. 65 near 157th Avenue in central Anoka County, is a good little trophy bass lake for the angler with a small boat. Every year at least one 7-pound bass is caught here. This lake warms up fast in the spring and offers good early-season panfishing. The clear water makes it a super night-fishing lake. An aerator on the lake prevents winterkill.

SPECIES	POPULATION	AVERAGE SIZE
Bass	Good	Medium to Large
Northern Pike	Good	Medium
Crappie	Excellent	Small
Sunfish	Excellent	Small

BASS The lily pads on the south side and the northeast bay attract June bass. Cast white spinnerbaits to the edge of the pads, or work the pockets of the pads with a Texas-rigged plastic worm or jig and pig. Also try the thickest weeds around the island. In the summer, fish the clumps of weeds around the entire lake with an orange-belly crankbait or plastic worm. Work both the weedy flats and weedy edges. Don't pass up the submerged cabbage weeds on the underwater point at the north end of the lake. Check out the same locations in the fall but use larger lures. In October when the frogs migrate back into the lake, the northeastern bay is productive. Use live frogs or green spinnerbaits.

NORTHERN PIKE For all-season success, fish the weedy areas around the entire lake. In early season, work the 2 to 7 foot depths with a spinnerbait. Move down to the 10 to 15 foot depths in the summer. Try trolling with a medium running crankbait (4 to 8 feet deep). A jig and pig in 8 to 12 feet of water works best in the fall. The north side of the lake is a popular ice fishing location.

CRAPPIE & SUNFISH The shoreline areas are alive with early-season crappies and sunfish, especially the northeast bay. In the summer, the crappies will be roaming the 10 to 20 foot depths in the basin of the lake. Summer sunfish will be in the bass areas. The bigger ones will be on the weedlines.

Information about this lake was provided by Larry Bollig and Bob McLean.

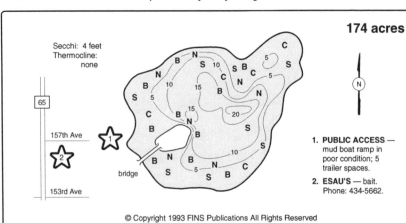

174 acres

Secchi: 4 feet
Thermocline: none

1. **PUBLIC ACCESS** — mud boat ramp in poor condition; 5 trailer spaces.

2. **ESAU'S** — bait. Phone: 434-5662.

Martin is one of the better lakes in the area for large crappies, especially in the winter and spring. This is a small, shallow, muddy lake that is subject to frequent winterkills. The crappie and carp populations are booming, but the supplies of sunfish, bass, northern pike, and walleye are meager. Bass and walleye fry were restocked after a partial winterkill in 1987/88.

Martin Lake is located in the Regional County Park one mile north of County Road 22 on East Martin Lake Drive in northeastern Anoka county.

SPECIES	POPULATION	AVERAGE SIZE
Bass	Fair	Medium
Northern Pike	Poor	Small
Walleye	Poor	Small
Crappie	Good	Medium to Large
Sunfish	Fair	Small to Medium

WALLEYE You'll find some early-season walleyes on the points and on both ends of the lake in about 5 to 8 feet of water. But by mid-June, the carp will drive you daft.

CRAPPIE Look for spring crappies in the weedy pockets in about 2 feet of water in front of the channels on both ends of the lake. As the water warms, move out to the deeper weedlines and breaks at the 10 to 12 foot depths. The crappies will stay here through early ice. You'll find most of the winter crappies off the point on the west shoreline, the round point above the boat launch, and the 16-foot hole. The lower west side of the lake is a good location in the morning and after dark. Glow-in-the-dark jigs or ice flies tipped with crappie minnows or wax worms are popular. Work the 10 to 15 foot depths about 1 to 5 feet off the bottom.

SUNFISH Spring sunnies will be in the shallow bays and channels, around the fallen trees, and in front of the dam.

Information about this lake was provided by Larry Bollig, Mike Hanson, Steve Larson, and Alex Lind.

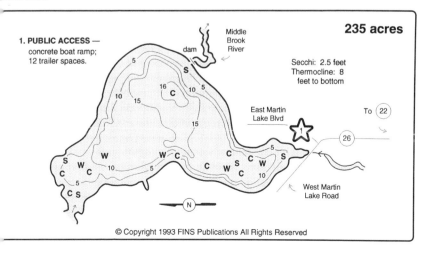

1. PUBLIC ACCESS — concrete boat ramp; 12 trailer spaces.

235 acres

Secchi: 2.5 feet
Thermocline: 8 feet to bottom

Middle Brook River

East Martin Lake Blvd

To 22

West Martin Lake Road

East Moore Lake, located just north of I-694 on Hwy. 65 in Fridley, is one of the better shore fishing locations in the metro area. In the mid-80's, retention ponds were built to divert storm sewer runoff, shallow areas were covered with plastic sheets to reduce the growth of weeds that choked the lake in the summer; and an aeration system was installed to prevent winterkill.

Huge numbers of largemouth bass, channel catfish, and walleyes were stocked in 1986 and 1987. No further stocking is anticipated.

West Moore Lake across the road also has an aeration system. Although this small lake is shallow and very weedy, DNR test nettings indicate nice sized bluegills and bass.

SPECIES	POPULATION	AVERAGE SIZE
Bass	Good	Medium
Walleye	Good	Large
Catfish	Fair	Medium
Crappie	Poor	Small
Sunfish	Excellent	Small

BASS & WALLEYE The west side of the lake by the culvert is the best early season shore fishing location. Walk in from the road and look for an opening in the cattails. The deep drop-off here close to shore produces fish in the summer and fall. If you cast over to the aerator, you'll be on the edge of the bar where you'll find the summer walleyes. The fishing dock shines in the summer and fall. Make long casts to the 17-foot hole.

CRAPPIE & SUNFISH The north side of the lake is a good spring location but it's difficult to reach because of the abundant cattails. The mouth of the culverts on East Moore Lake and West Moore Lake are good all-season spots.

Information about this lake was provided by Dave Genz.

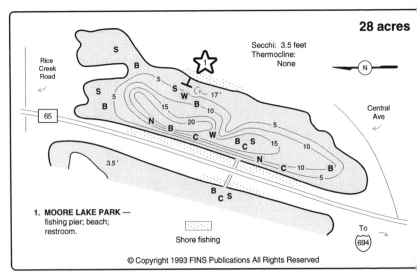

28 acres

Secchi: 3.5 feet
Thermocline: None

Rice Creek Road

Central Ave

65

3.5'

17'

1. **MOORE LAKE PARK** —
   fishing pier; beach; restroom.

Shore fishing

To 694

Courthouse Pond, located in Chaska behind the County Courthouse, is one of six lakes in the metro area that is stocked with trout. A favorite with the kids, this small clay-pit lake offers plenty of shore fishing territory and a new fishing dock accessible to handicapped anglers. No boating is allowed. Be cautious around this lake. In some places, the steep shoreline drops from 1 to 20 feet very quickly.

Rainbow trout are stocked here annually, and occasionally this lake receives adult rainbows that were displayed in the DNR pond at the State Fair. Courthouse Pond also contains lots of green sunfish and small bullheads. The green sunfish grow quite large in this lake but are not considered very tasty.

SPECIES	POPULATION	AVERAGE SIZE
Trout	Fair to Good	Medium
Sunfish	Good	Small to Large
Bullheads	Good	Small

TROUT Use a light graphite jig-stick with 2 to 4 pound test line. Spring and fall provides the most action. Put a miniature marshmallow (green color is best) on the eye of the hook and add a large inflated night crawler. Also experiment with a piece of red yarn on the hook. Put on a slip bobber and toss out as far as you can (10 to 25 feet). Or try a live-bait rig without a bobber; place the sinker about 4 feet from the hook. Don't drag your bait on the bottom or you'll catch bullheads. In the early season and early winter, the area where the lake narrows down on the south end of the lake is a good location. In the winter, the small pond is productive. Use a #2 Swedish Pimple.

You'll need a trout stamp, and be sure to heed the trout season dates.

Information about this lake was provided by Randy Barkley, Jeff Byrne, Dave Genz, Duane Shodeen, and Tiny Thomas.

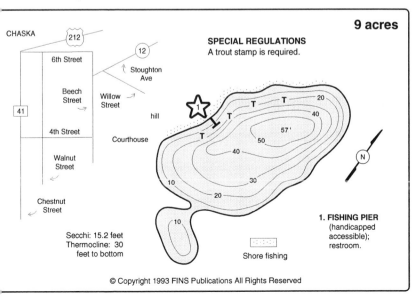

9 acres

CHASKA

SPECIAL REGULATIONS
A trout stamp is required.

Secchi: 15.2 feet
Thermocline: 30 feet to bottom

Shore fishing

1. **FISHING PIER** (handicapped accessible); restroom.

EAGLE LAKE

Carver County

Eagle Lake is a very shallow, calm, murky lake that's fun and easy to fish. The abundance of lily pads and floating bog islands provide prime sunfish and large-mouth bass habitat that is productive all summer. Muskies were first stocked in 1989 and stocking will continue every 3 years. An aeration device prevents winterkill.

SPECIES	POPULATION	AVERAGE SIZE
Bass	Good	Medium
Walleye	Poor	Small
Muskie	Fair	Small to Medium
Crappie	Fair	Small to Medium
Sunfish	Excellent	Medium

BASS For all-season success, work around the shoreline and the edges of the floating bogs. In the lily pads, throw a floating jighead with a weedless hook or a lightly weighted Texas-rigged plastic worm. Let it fall off the edge of the pad, give it a jerk, and pop it up on the next pad. This is a good technique when the sun is high.

To fish the floating bogs on sunny days, use a sinking-minnow lure. Adjust the diving bill (lip) so the lure swims left or right depending on which side of the bog you intend to fish. Toss it out, let it sink, and give it a jerk. The lure will swim under the bog. A crawdad pattern lure is best.

On cloudy days, work the edges or in front of the lily pads, cattails, or floating bogs with spinnerbaits or floating lures.

SUNFISH Work all the bass locations with worms or night crawlers on a plain hook and a bobber.

Information about this lake was provided by Ted Welch.

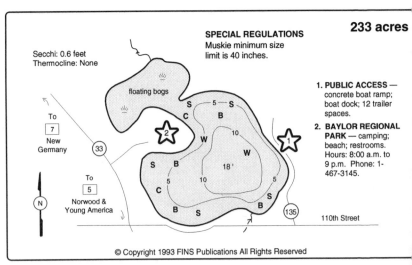

© Copyright 1993 FINS Publications All Rights Reserved

152

Hydes Lake, located southwest of Lake Waconia off Hwy. 5, is a popular spring and winter lake noted for its nice sized sunfish. Walleye fry were stocked in most years from 1972 to 1991. In the future, walleyes will only be stocked after a winterkill. This is a typical farm lake with little structure and very fertile water. It is subject to winterkill, and the size and quantity of the fish may vary from year to year. The lake has no aeration system and none is planned in the near future.

SPECIES	POPULATION	AVERAGE SIZE
Bass	Fair	Medium
Northern Pike	Fair to Good	Small to Medium
Walleye	Poor to Fair	Small to Medium
Crappie	Fair	Medium
Sunfish	Very Good	Medium to Large

BASS & NORTHERNS June bass are in the sunfish areas. Move to the weedline in the summer. Winter northerns can be found on the lip of the point on the northeast corner. Use a 4-inch sucker minnow.

SUNFISH & CRAPPIES In the spring, the east and south sides of the lake are the best crappie and sunfish areas. Stay in the 1 to 5 foot depths and use a 1/32 or 1/64 ounce jig with a crappie minnow or a very small hook with a piece of night crawler or wax worm. There is a good sunfish spawning bed on the southwest corner. When the weeds get high, move to the inside weedline. Tiny green shrimp are a local favorite bait on this lake. Stay in the same areas in the summer. This is also good territory for fly-fishing. For summer crappies, try drifting across the lake. Vary your depth. In the winter, the most productive sunfish areas are the 8 to 12 foot depths on the north and west sides of the lake. Also try the area in front of the spawning beds in 14 to 15 feet of water.

This information was provided by Evie Hedtke, Orrin Sechter, and Duane Shodeen.

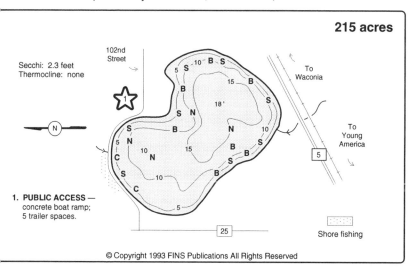

215 acres

Secchi: 2.3 feet
Thermocline: none

102nd Street

To Waconia

To Young America

1. **PUBLIC ACCESS —** concrete boat ramp; 5 trailer spaces.

Shore fishing

Parley Lake is located a mile and a half north of Hwy. 5 on Lake Township Roa
just south of the town of St. Bonifacius. It is known for its huge sunfish, especiall
in August. This is a very weedy, shallow mudhole with little structure. It has
history of winterkill but because Six Mile Creek connects it with Lake Minnetonka
Parley receives a steady supply of fish including a few walleyes.

SPECIES	POPULATION	AVERAGE SIZE
Bass	Poor to Fair	Medium
Northern Pike	Very Good	Small to Medium
Crappie	Very Good	Medium to Large
Sunfish	Very Good	Medium to Large

BASS When water levels are normal, start in the northern bay. Toss sma
spinners over the shallow weed growth. Then move to the area in front of the bi
rock on the east shoreline, and work the weedline up to the narrows.

NORTHERN PIKE In the early season, work the outside weedline around th
entire lake. Look for summer northerns in the weedy shallows on the north sic
of the 4-foot sunken island. Cast a spinnerbait here in the evening. Speedtrollin
down the middle of the lake is a good summer technique. Zig-zag back and forth

CRAPPIE For early-season action, fish the Six Mile Creek, the upper lake, an
the 17-foot hole. Use a slip bobber with a crappie minnow above the hole, an
stay 4 to 5 feet off the bottom. This is also a good summer and winter location
For more winter crappies, work the 14-foot depths on the point at the southea
end of the lake and in front of the big rock on shore on the east side.

SUNFISH Spring sunfish are in the warmer, muddy upper lake. Use a small j
tipped with a wax worm about a foot below a small bobber. Retrieve it slowly. Th
biggest sunnies are caught in August. Drift or troll very slowly in front of the b
rock on the east shore. Also try the north side of the 4-foot hump and the rock pi
in front of the point on the southeast side.

Information about this lake was provided by Jeff Byrne and Dave Gentz.

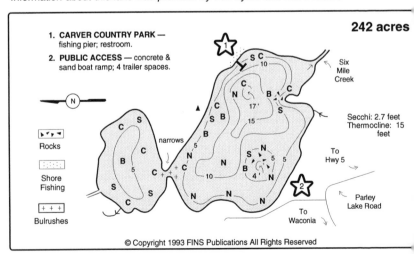

1. **CARVER COUNTRY PARK —**
   fishing pier; restroom.
2. **PUBLIC ACCESS —** concrete &
   sand boat ramp; 4 trailer spaces.

242 acres

Six Mile Creek

Secchi: 2.7 feet
Thermocline: 15 feet

To Hwy 5

Parley Lake Road

To Waconia

Rocks

Shore Fishing

Bulrushes

narrows

Kroon Lake, located 2-1/2 miles south of Lindstrom off County Road 85, is a very fertile panfish factory. But you'll have to be there early in the season before the prolific weed growth chokes out the prime areas. The water is very clear in the spring but frequently pea soup green in the summer from the heavy algae bloom.

SPECIES	POPULATION	AVERAGE SIZE
Bass	Good	Medium
Northern Pike	Fair	Medium to Large
Crappie	Excellent	Small to Medium
Sunfish	Excellent	Small to Medium

BASS Early June bass will be in the shallow, weedy areas on the south end of the lake. About mid-June, these areas become choked with weeds. Toss a weedless lure into the openings (holes) in the weeds. Or work a jig and pig on the weedline around the entire lake. In the fall, stay on the weedline, but use a plastic worm or shallow-running crankbait and try to tic the top of the weeds. When the shallow weeds die off, move down to the edge of the deepest weeds.

NORTHERN PIKE Start at the inlet at the south end of the lake and the outlet on the west side. As the season progresses, concentrate on the cabbage weeds on the south end of the lake. In the summer, work the weedline and the points with sucker minnows. Don't pass up the sunken island on the east side of the lake. In the fall, work all the same areas but keep moving and cover lots of water.

CRAPPIE AND SUNFISH You can catch early-season sunfish and crappies from shore around the boat launch and in the weedy area on the north end of the lake. Summer sunfish are in the weedy areas around the lake. In the fall, work the remaining green weeds in the southwest section of the lake where the weedline drops fast into deep water. When the weeds die off, the sunfish and crappies will move out and suspend off the breaks.

Information about this lake was provided by Frankie Dusenka.

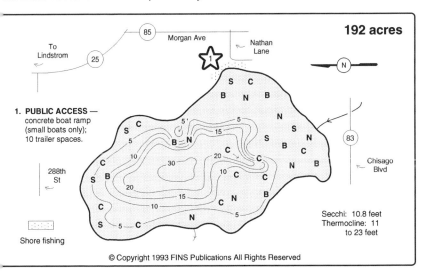

Little Lake, located 2-1/2 miles northeast of Center City, is known for producing decent-sized, early-season crappies and sunfish. This is a very weedy, murky, fertile lake, and trollers will appreciate the classic weedlines. Walleyes have been stocked periodically since 1986. This lake has a history of partial winterkill.

SPECIES	POPULATION	AVERAGE SIZE
Bass	Good	Small to Medium
Northern Pike	Good	Medium to Large
Walleye	Fair	Medium
Crappie	Excellent	Medium to Large
Sunfish	Fair	Medium to Large

BASS The bass will be in the same locations as the northerns. When both occupy the same locations, the bass will be in the thick weeds while the northerns are usually on the weedy edges.

NORTHERN PIKE Early-season northerns will be in the shallow weeds all over the lake. In the summer and fall, the weedline in the southeast bay is a good location. Also try the underwater point (bar) on the west side of the lake. In the winter, work the deepest holes on the flats in 15 to 20 feet of water.

CRAPPIE Spring crappies are in the shallow, dark-bottom bays on the west side of the lake. Summer crappies will be suspended at 6 to 15 feet in 10 to 25 feet of water. In the fall, check out the summer locations, and then try the shallower areas. Winter crappies will be in 15 to 20 feet of water in the center of the lake.

SUNFISH Spring sunfish will be in the weedy bays. In summer, fish the weeds and the weedline on the west side or in the southeast corner of the lake. In the fall, the deepest weeds in these areas will hold most of the population. Winter sunfish will be scattered in the sparse weeds in 8 to 20 feet of water.

Information about this lake was provided by Frankie Dusenka.

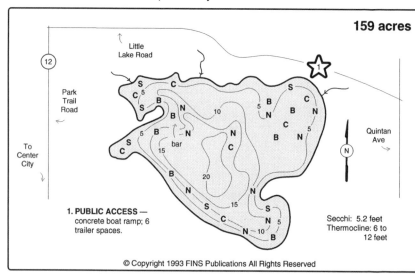

159 acres

Little Lake Road

Park Trail Road

To Center City

Quintan Ave

bar

1. **PUBLIC ACCESS —** concrete boat ramp; 6 trailer spaces.

Secchi: 5.2 feet
Thermocline: 6 to 12 feet

Sunrise Lake, located approximately 2 miles northwest of the city of Lindstrom, has received much attention in the past few years for its slab-sized panfish as well as big bass and northern pike, especially in the winter. However, over-harvesting of the larger fish has reduced the average size. Since the DNR does not restock this lake (no public access) and there is no inlet to allow fish to migrate in from other lakes, the supply of fish could be meager after a severe winterkill.

SPECIES	POPULATION	AVERAGE SIZE
Bass	Good	Medium
Northern Pike	Fair	Medium
Crappie	Good	Medium
Sunfish	Good	Medium

BASS June bass will be in the weedy, shallow areas all over the lake. In July, fish the inside edge of the cabbage weeds and lily pads with topwater lures or white spinnerbaits. Also work the bulrush point on the west side of the lake.

NORTHERN PIKE Early-season northerns will be in 1 to 4 feet of water in the shallow weedy bays in Little Sunrise; the far south end of the main lake; and the small bay on the west side in front of the outlet. In the summer and fall, move out to the outside edge of the cabbage weeds or the narrows. The east side of the narrows in 8 to 15 feet of water produces in winter.

CRAPPIE & SUNFISH Start the season in the shallow weedy bays in Little Sunrise. Emerging cabbage weeds and submerged timber on the west side of Little Sunrise are especially good for crappies. As the season progresses, crappies move out to the edge of the cabbage weeds and sunfish will be in the green weeds all over the lake. Work the deeper holes (8 to 15 feet) in the winter.

Information about this lake was provided by Frankie Dusenka and Orrin Sechter.

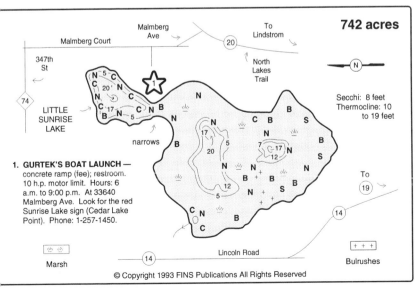

742 acres

Malmberg Ave
To Lindstrom
Malmberg Court
347th St
North Lakes Trail
74
LITTLE SUNRISE LAKE
narrows

Secchi: 8 feet
Thermocline: 10 to 19 feet

1. GURTEK'S BOAT LAUNCH — concrete ramp (fee); restroom. 10 h.p. motor limit. Hours: 6 a.m. to 9:00 p.m. At 33640 Malmberg Ave. Look for the red Sunrise Lake sign (Cedar Lake Point). Phone: 1-257-1450.

To 19

To 14

Marsh

Lincoln Road

14

Bulrushes

CRYSTAL LAKE

Crystal Lake, located in the city of Robbinsdale, is a very turbid, murky lake with a heavy summer algae bloom due to the many storm drains pouring nutrients into the lake. An aeration system prevents winterkill.

Crystal Lake is a northern pike and panfish oasis. Hybrid muskies were stocked in 1984 and will be restocked every 3 years. They have now surpassed the legal size limit of 40 inches. The reason for the good growth rate is the superior forage base including goldfish! Don't even think about using goldfish for bait — it's illegal!

SPECIES	POPULATION	AVERAGE SIZE
Bass	Good	Small to Medium
Northern Pike	Excellent	Medium to Large
Muskie	Fair	Medium to Large
Crappie	Excellent	Small
Sunfish	Good	Small

NORTHERN PIKE & MUSKIE   The lower half of the lake holds the major supply and some of the best spots can be reached from shore. Work the weedy flats no deeper that 5 feet. The west side of the 7-foot hole is a big-fish location. June and July are the most productive months. Try a gold or orange bucktail lure that resembles a goldfish. Bright flashy lures are best in this very murky lake.

CRAPPIE & SUNFISH   Early-season sunfish are on the shallow flats on the south end of the lake. The area in front of the drainage ditch on the northeast corner is an all-season crappie hotspot that can be reached from shore. The inside turn just north of the underwater point on the upper west side of the lake is productive in the summer, fall, and winter. More winter sunfish are in 10 to 15 feet of water, and crappies are at the 5 to 10 foot depths.

Information about this lake was provided by Tom Zenanko.

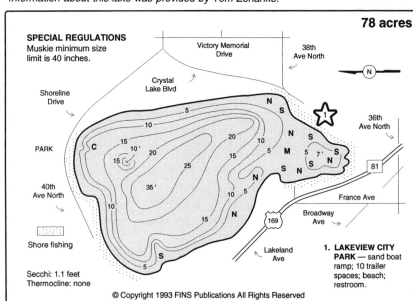

Haften is a small, quiet, easy-to-fish lake that's great for family fun. Mud and cat-tails plug up both sides of the boat launch. It can only accommodate a small boat, and in low-water years even that's impossible. The good news is that you won't be bothered by speedboats and water-skiers. This lake is crammed full of fish and has no history of winterkill in the past 10 years. It's also a popular winter lake.

Haften Lake is located on 75th Lane about a third of a mile north of County Road 50 near the city of Greenfield in western Hennepin County.

SPECIES	POPULATION	AVERAGE SIZE
Bass	Good	Medium
Northern Pike	Fair	Medium
Crappie	Good	Small
Sunfish	Excellent	Small

BASS   You'll find the bass in the weeds, lily pads, and rocky areas around the entire lake. The south end is especially good. Use a weightless plastic lizard and crawl it over the lily pads, giving particular attention to the pockets and edges. Also cast a dark colored spinnerbait or weedless surface lure to the weedy, rocky areas in 4 feet of water.

NORTHERN PIKE   You'll find some northerns at the entrance to the outlet on the northeast corner or the rocky areas on the south and southwest shoreline in 6 to 8 feet of water. Or try trolling the weedy edges around the lake with a red and white spoon, minnow strip-on, or minnow lure. In the winter, the northerns will be on the edges of the holes about 2 to 3 feet off the bottom.

CRAPPIE & SUNFISH   The crappies will be all over the shallow areas, espe-cially on the edge of the boggy bottom on the east and southwest sides of the lake. Look for sunfish in the bass areas and off the rocks on the north side of the lake. In the winter, the crappies will be suspended in 30 feet of water about 14 feet below the surface.

Information about this lake was provided by Ted Welch.

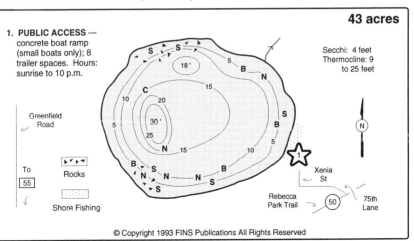

43 acres

1. **PUBLIC ACCESS** — concrete boat ramp (small boats only); 8 trailer spaces. Hours: sunrise to 10 p.m.

Secchi: 4 feet
Thermocline: 9 to 25 feet

Greenfield Road

To 55

Rocks

Shore Fishing

Xenia St

Rebecca Park Trail

50

75th Lane

HYLAND LAKE

Hyland is a small shallow lake in the Hennepin County Park Reserve in Bloomington that is geared for family fun. Parkland surrounds the entire lake and offers unlimited shore fishing opportunities.

Unfortunately, a defective aeration system resulted in a partial winterkill in 1988, 1989 and most of the bass were wiped out. More were stocked the following year and are now catching size.

Hybrid tiger muskies were stocked in 1988 and will be restocked every 3 years. They should reach the legal size of 40 inches about 1994 or 1995. Hyland Lake warms up fast in the spring for early-season action. In the summer, it becomes very weedy and difficult to fish.

SPECIES	POPULATION	AVERAGE SIZE
Bass	Fair	Small to Medium
Muskie	Fair	Small
Crappie	Poor	Small
Sunfish	Good	Small to Medium

BASS The flooded timber and overhanging branches on the south side of the lake hold bass in the spring. Also work west to the long land point and bar. Spinners and floating minnow lures are good producers on these spots.

SUNFISH For spring shore fishing, the most popular spot is at the north end of the lake between the public access and the dike. From a boat, cast under the overhanging trees on the south side of the lake. This is also a good location for fly fishing. Try a weighted wet fly or a white, black, or green sponge-rubber spider with the legs trimmed down. Don't pass up the flooded timber on the southwest shoreline.

Information about this lake was provided by Bob Gibson and Duane Shodeen.

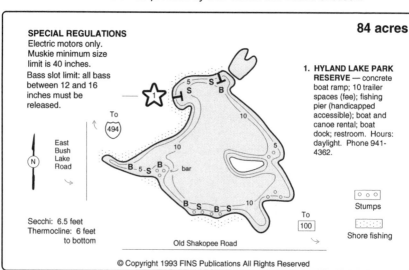

SPECIAL REGULATIONS
Electric motors only.
Muskie minimum size limit is 40 inches.
Bass slot limit: all bass between 12 and 16 inches must be released.

84 acres

1. HYLAND LAKE PARK RESERVE — concrete boat ramp; 10 trailer spaces (fee); fishing pier (handicapped accessible); boat and canoe rental; boat dock; restroom. Hours: daylight. Phone 941-4362.

To
494

East Bush Lake Road

N

B-5-S   B   bar

B   S   B   S

Stumps

Shore fishing

To
100

Secchi: 6.5 feet
Thermocline: 6 feet
to bottom

Old Shakopee Road

PARKERS LAKE

Parkers Lake is located on County Road 6 about a mile south of Highway 55 in Plymouth. This small shallow lake warms up fast in the spring and provides some good early-season panfish action.

SPECIES	POPULATION	AVERAGE SIZE
Bass	Fair	Small to Medium
Northern Pike	Fair	Small to Medium
Crappie	Good	Medium
Sunfish	Very Good	Small to Medium

BASS Trees and stumps on the south end of the lake will attract June bass. Use a small yellow beatle-spin or white spinnerbait with a copper blade and tipped with pork. Cast it to the base of the tree or stump, let the lure fall to the bottom, and retrieve it slowly. In the summer, move out to the 12-foot breakline in the same area. Fall bass are on the sharp drop-offs on the lower east side of the lake.

NORTHERN PIKE Start at the middle of the west side and work down to the south end. Troll the 6 to 8 foot depths with weedless spoons and shallow-running crankbaits. Stay above the weeds. In late summer and fall, move down to the 15 to 17 foot depths, and use live bait rigs. Winter northerns will be in about 30 feet of water around the deep hole. The west side of the hole is the most productive.

CRAPPIE Spring crappies are in 5 feet of water on the weedy mud flat on the northeast corner of the lake. In the summer and fall, move out to the 15 to 17 foot depths on the same side of the lake. In late fall and winter, they will be suspended 12 to 15 feet below the surface in 30 feet of water at the edge of the deep hole.

SUNFISH In the spring, work the stumps and weedy pockets in 5 feet of water on the south side of the lake. In the summer, move out to the 5 to 10 foot depths in the same area and the 12 to 15 foot depths in the fall. Winter sunfish will be at the 18 to 21 foot depths on the south side of the deep hole.

Information about this lake was provided by Tim Sonnenstahl.

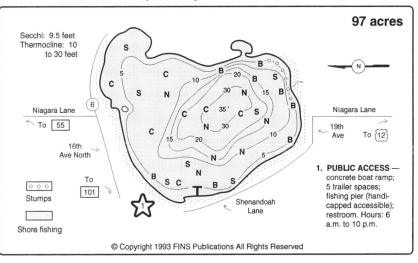

97 acres

Secchi: 9.5 feet
Thermocline: 10 to 30 feet

Niagara Lane
To 55

16th Ave North

To 101

Stumps

Shore fishing

Niagara Lane

19th Ave   To 12

1. PUBLIC ACCESS — concrete boat ramp; 5 trailer spaces; fishing pier (handicapped accessible); restroom. Hours: 6 a.m. to 10 p.m.

Shenandoah Lane

Spurzem Lake is located in the Baker County Park Reserve on County Road 201, one mile east of County Road 19. It has a history of winterkill but gets an adequate supply of fish from Lake Independence. Occasionally a muskie migrates in, but you'll seldom catch one that has reached the legal size of 40 inches.

SPECIES	POPULATION	AVERAGE SIZE
Bass	Good	Medium to Large
Northern Pike	Very Good	Medium
Crappie	Very Good	Small to Medium
Sunfish	Excellent	Medium

BASS Look for June bass at the outlet, in the stumps on the south side of the lake, and in front of the pump house on the east side. Try a small surface lure, a spinnerbait, or a bobber and night crawler. The same areas are productive in the summer. Cast a jig to the edge of the cattails, let it drop to the bottom, and retrieve it slowly.

NORTHERN PIKE Early-season northerns will be all over the lake. Cast a spoon to the 4-foot depths, and work it back across the drop-off into deeper water. The same technique works in the summer but on very hot days concentrate on the drop-offs around the holes. In the winter, the northerns will be 2-1/2 to 3 feet off the bottom in 12 to 22 feet of water. Ted's Bottom Rigs with sucker minnows work well here.

CRAPPIE & SUNFISH You'll find spring crappies and sunfish on the edge of the cattails out to about the 4-foot depths around the entire lake. In the summer move down to the 8-foot depths. In the winter, the 18 to 22 foot depths are the most productive. Crappies will be suspended 6 to 12 feet below the surface and sunfish 6 to 18 inches off the bottom.

Information about this lake was provided by Ted Welch.

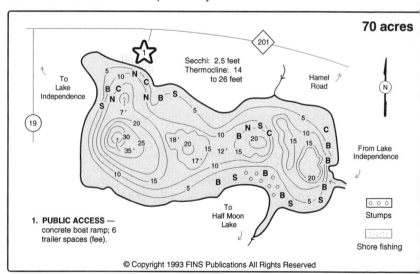

Staring is one of the first lakes in the area to warm up in the spring and provides lots of early-season panfish action. The best spots for all species are the areas in front of the inlet and outlet and the fishing pier on the southwest side of the lake. This lake becomes weed choked in the summer and is prone to winterkill. Winter-rescue northerns averaging 10 to 12 inches are added regularly.

SPECIES	POPULATION	AVERAGE SIZE
Bass	Fair	Small
Northern Pike	Poor to Fair	Small to Medium
Crappie	Good	Medium
Sunfish	Good	Small to Medium

BASS In June, start at the southeast shore, and work the weedy pockets to the southwest shore. In the summer, stay on the weedy edges. The June spots will produce again in the fall.

NORTHERN PIKE The all-season hotspots for northerns are the areas around the inlet and outlet, the Center Bar (the east side is best), and the weedy patch on the northwest side of the lake. Sucker minnows are a good choice.

CRAPPIE & SUNFISH The best supply of sunfish and crappies will be in the weedy areas on the southeast corner of the lake and around the entire southern shoreline. Stay in 5 to 8 feet of water and use a feather jig and wax worm with a bobber. The weeds choke out this lake in the summer, but the spring areas are productive again in the fall. In the winter, work the areas with dotted lines marked on the map.

Information about this lake was provided by Terry Hennon and Glenn Simons.

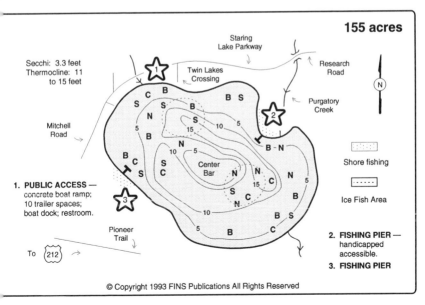

155 acres

Secchi: 3.3 feet
Thermocline: 11 to 15 feet

Staring Lake Parkway

Twin Lakes Crossing

Research Road

Purgatory Creek

Mitchell Road

Center Bar

Shore fishing

Ice Fish Area

1. **PUBLIC ACCESS —** concrete boat ramp; 10 trailer spaces; boat dock; restroom.

Pioneer Trail

To (212)

2. **FISHING PIER —** handicapped accessible.

3. **FISHING PIER**

WEAVER LAKE
Hennepin County

Weaver Lake, located in the community of Maple Grove on Hwy. 101, is a sunfish factory. According to the DNR, the population is 17 times the local average. Hybrid muskies were first stocked in 1984, and stocking continues every 3 years.

SPECIES	POPULATION	AVERAGE SIZE
Bass	Fair to Good	Small
Northern Pike	Fair	Medium
Muskie	Poor	Small to Medium
Crappie	Fair	Medium
Sunfish	Excellent	Small to Medium

BASS June bass will be in the two channels on the west side of the lake and around the north shore down to the beach. In the summer, fish the weedline and the pockets in the weeds down to 15 feet on the west and south sides of the lake. This is also a good night fishing lake. Cast a black spinnerbait in 6 to 10 feet of water on the north, west, and south sides of the lake. In early fall, work the summer locations in 2 to 4 feet of water. In late fall, fish the 10 to 15 foot depths.

NORTHERN PIKE & MUSKIE Early season northerns are in 2 to 5 feet of water on the north side and around the channels on the west side. In the summer and fall, troll or cast to the outside weedline around the entire lake. The best winter locations are the 15 to 20 foot depths on the north and northwest sides.

CRAPPIE & SUNFISH Spring sunfish and crappies will be in the cattails and emerging weeds on the north side. In the summer, sunnies will be on the deep weedline in 10 to 20 feet of water. Larger sunfish can be found on the eastern shoreline. Mid-summer and early fall crappies will be suspended in 20 to 30 feet.

Information about this lake was provided by Steve Carney and John Daily.

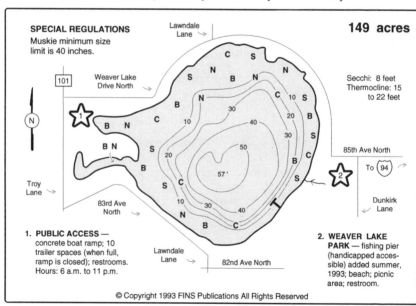

SPECIAL REGULATIONS
Muskie minimum size limit is 40 inches.

149 acres

Weaver Lake Drive North

Secchi: 8 feet
Thermocline: 15 to 22 feet

85th Ave North

To 94

Troy Lane

Dunkirk Lane

83rd Ave North

Lawndale Lane

82nd Ave North

1. **PUBLIC ACCESS —** concrete boat ramp; 10 trailer spaces (when full, ramp is closed); restrooms. Hours: 6 a.m. to 11 p.m.

2. **WEAVER LAKE PARK —** fishing pier (handicapped accessible) added summer, 1993; beach; picnic area; restroom.

Whaletail Lake, located just west of Lake Minnetonka, is known for big crappies. A state-record crappie weighing 2 lb. 14 oz. was taken from this lake in 1989. But you'll have to go through hundreds of tiny ones before you hit the slabs. The shallow, muddy water of the upper section warms up fast in the spring for good early-season action. The lower section has clearer water, a deeper weedline, and is a better producer in the fall.

SPECIES	POPULATION	AVERAGE SIZE
Bass	Fair	Medium to Large
Northern Pike	Fair	Medium
Crappie	Very Good	Small to Large
Sunfish	Excellent	Small

BASS   In June, fish the pockets and holes in the weeds in the upper section. Dark lures or bright fluorescent lures perform best in these dark waters. A good summer technique is to cast to the pockets in the lily pads and to the edges of the floating cattail bogs. In the fall, the trophy sized bass are in the deeper southeastern section on the deeper drop-offs or in the remaining patches of healthy weeds.

NORTHERN PIKE   Cast to the edges of the floating cattail bogs on the northern section with spinnerbaits, plastic worms, or spoons. Also try the edges of the deep holes. The south side of the 13-foot hole is a good summer trolling run. In the summer and fall, also troll the south side of the lower section. Start at the weedline, and troll over the top of the submerged weeds in 6 to 8 feet of water.

CRAPPIE & SUNFISH   The shallow upper lake warms up first in spring and provides an abundant supply of both species all year. Find them in the weeds or just off the edge of the weeds. Crappies spawn in the lower lake in 6 to 8 feet of water.

Information about this lake was provided by John Daily and Tom Zenanko.

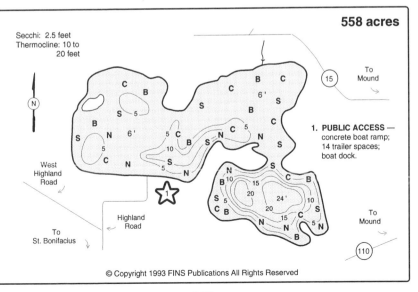

558 acres

Secchi: 2.5 feet
Thermocline: 10 to 20 feet

To Mound 15

1. **PUBLIC ACCESS** — concrete boat ramp; 14 trailer spaces; boat dock.

West Highland Road

Highland Road

To St. Bonifacius

To Mound

110

Wirth Lake, located on Hwy. 55 in Golden Valley, is recovering from a severe winterkill in 1991/92 which greatly reduced the supply of bass, walleyes, and catfish. The following year, the lake was restocked with walleyes and crappies and should provide good supplies of fish in a few years. The good news is that after a winterkill the crappies usually increase in size due to the reduced competition for food. The installation of an aerator to prevent future winterkills is planned before 1995. Bass will then be restocked.

SPECIES	POPULATION	AVERAGE SIZE
Bass	Poor	Small
Northern Pike	Poor to Fair	Medium
Walleye	Fair	Small
Crappie	Excellent	Small

BASS   The fishing pier on the lake's upper east side will hold bass throughout the season. Also work the western shoreline. Look for fallen timber and thick weeds.

WALLEYE   In the spring, early summer, and fall, walleyes will be on the east and west sides of the lake. The northeast corner is also a prime location. The beach area produces in the early season or during low-light periods.

CRAPPIE & SUNFISH   In early spring, you can get crappies from shore on the northeast corner of the lake, the fishing dock, and on the east and west sides. From early May until mid-June, work the submerged brush 75 to 80 yards north of the fishing pier. The fishing pier produces small crappies and sunfish most of the year. Sunfish are in the weeds. The entire north side attracts sunfish all season.

Information about this lake was provided by Jim Kirk.

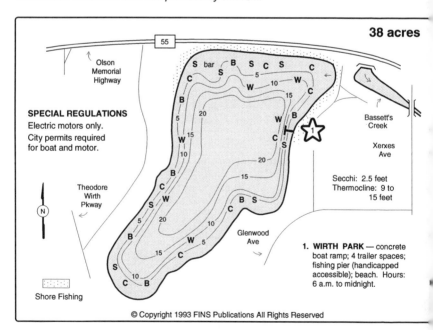

38 acres

55

↑ Olson Memorial Highway

SPECIAL REGULATIONS
Electric motors only.
City permits required
for boat and motor.

Bassett's Creek

Xerxes Ave

Theodore Wirth Pkway

(N)

Glenwood Ave

Secchi: 2.5 feet
Thermocline: 9 to 15 feet

1. **WIRTH PARK** — concrete boat ramp; 4 trailer spaces; fishing pier (handicapped accessible); beach. Hours: 6 a.m. to midnight.

Shore Fishing

ISLAND LAKE   Ramsey County

Island Lake is one of the most popular shore fishing lakes in the metro area, and there's a new fishing pier on the west side. On many weekends, water-skiing competitions are held on this small lake that can be disruptive to anglers.

Hybrid muskie fingerlings were added in 1984, and stocking continues every three years. Walleye fingerlings were stocked in 1979, 1982, and 1983 but no further stocking of this species is anticipated. An aeration system prevents winterkill.

SPECIES	POPULATION	AVERAGE SIZE
Bass	Very Good	Medium
Northern Pike	Excellent	Small to Medium
Muskie	Poor	Small
Walleye	Poor	Medium to Large
Crappie	Good	Small
Sunfish	Excellent	Medium

BASS In early June, look for the bass near last year's cattails in the bays on the north side of the highway. As the season progresses, move to the overhanging trees and heavy shoreline cover in the main lake.

NORTHERN PIKE & MUSKIE The northerns will be in the back bays until June. In the summer, work the main lake. Muskies are in shallow, open-water areas.

WALLEYE A few walleyes are with the bass on the inside and outside weedlines. Try a slip bobber with a jig and leech on the edges and pockets of the weeds.

CRAPPIE & SUNFISH In the spring, look in the back bays. Summer crappies will be suspended in the deepest part of the main lake. A small white jig is a good choice. Sunfish are in the channel and in the weedy areas.

This information was by provided by John Daily, Dale Glader, and Mike Schuett.

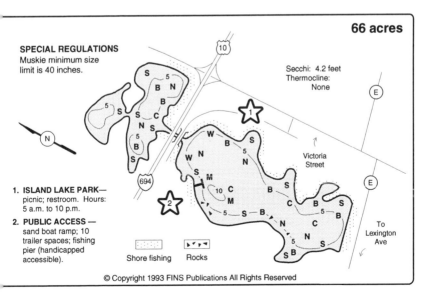

66 acres

SPECIAL REGULATIONS
Muskie minimum size limit is 40 inches.

Secchi: 4.2 feet
Thermocline: None

Victoria Street

To Lexington Ave

1. **ISLAND LAKE PARK—** picnic; restroom. Hours: 5 a.m. to 10 p.m.

2. **PUBLIC ACCESS —** sand boat ramp; 10 trailer spaces; fishing pier (handicapped accessible).

Shore fishing   Rocks

MCCARRONS LAKE   Ramsey County

McCarrons is known as a panfish paradise. Pure strain muskies were first stocked in 1983. Hybrid tiger muskies were added in 1986 and are restocked every 3 years. Walleyes have been stocked annually since 1980.

SPECIES	POPULATION	AVERAGE SIZE
Bass	Fair	Medium
Northern Pike	Good	
		Small
Walleye	Good	Small
Crappie	Very Good	Small
Sunfish	Very Good	Small

BASS   Look for the early-season bass in the lily pads and the weedy flat on the west side of the point on the southwest side of the lake and up to the inlet on the northwest corner. In the summer, look for docks with deep water nearby. Concentrate on the weedy edges. For fall action, go back to the spring locations.

NORTHERN PIKE & MUSKIE   Fish the mouth of the creek (inlet) and along the shoreline from the northwest corner down to the southwest corner. Move down to the 8 to 10 foot depths in the summer. In the fall, work the northern shoreline.

WALLEYE   Fish the mouth of the inlet and the east side of the point on the southwest side of the lake. In the summer, try the northern shoreline. In fall and winter, work the deep drop-offs on the points in 20 to 30 feet of water.

CRAPPIE & SUNFISH   All-season locations are the beach area; the southeast corner; the west side of the point on the southwest shoreline; and up the western shoreline to the inlet. In the winter, work the 20 to 30 foot depths on the west side of the lake and the 15 to 30 foot depths in front of the beach.

Information about this lake was provided by Dick McCarthy.

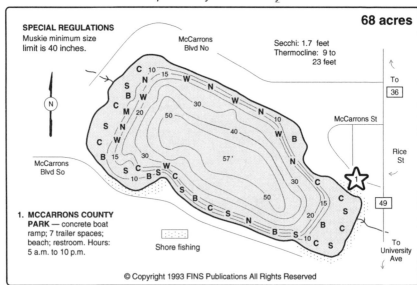

68 acres

SPECIAL REGULATIONS
Muskie minimum size limit is 40 inches.

McCarrons Blvd No

Secchi: 1.7 feet
Thermocline: 9 to 23 feet

To 36

McCarrons St

Rice St

McCarrons Blvd So

49

1. **MCCARRONS COUNTY PARK** — concrete boat ramp; 7 trailer spaces; beach; restroom. Hours: 5 a.m. to 10 p.m.

Shore fishing

To University Ave

OTTER LAKE   **Ramsey County**

Otter Lake, located one block east of I-35E in northeastern Ramsey County, is subject to frequent winterkills. Expect fluctuations in the size and supply of fish for several years after a winterkill. When water levels are normal, the supply of fish can be replenished through a channel from Bald Eagle Lake.

SPECIES	POPULATION	AVERAGE SIZE
Bass	Good	Small
Northern Pike	Excellent	Medium
Crappie	Fair	Medium
Sunfish	Excellent	Medium

BASS June bass are on the shoreline structures in 2 to 5 feet of water around the entire lake; the east side is best. Try a green or white spinnerbait. In summer, stay in the same locations but move deeper to 5 feet. If the area is too weedy, work edges and pockets with weedless surface lures. In fall, fish the weedlines around the deep hole and the remaining green vegetation at 7 to 10 feet around the lake.

NORTHERN PIKE Look for early-season northerns in 1 to 5 feet of water around the lake, especially on the southeast corner in front of the inlet. In the summer, they'll move onto the edge of the weeds in 7 to 10 feet of water around the deep hole. In the fall, go back to the spring locations. The northeast and southeast shorelines are especially good. Look for the green weeds. In the winter, work the 10 to 20 foot depths in the 20-foot hole.

CRAPPIE & SUNFISH Spring crappies and sunfish will be in 2 to 3 feet of water in the marshy areas at the entire south end of the lake, the west side of the lake, and the north end. The best summer areas are the open pockets in the weeds on the north end. In the fall, fish edges of the healthy green weeds. Winter sunfish are in 7 to 10 feet of water around the deep hole. Crappies will be suspended over the deepest part of the hole in 20 feet of water.

Information about this lake was provided by Brad Stanius.

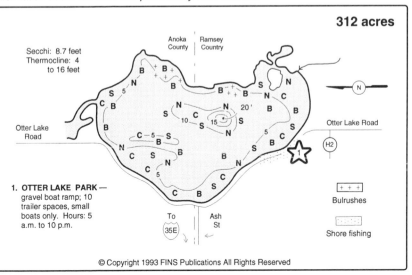

Silver Lake, located in North St. Paul on the border of Ramsey and Washington Counties, produces best in the spring, fall, and early winter (early ice). An aeration system was installed to prevent winterkill. The west side of the lake is the most fertile and holds most of the fish. Walleyes have been stocked annually since 1985, and hybrid tiger muskies have been added every three years since 1986. The muskies are expected to reach legal size (40 inches) in 1993.

SPECIES	POPULATION	AVERAGE SIZE
Bass	Good	Medium
Northern Pike	Fair	Medium
Muskie	Fair	Small
Walleye	Good	Medium
Crappie	Excellent	Small
Sunfish	Excellent	Small

BASS In June, try the fishing pier and the shallow weedy flats on the north side of the lake. For summer bass, work the weedless slot on the north side and the bays and shoreline on the upper west side.

NORTHERN PIKE Early-season northerns will be scattered around the shallow weedy areas. In the summer, try trolling the 10 to 12 foot depths around the 20-foot hole. Also check out the weedy flats.

WALLEYE Early-season walleyes are in front of the finger-shaped bay on the north end. At night, look for them here in 2 to 3 feet of water, and use a black jig or live bait rig. In the summer and winter, move out to the weedy flats and weedy edges around the 20-foot hole.

CRAPPIE & SUNFISH The fishing pier, the south shoreline, and the north side of the 12-foot hole are the prime locations. The weedy edge around the 20-foot hole will hold summer and winter sunfish. Crappies will be suspended over the hole.

Information about this lake was provided by Mike Bonn and Troy Driscoll.

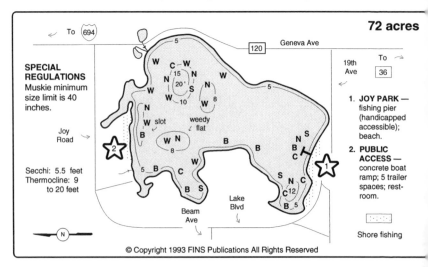

Snail, located in the city of Shoreview, was once a superb little fishing lake. But declining water levels in the 1980's resulted in oxygen deprivation and frequent winterkills. However, the heavy rains of recent years have improved the water quality. Look for more healthy populations of fish in future years. Walleyes were stocked in 1979 and 1983, but few remain, and no future stocking is scheduled.

SPECIES	POPULATION	AVERAGE SIZE
Bass	Fair	Medium
Northern Pike	Excellent	Small to Medium
Crappie	Fair	Small to Medium
Sunfish	Good	Small

BASS   The rocky point in front of the camp and the weeds all over the north end of the lake are prime spots for June bass. Also work the long land point on the west side down to the south end of the lake. In the summer, the entire north and northeastern section is productive. Also work the docks on the north and northwest sides. In the fall, fish the deeper weedlines, particularly in front of the camp.

NORTHERN PIKE   The thick weedbeds in the northwest, north, and east sections of the lake are good all-season locations. Don't pass up the deep weedline in front of the pump house on the northeast corner. In late fall after turnover, fish the hole in front of the long point on the upper west side.

CRAPPIE & SUNFISH   Spring crappies and sunfish are in the shallow weeds in the northwest bay. In early June, spawning sunnies are on the mid-east side of the lake. Summer sunfish are scattered throughout the weedy areas, and crappies will move out to the deep weedlines.

Information about this lake was provided by Ken Matheson.

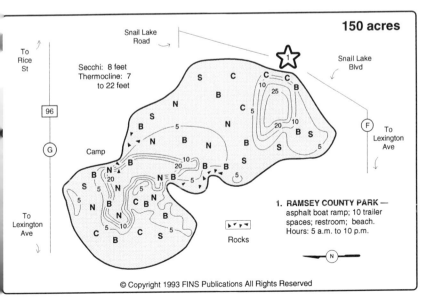

150 acres

Snail Lake Road

To Rice St

Secchi: 8 feet
Thermocline: 7 to 22 feet

Snail Lake Blvd

96

Camp

To Lexington Ave

To Lexington Ave

Rocks

1. RAMSEY COUNTY PARK —
asphalt boat ramp; 10 trailer spaces; restroom; beach.
Hours: 5 a.m. to 10 p.m.

MCMAHON (CARL'S) LAKE

Scott County

Located about 10 miles south of Prior Lake on Hwy. 87, McMahon Lake is one of the best spring bluegill lakes in the area. Because it is small and shallow, it warms up fast and provides plenty of early-season action.

An aerator was installed after a severe winterkill in 1984, and the lake was restocked. Walleyes were also added but few survived.

SPECIES	POPULATION	AVERAGE SIZE
Bass	Good	Medium to Large
Northern Pike	Very Good	Small to Large
Crappie	Good	Medium to Large
Sunfish	Excellent	Small

BASS   In the early season, the northwest bay is a good place to start. Plastic worms with sparkle will be more effective in this murky water. In the summer, work the weedy areas round the lake. Use a yellow spinnerbait with a nickel blade or try shallow-diving crankbaits. The submerged brush on the northeast and east sides of the lake will attract fish.

NORTHERN PIKE   Troll around the entire lake with red and white spoons, or try still-fishing in the weeds with a bobber and a golden shiner minnow. In the summer and fall, stay in the 5 to 10 foot depths.

CRAPPIE & SUNFISH   The northwest bay holds crappies and sunfish most of the year. Sunfish are also abundant on the west and southwest sides of the bay. This is also a popular location for fly fishing. The submerged brush on the east side of the lake attract sunfish and crappies. In the summer, look for crappies in the 15-foot hole in the center of the lake. They'll be suspended 10 to 15 feet below the surface.

Information about this lake was provided by Jim Picka.

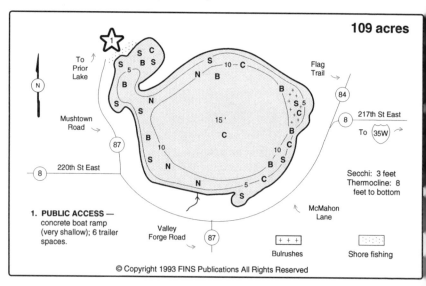

109 acres

To Prior Lake

Flag Trail

Mushtown Road

217th St East

To 35W

220th St East

Secchi: 3 feet
Thermocline: 8 feet to bottom

McMahon Lane

1. PUBLIC ACCESS — concrete boat ramp (very shallow); 6 trailer spaces.

Valley Forge Road

Bulrushes

Shore fishing

BATTLE CREEK (MUD) LAKE

Washington County

Battle Creek Lake is located in the northwest corner of Woodbury just south of I-94. In the winter of 1987/88, a malfunctioning aeration system resulted in a partial winterkill and reduced the supply of fish. Huge quantities of sunfish, largemouth bass, and walleyes were restocked in 1988/89 and are now catching size. The walleyes had a poor survival rate and will not be stocked in the future.

The best time to fish this lake is in the early season before it becomes difficult to work through the heavy weeds. Otherwise you'll have to concentrate on the weedy edges or look for openings in the weeds. Early ice is also a prime time.

SPECIES	POPULATION	AVERAGE SIZE
Bass	Fair	Small to Medium
Northern Pike	Very Good	Small to Medium
Crappie	Fair	Medium
Sunfish	Good	Small to Large

BASS & NORTHERNS Look for early-season fish around the outlet in the middle of the west side of the lake. The rest of the year, stay around the edge of the holes in the center of the lake. The meager supply of walleyes will be here too.

SUNFISH & CRAPPIES The best spring locations are around the outlet, the boat launch, and the fishing dock. Also look for spawning sunfish around the bog on the lower end of the lake. As the water warms, move to the edge of the holes in the center of the lake. In the winter, especially during early ice before the aerator is turned on, crappies will be suspended in 13 to 14 feet of water at the edge of the holes, and the sunfish will be just off the bottom of the hole. Perch are here too.

Information about this lake was provided by Mike Bonn and Troy Driscoll.

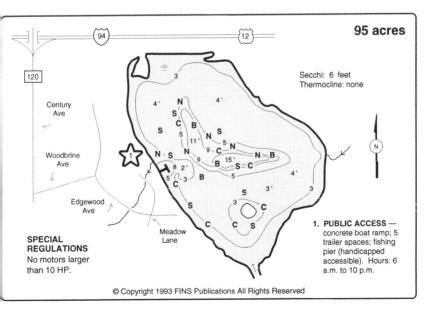

95 acres

Secchi: 6 feet
Thermocline: none

Century Ave

Woodbrine Ave

Edgewood Ave

Meadow Lane

SPECIAL REGULATIONS
No motors larger than 10 HP.

1. **PUBLIC ACCESS —** concrete boat ramp; 5 trailer spaces; fishing pier (handicapped accessible). Hours: 6 a.m. to 10 p.m.

Lake Jane, located near the city of Lake Elmo, is a super bass and sunfish hatchery. The bass are hard to catch because of the very clear water and the abundance of stunted sunfish which provide plenty of food. Nighttime is best.

SPECIES	POPULATION	AVERAGE SIZE
Bass	Very Good	Medium
Northern Pike	Fair	Small
Crappie	Fair	Very Small
Sunfish	Excellent	Very Small

BASS You'll find early-season bass on the southeast, south, and west shorelines in 2 to 8 feet of water. The underwater point on the northeast side of the lake is a good all-season location. On sunny days, use a white spinnerbait tipped with red and white pork. When the skies are overcast, switch to an orange or chartreuse spinnerbait. In the summer, try the 8 to 10 foot depths on the south, west, and north sides of the lake and the little 5-foot hump on the north side. For fall bass, work a jig and pork frog (#2) slowly along the weedline on the south and southwest sides of the lake.

NORTHERN PIKE Northerns are all over the lake, but mostly on the weedline. You'll also find them with the bass on the west side of the lake or on the underwater point on the northeast side. Use a spinnerbait or sucker minnow. This is a tough lake to troll because of the irregular weedline.

CRAPPIE & SUNFISH The east side of the lake has a good all-season supply of sunfish. Look for the underwater root system surrounded by brush about 100 feet out from shore. Bass are here too. Crappies can be found on the breaklines throughout the lake, especially on the south and west sides.

This information was provided by Ken Evanoff, Tina Outlaw, and Joe Unger.

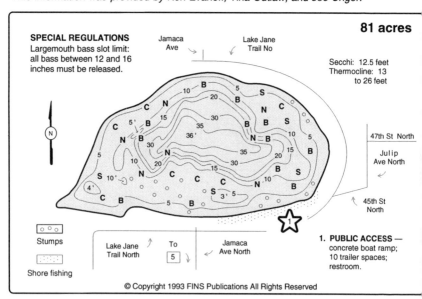

Lily, located in the community of Stillwater, has a fishing pier and a new public boat launch. Northern pike yearlings are stocked in most years to boost the meager population. Walleye fingerlings were stocked in 1989.

SPECIES	POPULATION	AVERAGE SIZE
Bass	Fair	Small to Medium
Northern Pike	Fair	Small
Walleye	Poor	Small
Crappie	Good	Small
Sunfish	Excellent	Small

BASS In June, you'll find bass on the upper west side of the lake, especially in front of the area where the paved road leads down to the lake. In the summer, work around the pads on the west side. Stay in the same area in the fall but move deeper to the weedline and use a crankbait or jig and pig.

NORTHERN PIKE A good supply can be found around the end of the long round bar. Work down deeper from here, then across and back up to the weedy edge on the west end of the lake.

WALLEYE A few walleyes have been caught off the fishing dock. In the winter, try the crappie locations on the long bar.

CRAPPIE & SUNFISH You can catch crappies and sunfish from the fishing dock throughout most of the season, especially in the evening. In the spring and summer, look for sunfish around the edge of the lily pads in 3 to 4 feet on the south and west sides of the lake. Try a wax worm on a plain hook or a chartreuse ice fly and a bobber. Summer crappies will be suspended off the weedline around the 20-foot hole on the west side. In the winter, fish the top of the long bar. Winter sunfish will be on the weed flat on the west side of the lake.

Information about this lake was provided by Bill Tomberlin.

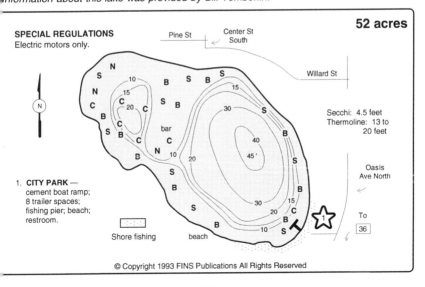

Tanners Lake is located at the northeast corner of Century Avenue (Hwy. 120) and I-94 in Oakdale. It's a super panfish lake and walleyes are stocked periodically. Tanners Lake has few healthy weedbeds and is not a good trolling lake.

SPECIES	POPULATION	AVERAGE SIZE
Bass	Good	Small
Northern Pike	Poor to Fair	Medium
Walleye	Fair	Small
Crappie	Very Good	Small to Medium
Sunfish	Very Good	Small to Medium

BASS   The north end of the lake will attract June bass. Look for the healthiest weeds in 2 to 4 feet of water. In summer and fall, fish the point (willow tree) on the west side of the lake down to the south end. Concentrate on the weedline.

NORTHERN PIKE   The best all-season spot is from the willow tree on the west side down to the south end. Also fish the drop-offs above and below the boat launch. Winter fish are on the weedline on the north end or south of the beach.

WALLEYE   For early-season walleyes, start at the point on the west side in front of the willow tree and work down to the southwest corner. During the day, work the 15 foot depth at the end of the break. In the evening, move up onto the point. Fish the deep side of the weedbed on the southwest corner. In the fall, stay in the summer areas but start at the edge of the weeds and work down to 30 feet.

CRAPPIE & SUNFISH   In late winter and spring, sunfish are on the far north end. Sunfish and crappies are found most of the season in front of the willow tree, the nursery, and the muddy bay by the boat company. Winter crappies suspend about halfway down in 26 to 42 feet; sunfish will be in 3 to 6 feet in weedy summer spots.

This information was provided by Mike Bonn, Troy Driscoll, and Chuck Hamer.

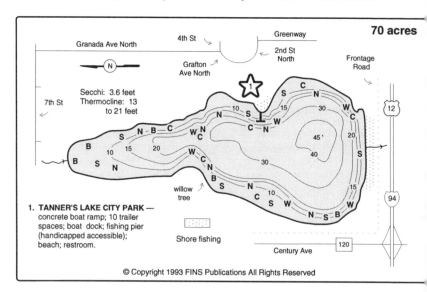

70 acres

1. **TANNER'S LAKE CITY PARK —** concrete boat ramp; 10 trailer spaces; boat dock; fishing pier (handicapped accessible); beach; restroom.

Shore Fishing

Shore fishing can be amazingly effective if you pick your spots carefully according to shoreline features, season, and time of day.

SHORELINE FEATURES   Weedbeds are natural fish-holding territory providing plenty of food, shade, and security.   Also look for any place where water empties into the lake, such as storm drains, the mouths of creeks and channels, and the area below dams and waterfalls.   Brushy areas, sunken trees, stumps, and overhanging banks also attract fish.   Bridge pilings or cement pillars offer protected quiet areas as the current goes by.   The shady side will be best.

Frequently, you can tell whether deep water comes close to shore by looking at what's above the surface.   A steep bank will probably continue beneath the surface of the water.   A flat shoreline, on the other hand, usually indicates that shallow water extends quite some distance from shore.   Darker patches of water near the shore indicate deeper holes or slots.

Whenever possible, select a shoreline that is facing the wind.   The wave action stirs the bottom materials and makes the water more murky.   This allows the bait fish to move in close to shore, and the game fish will follow the bait fish.

Polaroid sunglasses can help you spot the weedbeds and other shallow underwater cover — and sometimes even fish.

SEASON   Shore fishing is best in the spring and fall.   In the spring, most species of fish will spawn in shallow water in both lakes and rivers.   For summer shore fishing, look for areas that have deep water close to shore.   Try to cast to the inside weedline in the early morning and evening and to the outside weedline during the day.   The outside weedline is home to most species.   Use a weighted bobber to reach to the deeper weedlines.

In September and October, the big fish move into the shallows for their final feeding spree before the ice comes in.   Huge northerns have been known to hang just inches off shore waiting for frogs to migrate back into the lakes.   Areas that have noticeable current flow such as inlets and culverts will be key attractions in the fall.   Areas below dams are also fish magnets at this time of the year.

TIME OF DAY   Low-light periods such as dawn, dusk, and cloudy days are best. In the summer when the bright sunny days drive the fish into deep cover, night fishing may be best, especially on lakes with clear water.

FISHING FROM DOCKS   The best docks are those that have a good supply of weeds nearby and quick access to deep water.   Before you step on the dock and spook the fish underneath, try casting alongside parallel to the dock.   Let your lure flutter down at the end of the dock and at the deeper posts.   The shady side of the dock is best.   Also cast to the sides of nearby moored boats.   You'll also often find a fish in the hole created by the turbulence of starting a boat motor in shallow water; the bigger the motor, the deeper the hole will be.

SHORE FISHING HOTSPOTS

Here is a list of some of the best shore fishing hotspots in the metro area. Locations marked with an asterisk (*) in this list are shown on the maps in this book. Check the maps to see if there are "Special Regulations" for these lakes. Fishing piers marked with (H) are handicapped accessible. See the Children's Ponds section of this book for more shore fishing sites.

Most of the public boat launches on metro lakes can be good spring locations, especially where there is a boat dock (see the facilities data on the maps). But step aside for boaters. Periods of minimal boat activity will be best. Some of the new public assesses have rock jetties around them to prevent erosion. These can also be fish attractors. The shading around the shoreline on the maps indicate proven shore fishing areas or fishing piers.

ANOKA COUNTY

Cenaiko Lake is a small trout lake (rainbow and brook) in the Coon Rapids Regional Park next to the Mississippi River in Coon Rapids. The fishing pier (H) on the southwest side of the lake is the most productive of the two piers. The southern shoreline is also very good. Fishing with minnows is prohibited.

On **Centerville Lake*** in Lino Lakes at the north end of the lake, the 4-foot hole (see map) is a very good all-season crappie spot. The culvert from Lake Peltier holds sunfish and crappies right after ice-out. Early season northerns and walleyes are here too. Big northerns are caught here in the fall.

On **Coon Lake***, for a small fee, you can fish from a dock at Olson's Resort (434-5831) on the west side of the lake.

Andover's **Crooked Lake*** has a fishing pier (H) in Crooked Lake Beach Park.

Moore Lake* in Fridley has a fishing pier. See the lake description.

Peltier Lake* in Lino Lakes will receive a fishing pier (H) in summer, 1993. You can catch northerns all year on both sides of the dam, particularly in the spring and fall. You'll also find crappies, walleyes, and bullheads here. Try the cement slab at the culvert between Peltier and Centerville Lakes. You'll find crappies on the Centerville side of the culvert and northerns on the Peltier side.

CARVER COUNTY

On **Ann Lake*** in the City Park in Chanhassen, you can catch panfish, northerns, and bass from the fishing pier (H) and along the shoreline on the south side.

Lake Auburn* in Victoria has a fishing pier (H) on the southeast corner in the Carver Park Reserve off Hwy. 11.

Courthouse Pond* in the city of Chaska behind the County Courthouse has a fishing pier (H). See the lake description.

Lotus Lake* in Chanhassen offers a fishing pier on the south side. Also try the inlet on the middle of the western shoreline and the shoreline from Carver Beach up to the old public access.

Parley Lake* in the Carver Park Reserve has a fishing pier (H).

Steiger Lake* in the Carver Park Reserve offers shore fishing on both sides of the public access until the weeds get too thick. This is a popular fly fishing location.

Lake Susan in Chanhassen has a fishing pier (H) at the Lake Susan Park.

On **Virginia Lake** near the city of Excelsior, fish below the public access and around the channel area for sunfish and crappies. Park at the public access and walk down.

On **Zumbra Lake*** in Victoria, the north end is a good all-season location for all species. It's especially good for spring crappies. Parking is difficult. Spring sunfish and crappies can be caught at the boat access.

DAKOTA COUNTY

On **Lake Byllesby***, work the area around the long land point in the Regional Park, especially where the main lake narrows into the channel. Also try the park.

On **Crystal Lake*** in Burnsville, the fishing pier attracts crappies and sunfish.

On **Fish Lake** near Eagan, try the fishing pier (H) for sunfish and crappies.

Lac Lavon Lake in Apple Valley, will receive a fishing pier (H) summer, 1993.

On **Marion Lake*** in Lakeville, try the fishing pier (H) in Casperson Park for sunfish and crappies. The channel provides sunfish, crappies, northerns, and bass.

Rebecca Lake in the city of Hastings has a fishing pier (H).

Valley Lake in Lakeville will receive a fishing pier (H) in summer, 1993.

HENNEPIN COUNTY

Bush Lake* in the Bush Lake Park Reserve off West Bush Lake Road has 3 fishing piers (H). A new fishing pier will be built in summer, 1993.

Lake Calhoun* in Minneapolis has 2 handicapped accessible fishing piers. The fishing pier at 36th Street on the east side of the lake offers sunfish and crappies all season. The left side of the pier is especially productive for northerns and muskies from early season until mid-June. Cast out about 30 feet to the 16-foot depth. The fishing pier (H) on the west side of the lake produces walleyes in the evening until early June. You'll also find lots of small crappies under the fishing pier and along the shoreline on both sides of the pier between April and June.

Cedar Lake* in Minneapolis has a fishing pier (H) on the west side that produces all-season bass, and sunfish. For muskies and northerns, use long casts from the center of the pier to reach the weedline of the 10-foot sunken island and the saddle at the 12-foot depths. The bay in the middle of the west side of the lake has a storm drain that attracts early-season northerns and panfish. The fast drop-off just east of the channel on the north side is a good all-season location for northerns and muskies. You'll find big northerns here in the fall.

On **Crystal Lake*** in Robbinsdale, the south end is a good location for spring crappies and sunfish. The storm duct on the northeast corner attracts crappies throughout the season. For northerns, try the storm duct at 38th Street on the lower eas side of the lake or the west side of the 7-foot hole on the lower west side.

On **Eagle Lake*** in Maple Grove, you'll find spring crappies in the boat channel or the west side of the lake. Also work the channel to Pike Lake.

Gun Club Lake is in the Fort Snelling Park. You can walk in from the parking lo under the I-494 bridge on Hwy. 13. On the west side of the parking lot, take the footpath about 3/4 of a mile to the lake. The entire shoreline is open for shore fishing. Cast to both lakes. The best area is where the channel connects the two lakes. This area is notorious for jumbo crappies and sunfish as well as huge northerns in the spring. Even the bullheads are humongous.

Lake Harriet* in Minneapolis has 2 fishing piers (H). For all-season crappies and sunfish, the best locations are the fishing piers, boat docks, and around the storm drains on the east side (near 43rd Street). This area is especially good for bass and walleyes when rain water is draining into the lake. Start at 43rd Street and work down to 46th street. For June bass, start at the fishing dock on the northeas corner and work the sandy, weedy areas down to 46th Street. Also try the wes side from the drain pipe at 44th Street down to the tennis courts. The sunken trees just north of the fishing pier on the southwest corner provide good midsum mer bass territory. The moored sailboats on the north and west sides of the lake offer shady hangouts for muskies all season.

On **Lake Hiawatha*** in Minneapolis, the fishing pier produces northerns and crappies all season. Also fish the channel to Lake Nokomis.

On **Hyland Lake*** at the Hyland Lake Park Reserve in Bloomington, try the nortl end of the lake between the public access and the dike for spring bass and sunfish. Also fish the flooded timber and overhanging branches on the south side of the lake. This is a popular fly fishing area. There is also a fishing pier (H).

On **Lake of the Isles*** in Minneapolis, the long arm on north side warms up firs and offers all species. You'll also find sunfish along the southern shoreline where the deep water comes close to shore (see the map). The west side of the lake jus below the channel to Cedar Lake produces bass and walleyes.

On **Little Long Lake*** near Mound, look for sunfish at the canal on the north enc off Game Farm Road. Park at the public access and walk up.

For **Long Lake*** in the city of Long Lake, see the lake description.

Medicine Lake* in Plymouth has a fishing pier (H). See lake description

On **Lake Minnetonka*** the west side of Hwy. 101 near the channel to Grays Ba produces northerns, sunfish, crappies, walleyes in all seasons. Park at the boa launch. The area from the Railroad Depot to the cafe on Wayzata Bay is a good all-season location for northerns and walleyes. The narrow channel between Eas Upper Lake (Carman's Bay) and Lafayette Bay known as "The Narrows" provide the most consistently productive shore fishing for all species in all seasons.

In Halsted's Bay, work the channel between Priest Bay and Eagle Bluff for good sized northerns all season. There's no parking here but you can park about a block and a half away and walk up on County Road 44 underneath the bridge The east side is best.

On North Arm Bay, the 2 channels that lead to Crystal Bay and to Maxwell Bay both produce sunfish, crappies, bass, and northerns in the spring and summer. Coffee Bridge on County Road 19 between Crystal Bay and West Arm Bay produces all-season northerns, crappies, and sunfish.

The railroad bridge on Tanager Lake is a good spring and summer location for sunfish and crappies. You'll also find bass and northerns here in the summer. The channel on the southeast side is a prime all-season location. The shoreline from the bridge up to Brown's Bay often yields large muskies. Park further up on County Road 15. Above the boat launch in Carson's Bay is a bridge that separates Carson's Bay and the lagoon. You can catch sunfish, crappies, and bass here in the spring and fall. Park by the old railroad tracks. At the Excelsior Yacht Club, fish off the railroad trestle for all species. Park in the public parking lot south of the Yacht Club.

On **Lake Nokomis*** in Minneapolis, The northeast side of the Cedar Avenue bridge is notorious for small crappies and a few walleyes. Other good crappie locations are the fishing piers (H), the north side of Lake Nokomis, the southeast corner of the lake, Minnehaha Creek, and the channel to Lake Hiawatha. At the northeast corner in front of the concrete wall, try wading at sunset for all-season walleyes. The lagoon is good for early-season sunfish, crappies, and walleyes.

On **Parkers Lake*** in Plymouth, the best locations for all species are the northwest corner and the fishing pier (H). Also look for bass in the stumpy area near the outlet on the south end.

The pond in **Powderhorn Park** in Minneapolis produces spring sunfish.

On **Riley Lake***, you can catch panfish from the park on the east side.

Round Lake in Eden Prairie has a fishing pier (H).

On **Lake Sarah***, there are early-season sunfish and crappies in the boat channel off Sunset Drive on the east side of the lake. Other good locations are the area where the shoreline parallels South Lake Sarah Drive, and by the old boat launch on the north side of the lake.

Snelling Lake in Fort Snelling State Park has a fishing pier that produces early season panfish. After the weeds get too high in late spring, try the culvert between the lakes. The shoreline from the pier east to the beach is good spawning territory for sunfish and crappies. Wade out to the 2 to 3 foot depths and cast for bass and northerns.

Staring Lake* in Eden Prairie has three fishing piers (H). The best one is on the southwest side of the lake.

On **Twin Lakes* in** Robbinsdale, the action is on the lower lake. Fish both sides of the channel for sunfish, crappies, northerns, and bass. These areas are good in the early morning when boat traffic is minimal. The inside turn on the northeast corner holds a good population of summer crappies and sunfish.

Weaver Lake* in Maple Grove, will receive a fishing pier (H) in summer, 1993.

On **Wirth Lake*** off Hwy. 55 in Golden Valley, the new fishing pier (H) produces sunfish, crappies, and walleyes most of the season. The outlet on the northeast corner attracts crappies. The north side of the lake is a good sunfish location.

RAMSEY COUNTY

On **Bald Eagle Lake*** in the city of White Bear Lake, look for early-season sunfish and crappies on the north end and at the Regional Park on the lower east side.

Beaver Lake in Maplewood has a fishing pier (H) on the west side.

On **Lake Como**, the fishing pier (H) is a good location for sunfish and crappies

On **Gervais, Kohlman, and Keller Lakes*** in Little Canada, you'll find early-season crappies at the Gervais-Kohlman channel off Keller Parkway. Both sides of Spoon Lake produce sunfish, crappies, and early-season bass. The east shore of Keller Lake produces sunfish and crappies.

Island Lake* in Shoreview has a fishing pier. For crappies, the channel under the highway is very popular; or move a little further north into the bay for spring panfish. Summer bass can be caught on the upper east side of the main lake.

On **Lake Johanna*** in Arden Hills, you'll find crappies, sunfish, northerns, and bass on the northwest corner at Schmidt Park and around the boat access.

Long Lake* in New Brighton has a fishing pier (H) on the south side that produces bass, northerns, sunfish, and crappies. Walleyes and northerns can be caught around the inlet on the southeast corner and around the public access. These are good summer and fall locations.

On **McCarron's Lake*** in Roseville, you can catch panfish at the County Park on the east side of the lake. The southeast corner is best. The west side of the land point on the southwest side of the lake is popular for bass, northerns, and panfish

Lake Owasso* in Shoreview provides shore fishing for sunfish and crappies at the railroad bridge on the southeast corner of the lake between the main lake and the pond. Walk in from Rice Street or South Owasso Boulevard.

Lake Phalen* has a fishing pier (H) on the west side of the lake. The north side of the pier is close to the channel and has a deeper drop-off. This is an all-season location for crappies, sunfish, and northerns. The east side of the upper section of the lake has deep water close to shore that attracts walleyes and crappies.

On **Round Lake*** in Maplewood, there is a new fishing pier (H) on the north side. Entrance to the pier is from Frost Avenue. Both sides of the channel to Lake Phalen are productive in the spring. Also try the shoreline around Round Lake

On **Silver Lake*** in North Saint Paul, you can catch panfish and bass from the beach and the fishing pier (H) on the south end or around the public access on the north end. In the summer, try casting to the "weedless slot" (see map) for bass

On **Sucker Lake** in Vadnais Heights, the channel on the north side leading into Sucker Lake offers the best fishing in the spring. The entrance is off Hwy. 95.

On **Vadnais Lake** in Vadnais Heights near Rice Street and I-694, boating, wading, and ice fishing are prohibited. The point and the area close to the pumphouse on the east lake are the most popular locations for crappies, sunfish, perch, and an occasional large walleye or northern. The western section is very shallow and contains bullheads and small panfish.

SCOTT COUNTY

Cedar Lake* near New Prague offers shore fishing east of the outlet on the north end where the lake parallels the road. In the spring and early summer, you'll find crappies, sunfish, walleyes, and bullheads.

Cleary Lake is located southeast of Prior Lake. There is a fishing pier (H) in the Regional Park on the southeast side. Enter from County Hwy. 27.

Gilford Lake is located just south of the Minnesota River off Hwy. 41 (Chestnut Boulevard). Take the first turn before the river and follow the road back to Gilford Lake. Both sides of the culvert are good for crappies all season. Northerns are attracted to this spot in early season.

On **Prior Lake***, the channel between the upper and lower lakes attracts sunfish and crappies as well as an occasional bass or northern pike. Also try Sand Point Beach and the boat launch area for walleyes, northerns, sunfish and crappies.

O'Dowd Lake* near Shakopee is the best shore fishing lake in the county for big northerns, bass, sunfish, and crappies. The best spots are at O'Dowd Lake Park on the west side of the lake and the long point on the upper west side. Fish the submerged brush along the shoreline or try the fishing dock on the point.

Thole Lake* near Shakopee has a fishing pier (H) on the northeast shore. The upper half of the eastern shoreline attracts crappies, sunfish, and northerns.

WASHINGTON COUNTY

At **Battle Creek Lake*** in Woodbury, you can catch crappies from the fishing pier (H). There are reports of good sized sunfish.

Big Carnelian Lake* has sunfish and crappies at the public access in early spring. You'll also find some early-season bass here.

Clear Lake* offers shore fishing on both sides of the public access on the northwest side of the lake. You'll find plenty of panfish and an occasional walleye or northern pike. For more consistent success, try wading out to the lily pads.

On **Lake Demontreville***, the best all-season location for bass, northerns, sunfish and crappies is the shoreline below the public access off County Road 13. On **Olson Lake**, you can catch the same mix of fish from the eastern shoreline. Look for the brushy areas. Parking is scarce.

Lake Elmo* has a fishing pier (H).

On **Forest Lake***, you can catch some early spring crappies from the Park on the west side of Lake #1, especially around the outlet north of the park.

Half-breed Lake is located near the southeast corner of Forest Lake off of County Hwy. 97. The north end produces very early sunfish and crappies until early May.

Lily Lake* in Stillwater has a fishing pier where you can get sunfish, crappies, and bass throughout most of the season, especially in the evening. The lights from the tennis courts attract the crappies and bring them close to shore in early spring.

On **Square Lake***, the southeast corner is a popular fly fishing location fo sunfish. Work both sides of the cattails and from the east side of the cattails to the beach. You'll find trout here in the early season.

Tanners Lake* borders I-94 in the city of Landfall. Try the fishing pier (H) on the park's east side. Fish the south shoreline for sunfish, crappies, northerns, and bass

On **White Bear Lake***, you'll find crappies and bass in front of the Ramsey County beach. For fall walleyes, try fishing late at dusk from the boat dock in the county park. You can also catch sunfish and crappies from the fishing pier in Lion's Park and from the old boat access on the south end.

RIVERS

On the **Rum River**, the River Bend Park in the city of Ramsey has a fishing pie (H). From Hwy. 47, take 142nd Avenue to the park entrance. Riverside Park in Anoka also has a fishing pier (H). From East River Road, take 4th Avenue South to Madison and turn west to the park.

On the **Mississippi River**, you can catch smallmouth bass, walleyes, northerns crappies, carp, bullheads, and rock bass at the Coon Rapids Dam. There are numerous shore fishing areas and a fishing platform at the Regional Park off Hwy 12 in Brooklyn Park; or from Coon Rapids Boulevard NW in the city of Coon Rapids, take Egret Boulevard South to the park.

At Islands of Peace Park about a half mile north of I-694 in Fridley, fish both ends of the small island or the main Mississippi River channel.

The stretch of the Mississippi from the Ford Dam to the confluence of the Mississippi and Minnesota Rivers (where the 2 rivers join) offers some of the bes shore fishing on the river. You can catch walleyes, saugers, smallmouth bass carp, catfish, crappies, and muskie in mid-summer. Give special attention to the area beneath the locks, where Minnehaha Creek empties into the Mississipp River, and the first main bend above Hidden Falls.

At the confluence of the Mississippi and Minnesota Rivers, the best spot is on the Minnesota River (east side of Pike Island) in Fort Snelling State Park. Stand on the tip of the island, and cast out to the right side about 15 or 20 yards. There is a hole here that holds smallmouth bass, walleyes, carp, and catfish. From Hwy 5/I-494, take Post Road and follow the signs to the park.

There is a fishing pier on the north side of Lower Gray Cloud Island in Cottage Grove where Gray Cloud Trail crosses the channel (Mooer Lake).

On the **Minnesota River** in the city of Chaska where Chaska Creek flows into the Minnesota River, you'll find silver bass, sheephead, walleyes, and northerns This area is especially good in early season.

On the **St. Croix River**, you'll find crappies and sunfish in the quiet water near the discharge area of the King Power Plant off Hwy. 95 north of Bayport. In the spring and fall, you'll find silver bass in the warm-water discharge. At Point Douglas Park, where the St. Croix River flows into the Mississippi River, you can catch smallmouth bass and walleyes in the spring and fall.

On the **Crow River**, the dam in Hanover is known for big crappies.

Rivers

The Mississippi, St. Croix, and Minnesota Rivers consistently produce some of the largest fish caught in the metro area. There is a small army of anglers out there who regularly pound these rivers in search of the next state-record walleye. Here are some good reasons for fishing the rivers in the Twin Cities.

* In spring, rivers warm up faster and offer good fishing earlier than most lakes.

* When lake fishing blows hot and cold as dreaded "cold front" weather systems arrive, rivers offer amazingly consistent fishing action.

* When area lakes are buzzing with people, nearby rivers are usually underfished.

* You never know what you're going to catch. These rivers offer a smorgasbord of fish: smallmouth bass, walleyes, sauger, northern pike, muskies, largemouth bass, catfish, gar, sunfish, crappies, silver bass, perch, bullheads, carp, sturgeon, redhorse, sheephead, and rock bass.

WHERE TO FIND HELP

If it's your first trip out, a guide recommended by a local bait shop can show you some good spots and teach you river techniques that will last you a lifetime.

The DNR Information Center offers free river publications. Contour maps of most sections of the Mississippi, and St. Croix Rivers are available from the Minnesota Bookstore of the State of Minnesota (see the "Where to Get Help" section of this book). For recommendations on fish consumption from lakes and rivers, request a free booklet from the Department of Health (627-5046) or the DNR (296-2835).

For some top-notch tips on river fishing, read *Rivers* published by the Hunting & Fishing Library; *Stream Smallmouth* by Tim Holschlag; and the many river publications by Dan Gapen, a true river rat.

SPECIAL REGULATIONS ON THE RIVERS

All walleye, sauger, smallmouth bass, and largemouth bass must be returned to the water in the following stretches.

* Minnesota River downstream from the Mendota Bridge.

* Minnehaha Creek downstream from Minnehaha Falls.

* Pool 2 of the Mississippi River between the Hastings Dam and the Ford Dam, including all backwater lakes and connecting waters except Crosby Lake, Pickerel Lake, and Upper Lake. This stretch of the river (excluding lakes) is now open to angling all year from 1993 to 1998. The DNR will monitor the fish populations annually and review these regulations in 1998.

* On the Mississippi River from the Hwy. 101 bridge at Elk River upstream to the Hwy. 24 bridge at Clearwater, the possession limit for smallmouth bass is 3, with not more than 1 over 20 inches. All smallmouth bass between 12 inches and 20 inches must be returned to the water immediately.

MISSISSIPPI RIVER

The best surprise on the Mississippi River in the 1990's is the improvement i water quality. The improvement is especially noticeable from the Ford Dam in S Paul down to Lock & Dam #2 in Hastings. According to the DNR, the average siz of the walleyes in this stretch of the river is twice the size of the state's average (See Special Regulations.)

The key spots are below the Ford Dam at Hidden Falls; the mouth of th Minnesota River; the rocky areas under the I-494 bridge; and down to Holma Field. This stretch attracts some of the largest walleyes, especially in the fall.

These are great spots to fish on the Minnesota Fishing Opener. Look for holes a the 8 to 24 foot depths in the main river channel or below the dams. Use jigs wit minnows, and try vertical jigging while moving slowly with the current.

Wing dams are also good walleye ambush points, especially near Hasting Other good locations are the holes on river bends and the points of islands. A night, anchor about 10 yards upstream from the point and cast toward the tip.

Don't overlook the upper stretches of the Mississippi from the Hwy. 24 bridge a Clearwater down to the Hwy. 101 bridge at Elk River. The smallmouth bas fishery here has been written about in every national and local outdoor publicatio across the country. Make short casts to every rocky point, current breaks aroun the rocks, shallow rapids and riffles, or depressions as you float by. Remembe fish will face into the current.

The river bottom in this area is mostly shallow rock, gravel, and sand unlike th deeper waters of the lower Mississippi. In low-water years, it is hard to motor bac upstream to your put-in access. You'll need to use two cars; one at you launching point, and another at your destination.

Most anglers use a short-shaft motor on their boat for greater mobility and to allo more precise casting to the best spots. The bigger fish are in the depressions c troughs through the shallow areas. Work the edges of the current breaks. Als check river bends and shoreline structure such as fallen trees, logs, docks, et Cast upstream so the current pulls your bait down and over or around th structures. Don't hesitate to cast into 6 inches of water. Be prepared to lift yo motor as you float over the shallow rocky areas. Troll a live-bait rig or lon crankbait.

Other notable smallmouth locations on the Mississippi River are the Coon Rapid Dam (good shore fishing here) in Coon Rapids; where the Rum River dumps int the Mississippi River in Anoka; the I-694 bridge; and from St. Anthony Falls dow to Hidden Falls.

For largemouth bass, fish the quieter backwater areas throughout the river; th channel behind Pike Island (west side); Gun Club Lake; Snelling Lake; Pig's Ey Lake; and the lakes around Upper and Lower Grey Cloud Island — Spring Lak Baldwin Lake, Mooers Lake, and River Lake. Flip a jig and pig to the stumps an fallen trees.

MINNESOTA RIVER

Most anglers write off the Minnesota River as a polluted, muddy waterway not capable of supporting decent populations of game fish. But those who fish these waters regularly know that using a little savvy will result in enviable catches.

The most productive part of the Minnesota River is from Carver Rapids near Carver up to the Shakopee-Savage area. Numerous creeks empty into this section of the river, and the abundance of clear, fresh, oxygenated water at the mouths of these creeks attracts walleyes most of the season. Rice Creek and Eagle Creek near I-35W and Chaska Creek in Chaska are good examples.

When the water is high, especially in the early season, you can motor a short distance up into the creeks. Cast up to the center of the channel over the holes, and let your lure bounce back down to you. Avid Minnesota River anglers ("river rats") use a small hook tipped with a minnow and add a lead split-shot sinker.

In low-water periods, move back out to the mouth of the creek and fish the sides. A jig with a 3-inch tail or minnow is a good all-season technique. Fathead minnows are the hottest baits on the river, and the best jigs are chartreuse, hot pink with a white tail, or white with a pink tail.

In the summer, also try trolling with a deep-diving crankbait. Look for the ledges and deep-water drop-offs, especially on the inside bends. The mouths of the creeks are also good fall and winter locations. But don't even think about standing on the ice. It's totally unsafe, and it's a dumb way to end your life.

You'll find northern pike in the same locations as the walleyes in all seasons.

Crappie hunters will find a good supply at the mouth of Eagle Creek by the I-35W bridge or in the adjacent backwaters.

Catfish as large as 50 pounds hang around the deep holes on the sharp bends of the river. Good locations are the Carver bridge, Ollie's Bend, Spearhead, Shakopee bridge, and the three bends between Valley Fair and Murphy's Landing. These spots are especially good in the heat of the summer. Big sucker minnows on bottom rigs are the key. Anchor and cast to the center of the hole. When the action slows for the larger fish, there are plenty of silver bass, carp, and sheephead to keep you entertained.

ST. CROIX RIVER

The fishing season opens 2 weeks earlier on the St. Croix River than on Minnesota lakes. It's the cleanest of the 3 rivers, and you can eat the catch. It can also offer some very good walleye, sauger, and smallmouth bass fishing.

The "Lower St. Croix", beginning at Stillwater and ending about 25 miles downstream at Prescott, is considered the best walleye fishery of the entire river. Walleye and sauger hunters on this stretch seek out the major points: the holes above the points, the eddies, and the sandbars.

The pilings under the bridges that span Minnesota and Wisconsin are productive spots that are easy to find. Give special attention to the current breaks (seams where fast water and quiet water meet) on the downstream side of the pilings.

The drop-offs just upstream from the Kinnickinnic Narrows are good all-season walleye locations. You can troll through the narrows for more action. The area where the St. Croix flows into the Mississippi River is especially good in the spring and fall. Winter walleye anglers do well in the warm-water discharge at the King Power Plant near Bayport.

Smallmouth bass are attracted to the same habitat as walleyes but usually in faster currents. Try the rocky shoreline under the I-94 bridge or just north of the mouth of the Kinnickinnic River about 7 miles north of Prescott. The best area is the 12-mile stretch from Stillwater north to Copas. Look for shorelines covered with rocks or pebbles, and cast an orange jig or shallow-running crayfish lure. Don't hesitate to cast into 6 inches of water next to the rocks.

Sunfish and crappies can be found at the Park in Stillwater, the shallow back-water areas above Stillwater, the quiet water around the warm-water discharge at the King Power Plant, the pilings by the railroad bridge across from Hudson, and at the mouth of the Willow River (Lake Mallalieu).

Mid-August is the time for giant catfish up to 60 pounds. The Hudson bridge is a popular location, but the biggest catfish come from the Stillwater area. They can be found in the deeper holes (30 to 40 feet) during the day and around the edges of the holes at night. They're easier to catch at night.

A 4-pound silver (white) bass that tied the Minnesota state record was taken from the St. Croix River. In the spring, the Stillwater area is the best location. You'll find silver bass in slower water off the eddies, below points, near current breaks, or slightly off the main channel. White jigs are best — they're easier to see in the summer. When bass are feeding in schools, they will force the minnows to the surface, causing a slight splashing sound. In addition, gulls will be circling over-head, attracted to an easy meal by the commotion on the water. The areas around the Kinnickinnic River and down to the mouth of the river at Hastings are prime summer locations. Fish may even roam downstream to the Mississippi River.

This information was provided by Jeff Byrne, Pat Buchanan, Steve Carney, John Daily, Steve Fisher, Dave Genz, Dale Haven, Tim Holschlag, Duane Melchnior, Butch Noterman, Orrin Sechter, Bill Tomberlin, Ted Welch, and Tom Zenako.

Children's Fishing Ponds

Children's fishing ponds in the Twin Cities provide fantastic fun for small anglers and for big kids of any age. Most of these ponds are small and fairly shallow. They are usually stocked with bluegills, crappies, and bullheads, but many of them contain other species too. In some ponds, an aeration system has been installed to reduce winterkill and the fish will fish survive from year to year. These waters are usually stocked in the spring (late April to mid-May) and may be fished out by mid-summer. The average size of bluegill and crappies in these ponds is 6 to 9 ounces.

The status of these ponds and the species that are stocked may change from year to year. Before you head off to your favorite pond in the spring, call the DNR (296-0131) to make certain stocking has been completed.

ANOKA COUNTY

- LOCH NESS PARK — Co. Rd. 12 and Lexington Ave. NE. (111th Ave.), Blaine. Stocked with bluegills and crappies. Has fishing dock.

- NATIONAL SPORTS CENTER POND — 105th Ave. NE. (east of Central Ave.), Blaine. Stocked with bluegills and crappies.

CARVER COUNTY

- CHASKA POND (Fireman's Park) — corner of Hwy. 212 and Hwy. 41 NW. (Chestnut Street), Chaska. Stocked with bluegills and crappies. Has fishing dock.

DAKOTA COUNTY

- SCHWANZ POND — in Trapp Park Farm on Wilderness Run Road, Eagan. Stocked with crappies.

- MARTHALER POND — Wentworth Ave. and Marthaler Lane, West Saint Paul. Stocked with bluegills, crappies, and bullheads.

- SIMLEY POND — Cahill Ave. E. and Co. Rd. 28 (80th St.), Inver Grove Heights. Stocked with bluegills, crappies, and bullheads.

- VALLEY LAKE — Cedar Ave. and 160th St., Lakeville. Stocked with bluegills and crappies.

HENNEPIN COUNTY

- BIRCHCREST POND — in Birchcrest Park northwest of Hwy. 100 and Co. Rd. 62 (Crosstown Hwy.) at Bernard and W. 60th St., Edina. Stocked with bullheads only.

- BOUNDARY CREEK POND (Mallard) — Boundary Creek Terrace and 105th Ave. N. (northeast of 101st Ave. N. and Zachary Lane N.), Maple Grove. Stocked with crappies and bullheads.

- CIVIC CENTER POND — on Shingle Creek Parkway southwest of I-94 and Hwy. 100, Brooklyn Center. Stocked with bluegills and crappies.

- CHAMPLIN MILL POND — Hwy. 52 and Hwy. 169, Champlin. Stocked with bluegills and crappies.

- LOWER PENN LAKE — 86th Street W. and Penn Avenue S., Bloomington. Stocked with bluegills and crappies. Has aeration system.

- POWDERHORN LAKE — in Powderhorn Park at E. 35th St. and 15th Ave. S., Minneapolis. Stocked with bluegills and crappies. Has fishing dock.

- TAFT LAKE — in Taft Park at Bloomington Ave. S. and Co. Rd. 62 (Crosstown), southwest of the Hwy. 36 interchange (Cedar Avenue South), Richfield. Stocked with bluegills and crappies. Has fishing dock and aeration system.

- WEBER POND — in Camden Park at Lyndale Ave. and Weber Parkway, Minneapolis. Stocked with bluegills and crappies. May not be stocked in low-water years.

- WIRTH LAKE — in Wirth Park at Wirth Parkway and Glenwood, Minneapolis. Stocked with crappies and walleyes. Has fishing dock.

RAMSEY COUNTY

- BENNETT LAKE — in Central Park at Lexington Ave. and Co. Rd. C, Roseville. Stocked with bluegills, crappies, and bullheads. Has fishing dock and aeration system.

- KERRY POND — east of Hwy. 49 at Elaine Ave. and MacKubin, Shoreview. Stocked with bluegills and crappies.

- LOEB LAKE (GERANIUM) — in Marydale Park at Maryland Ave. and Dale St., Saint Paul. Stocked with bluegills, crappies, and bullheads. Has fishing dock.

- SILVERVIEW LAKE — in Oak Lake Park at Co. Rd. H2 and Silver Lake Rd., Mounds View. Stocked with bluegills and crappies.

SCOTT COUNTY

- BEASON LAKE — at the St. Lawrence Wayside (Minnesota Valley Trail), Belle Plaine. Stocked with bluegills and crappies.

- JORDAN MILL POND — 2 blocks west of Hwy. 21 at Sunset Dr. and Park Dr., Jordan. Stocked with bluegills, crappies, and bullheads.

WASHINGTON COUNTY

- ALICE LAKE — in William O'Brien State Park on O'Brien Trail N. (west of Hwy. 95), Marine on St. Croix. Stocked with bluegills and crappies.

- LOST LAKE — in Wildwood Park on Old Wildwood Rd. (south of Co. Rd. 244), Mahtomedi. Stocked with crappies and bullheads.

Seasonal Fishing Patterns

Have you ever noticed that your favorite spring hotspot doesn't even produce a nibble in mid-summer; or that the same bait that drove the fish crazy in May doesn't interest them in August? To catch fish consistently, you'll need to understand the seasonal changes that take place in lakes and rivers and the way each species reacts to those changes.

The location of the fish at any particular time is determined by their need for food, security, and comfort. As water conditions change in response to the seasons, weather, and other factors, the fish will move to the area that provides the best combination of conditions to meet their needs.

Some of the factors that determine where the fish will be and what baits they will prefer are water temperature, water level, light penetration, turbulence, weed growth, food supply, and the availability of oxygen. A significant change in any of these factors can cause the fish to move in search of more favorable territory.

To help you locate your favorite species throughout the fishing season, we have summarized fish movements by calendar periods for each species and provided a few tips on lures and techniques for each period. Keep in mind that the time frames shown in these charts are very elastic. As the weather varies from year to year, so too will the time frames for each period. An early spring warmup can send the fish into their summer haunts in mid-June rather than mid-July. A late fall can keep them in the summer pattern long after Labor Day. Keep an open mind, and try a variety of techniques and spots.

The following charts have been tailored to reflect water conditions in metro-area lakes and rivers. Most of the lakes in this area are classified as late mesotrophic (late middle age) or early eutrophic (old age). Younger lakes in other parts of Minnesota may not have the same seasonal fishing patterns.

Seasonal patterns can also vary within the metro area, depending on size, depth, and water clarity of a lake. Small, dark lakes tend to warm up faster than large clear ones. So, lakes across the street from each other will not necessarily have the fish following the same pattern. Anyone who has fished both Lake Gervais and White Bear Lake knows that the "summer pattern" starts much earlier in the murky waters of Lake Gervais.

It is also possible for seasonal patterns to vary considerably within the same lake. Lake Minnetonka is a prime example. Because of great variations in bottom content, water temperature, light intensity, etc., a bay located on the west end of the lake will have totally different patterns from a bay at the east end of the lake. It is quite possible for spawning to be completed in one part of the lake before it begins in another part of the same lake.

The seasonal patterns shown in the following charts should simply be regarded as "guidelines". The time frames for each chart should be "stretched" to fit the water conditions of the lake you intend to fish. Above all, don't expect that every spot that is marked "C" on the map of a particular lake will produce crappies every day of the fishing season. Remember that most of the fish will move to an area that offers the best combination of factors to meet their need for food, security, and comfort.

SUNFISH

SEASON	FISH LOCATION	LURES & TECHNIQUES
EARLY SPRING April-May	Sunfish will be tightly schooled in the warmest water in both lakes and rivers. Look for them around brush, wood, or docks in backwater bays or canals.	Use a plain small hook, very small jigs or ice flies tipped with a piece of wax worm, Eurolarvae, angleworm, night crawler, or a small leech. A small slip-bobber will keep the bait at the right depth.
LATE SPRING May-June	Spawning begins when the water temperature reaches 68 to 72 degrees and may continue until mid-summer. Look for clusters of circular nests along shallow shorelines. The smaller fish will spawn close to shore. The larger fish prefer the 4 to 8 foot depths. Also check out the docks.	Use the same lures as early spring, but also try small spiders, poppers, or wet flies and nymphs on a fly rod. During spawning, the fish aren't actively feeding but will strike if the bait is dropped on the nest.
EARLY SUMMER June-July	The smaller fish stay in the shallows. The larger fish move to deeper water. Look for deep weedbeds, weedy points, sunken islands, submerged brush, or fallen timber. Also look for overhanging trees near a creek or boat channel or an entrance to a small bay.	Use the same lures as before, but also try larger live baits such as crickets, grass-hoppers, night crawlers, and minnows. Troll along the weeds or brush until you locate the school. Then anchor and cast into the fish.
LATE SUMMER July-August	As the water temperature climbs, the jumbo sunnies head for deep water. The biggest fish prefer rock or gravel humps, points, and flats in 15 to 30 feet of water. Smaller fish can be found in the early summer haunts.	Use a slip bobber and live bait in deep water, or try vertical jigging with small jigs tipped with live bait. Keep the bait within a foot off the bottom. Fish various depths along the weedline until you locate the fish.
EARLY FALL September-October	Look for submerged weeds in 8 to 15 feet of water, especially where the water temperature is 68 to 72 degrees. Large sunfish will return to the shallow bays.	Use the same live baits as before with jigs or a plain hook. Spinners are effective, too.
LATE FALL October-November	The fish will scatter over weedy bars and points or in shallow bays with a relatively hard bottom. Try water that is less than 15 feet deep and move around until you find the fish.	Many of the same baits used in the warmer months will work well. Also use ice flies or tiny ice fishing jigs tipped with mayfly larvae or corn-borer worms.
WINTER November-April	The fish will be scattered over weedy bars and points or in shallow weedy bays, particularly those with a hard bottom. Most of the fish will be found near weed growth in less than 20 feet of water. In the middle of the winter, the fish may move deeper depending on oxygen levels.	Use ice flies or tear-drop hooks with grubs, mousies, silver wigglers, wax worms, or very small minnows. All of these can be fished below a bobber.

CRAPPIES

SEASON	FISH LOCATION	LURES & TECHNIQUES
EARLY SPRING April-May	The fish will be attracted to the areas that have the warmest water. Look for them along the west and northwest sides of the lake around brush, wood, or docks in backwater bays or dark-bottom canals. Also fish the bulrush beds along the north shore.	Use very small marabou jigs in white and pink or pink and yellow, ice flies tipped with pieces of worms, or a small minnow on a jig or a plain hook. All of these should be fished below a slip bobber to change depths quickly.
LATE SPRING May-June	The fish spawn when the water temperature reaches 62 to 65 degrees. Look for dark bottom bays with cattails or lily pads. Shoreline bulrush flats are preferred. After spawning, the fish move into thick weeds near the spawning areas.	Use the same lures as in early spring. In-line spinnerbaits also work well. The fish aren't actively feeding during the spawn but will strike if the bait is dropped over the nest. Fly fishing can be effective. Use subsurface flies, poppers, floating bugs.
EARLY SUMMER June-July	Fish will be suspended well off the bottom just outside the weedline. Also try weedy underwater points, brush piles, docks, and rock piles near the weeds. The fish will often relate to the top of the thermocline. In early morning and evening, they will also suspend above a patch of weeds 6 to 7 feet below the surface.	A slip bobber with live bait works best. Use a small jig (1/16 to 1/8 oz.) or plain hook with angleworms, Eurolarvae, night crawlers, small minnows, or a plastic tail. To locate suspended fish, troll slowly with a small in-line spinnerbait.
LATE SUMMER July-August	Fish will be suspended over deep water (15 to 50 feet) some distance outside their early summer haunts. Pay attention to weedline drop-offs. In the evening and early morning, check the shoreline weedbeds and bulrush flats. Night fishing can be productive in clear lakes.	Early summer lures work well. Also try streamers, small spoons, and spinners. Trolling can be effective too. Night fishing works best on clear water lakes.
EARLY FALL September-October	Fish are still suspended in deep water but will move onto the rocks and remaining patches of green weeds for feeding.	Use jigs, jig spins, spinners or slip bobber with live bait.
LATE FALL October-November	Fish will be suspended off the weedline. A deep cabbage bed on a rocky bottom is ideal. Also check out rock piles, underwater points, bars, and sunken islands.	Use same lures as early fall. Crappies are now fattening up for the winter and will feed aggressively.
WINTER November-April	Check out the late fall spots. Fish will be suspended over deep weed growth, outside of cabbage weed points, on weedy flats, or over open water near a deep hole. Locate crappie resting areas in winter by following the direction that the bobber moves. When bobber goes straight down, you're on target.	Use ice flies or tear-drop hooks with grubs, mousies, silver wigglers, wax worms, or small minnows. Very small jigs work well too. All of these can be fished below a bobber.

NORTHERN PIKE

SEASON	FISH LOCATION	LURES & TECHNIQUES
LATE SPRING May-June	The fish will be scattered. In rivers, fish the backwater areas and the backwash areas created by wing dams. In lakes, look for fish on weedy bars, especially those adjacent to bulrush beds.	Try bobber fishing with sucker minnows or shiners. Large spinnerbaits, spoons, and small bucktail spinners are productive. Also try injured-minnow lures or jigs tipped with minnows
EARLY SUMMER June-July	Concentrate on the weedline drop-offs, bulrush points, and weedy flats and points. In rivers, look for fish in backwash areas near the dams or behind wing dams down river. Larger fish will move into the 15 to 30 foot depths. Small northerns prefer water temperatures of 65 to 70 degrees. Large northerns seek 50 to 55 degrees temperatures.	Use large gaudy spinnerbaits, spoons, spoonplugs, and vibrating crankbaits. Also try a jig and minnow or a slip bobber with a large sucker minnow or golden shiner.
LATE SUMMER July-August	Some fish will stay on the weedline but most of the big ones will move to very deep water except where there is a thermocline. In rivers, the cold-water springs will also attract large fish along the shoreline.	For the weedline, use same lures as early summer. For the deeper structures, try speedtrolling with spoonplugs or other large crankbaits.
EARLY FALL September-October	Fish the drop-offs at the 15 to 25 foot depths. Look for the remaining patches of green weeds along the sharp weedline drop-offs, underwater points, and shoreline flats.	Try vertical jigging, back-trolling or drifting with jigs tipped with large sucker minnows or pork rind. Spoons, spinnerbaits, jerkbaits, and crankbaits also work.
LATE FALL October-November	Some fish will stay on the flats near the remaining patches of green weeds. Also look along the steep dropping bars. During frog migrations, the big fish move in very close to shore and will be actively feeding.	Use live frogs in the weedy areas. For the deep drop-offs, use a jig and minnow combination or a live-bait rig with chubs. Injured-minnow lures, jerkbaits, or spinnerbaits work well too.
WINTER November-April	In early winter, look for them on the weedy flats and bars that drop off into deeper water. As the days get shorter, the fish will move further from shore. Submerged islands and humps with weeds or rocks are very good. At times, the northerns may be suspended with schools of crappies or cisco. Several weeks before ice-out, they will move into the shallow backwater bays.	Use a tip-up with dacron line and a braided wire leader. A jig or plain hook with a large shiner or sucker minnow works best. Dead bait fished on the bottom is effective during the later part of the season.

WALLEYE

SEASON	FISH LOCATION	LURES & TECHNIQUES
LATE SPRING May-June	River sections within 5 miles of a lock or dam are best . Check backwash areas, especially those created by wing dams (fish are usually found in the front depression of the wing dam and on the top). In lakes, look for windswept shorelines with gravel flats, rocks, and rubble. Fish the edge of the flats and look for gradually sloping points that drop into deep water.	Back-troll or drift using a jig or a live-bait rig with a minnow, leech, or night crawler. Injured-minnow lures can also be trolled with a bottom bumping rig. At night, troll over shallow bars with injured-minnow lures or crankbaits.
EARLY SUMMER June-July	Concentrate on underwater points, bars, and sunken islands. The saddles between islands are also productive. Look for submerged weedbeds, especially cabbage weeds.	Use the same baits and techniques as in late spring. To fish the top of submerged weeds, use a jig and minnow with a slip bobber.
LATE SUMMER August	Some fish will stay in the weeds. Irregular breaklines along shore will hold more walleyes in summer than a breakline with few points or pockets. Also check out the sharper drop-offs on rocky points, bars, and sunken is-lands. The fish will use the drop-offs during the day and move up to the shallow areas to forage at night. In fertile lakes, the thermocline limits the use of deep water for walleyes.	Continue to use jigs and live-bait rigs with leeches and night crawlers. Use a heavier weight to keep the bait near the bottom. During the day, try crankbaits or spinnerbaits with a minnow along the edge of the weeds. Broad-leaf weeds will usually hold more walleyes than narrow-leaf weeds. At night troll over the weeds with a crank-bait or spinner and night crawler combination on a very long line.
EARLY FALL September-October	Fish the same areas as late summer. The walleyes will be scattered. The migration of frogs back to the lakes attracts walleyes to the shallows, particularly near to inflowing water. Night fishing may be best.	Trolling with a live bait rig is the best way to locate scattered fish. Once located, use a jig tipped with a minnow. A slow presentation is recommended this time of the year.
LATE FALL October-November	During the day, the fish will concentrate on sharp drop-offs on inside turns and on rocky bars and points adjacent to very deep water. At night, they will forage on shallow, rocky bars or near inlets and outlets on lakes. Look for river fish in the same areas as in late spring.	In clear-water lakes, night fishing may be your best bet. Use the same lures and techniques as early spring. Also try jigs, flash lures, or jigging minnow lures. Use a slow presentation.
WINTER November-April	Walleyes are usually more shallow in early and late winter than in mid-winter. They will remain near their late fall feeding areas until March when they begin to move toward their spawning areas.	Use a tip-up with dacron line, monofilament leader, plain hook, and small golden shiner minnow. Also try jigs, or jigging minnow lures. Fish about a foot off the bottom.

LARGEMOUTH BASS

SEASON	FISH LOCATION	LURES & TECHNIQUES
LATE SPRING May-June	Spawned-out females will scatter and go off their feed for about 2 weeks. Males will be concentrated in and around weed growth (4 to 12 feet) adjacent to the spawning grounds. Fish the inside edge of the thick weeds in the early morning, and move to the outside edge around mid-day.	Spinnerbaits tipped with pork rind are excellent. Top-water lures, slow-falling jigs, small Texas-rigged worms, or live bait fished below a bobber will also produce. Also try jigs tipped with pork rind or minnow.
EARLY SUMMER June-July	The fish will scatter into three types of areas: very shallow weed-choked bays; the deep edge of the weeds; and the weedy flats between these areas. Also fish the thick cattail or bulrush banks, docks, riprap, bridges, piers, channel walls, and any odd type of shoreline debris. In clear-water lakes, night fishing is best.	For shallow fish, use buzzbaits, spinnerbaits, weedless spoons, and top-water lures such as jitterbugs and rubber frogs. For the weedlines and the weedy flats, use spinnerbaits, crankbaits, weedless spoons, and Texas rigged plastic worms.
LATE SUMMER July-August	Some of the fish will stay in the shallows. Most of them will move to the deep weedlines and drop-offs. Look for heavy cover near deep water. Fish the sunken islands, weedy points and bars, and rock piles. In rivers, fish backwaters, chutes, bridges, riprap, points, and wing dams.	For shallow fish, use the same lures as early spring. For the weedlines and deeper drop-offs, use jigs, vibrating crankbaits, plastic worms, or trolled spoon-plugs. Mark productive areas with floating markers and return to these locations about a half hour later.
EARLY FALL September-October	Fish the bulrush flats and weedlines near sharp drop-offs. Some of the bass will be suspended over deep water adjacent to mid-lake humps. Look for schools of sunfish on the surface; the bass will be underneath. In early September, work the docks, channels, and shallow points.	For suspended bass, swim small crankbaits underneath the sunfish. For the weedline drop-offs and bulrush flats, use spinnerbaits, jigs with minnows, or plastic worms.
LATE FALL October-November	Concentrate on the remaining patches of green weeds, rock piles, and rock flats adjacent to sharp drop-offs. Also check out the shoreline brush piles, bulrushes, cattails, stick-ups, and docks.	On warm days, use crankbaits or spinnerbaits on the flats or along the shoreline. When the fish are on the drop-offs, use small plastic worms, or jigs tipped with pork rind or golden shiner minnows.
WINTER November-February	Bass will remain in their late fall locations for a short period after the lake freezes over. As the temperature drops, the fish move deeper and become less active. Sometimes you'll find the bass in the same areas as the sunfish but they're harder to catch. Just before ice-out, the bass will begin to move onto the weedy flats adjacent to the spawning areas.	A small minnow fished below a bobber works well. Also try a teardrop jig or a large ice fly tipped with Eurolarvae.

SMALLMOUTH BASS

SEASON	FISH LOCATION	LURES & TECHNIQUES
LATE SPRING May-June	Spawning begins when the water temperature reaches 60 to 65 degrees. After spawning, the fish will scatter out into the surrounding area. In lakes, look for docks, logs, boulders, or rock-based weeds near the spawning beds. In rivers, the fish will use rock riffles, flats, pools, and rip-rap areas.	In the shallows, use small (1/4 oz) spinnerbaits or shallow-running crankbaits. For deeper water, use deep-diving crankbaits, jig and eel combinations, or live-bait rig with small minnows or night crawlers. As the water warms, use crayfish pattern crankbaits.
EARLY SUMMER June-July	As the water in the lakes gets warmer, the fish will move deeper. Look for rock reefs, underwater points, sunken islands, and boulder-strewn tapering shorelines. Logs, cabbage weeds, and docks that extend out to deep water can be very productive. The bigger fish will stay in the deep water during the day and roam the shallows after dark. In rivers, the fish continue to use the same areas as late spring and are usually in less than 5 feet of water.	Use the same lures and techniques as in late spring. At night, try a black spinnerbait over the tops of submerged rock piles. Use a stop-and-go retrieve. Jigging type lures are a good choice for fishing in murky water.
LATE SUMMER August	In lakes, the fish may be as deep as 25 feet. In rivers, try the 2 to 6 foot depths on flat, sandy sections with rocks and slow current.	Live bait is best. Try a live-bait rig with night-crawler, leech, hellgrammite, or crayfish. Jig-spins and in-line spinnerbaits also work.
EARLY FALL September-October	The fish will again be foraging in shallow water. Rocks where the crayfish hide are the main attraction. Look for deep-dropping rock or gravel points.	Use same lures as in late summer.
LATE FALL October-November	As the water cools, the fish will move in toward shore and stack up on rocky points or boulder areas. In rivers, look for areas with swift current with logs, rocks, or other obstructions. Fish feed actively until water temperatures drop into the low 40s.	Shiner minnows and redtail chubs work well. Also try crayfish pattern crankbaits.
WINTER November-April	The fish will remain in their late fall locations for a short period after the lake freezes over. As the temperature drops, they will move deeper. Several weeks before ice-out, the fish become more active and move onto the rocky reefs and drop-offs near the spawning beds.	Use "flash" lures or small lead-head jigs tipped with a small minnow or a piece of minnow. Also try a jigging lure with some type of scent added.

MUSKIE

SEASON	FISH LOCATION	LURES & TECHNIQUES
LATE SPRING May-June	After spawning, river muskies will retreat to the deeper pool areas that they will inhabit for the rest of the year. Concentrate on fallen trees and bank projections at the edge of the pools. In lakes, the fish will be in the backwater areas, suspended over open water, or use bars or underwater points with emerging weed growth.	Use spinnerbaits, wobbling plugs, jigs with minnows, or jerkbaits. Bucktail spinners are also a good choice. Muskies bite best on overcast days. Note: Split "O" rings on plugs should either be removed or soldered to increase strength and reduce line fraying.
EARLY SUMMER June-July	Continue to fish the weedbeds on underwater points and the sand flats near the weedbeds. Also check out the weedy sunken islands, rock piles, boulder reefs, and flooded timber in 5 to 20 feet of water. In clear lakes, night fishing can be productive from early summer through fall.	Baits can be larger now. Use bucktail spinners, spinnerbaits, top-water lures, and 5 to 7 inch crankbaits and jerkbaits.
LATE SUMMER August	Concentrate on the deeper submerged weedbeds, sharp weedline drop-offs, sunken islands topped with weeds, rock piles, or boulder reefs. At dusk and dawn, fish the bulrushes and the weedy bays. Muskies spend most of their time in deep water (30 feet or deeper) and most of them are inactive.	Use large noisy lures at fast speeds. Vary the speed occasionally, or pause and change direction to induce a strike. Use the early summer lures or try a bucktail jig with a trailer hook.
EARLY FALL September-October	Work the remaining patches of green weeds adjacent to sharp drop-offs. Rock piles in combination with green cabbage weeds are the best bet. Also fish the river mouth.	Use very large bucktail spinners, jerkbaits, vibrating crankbaits, spinnerbaits with pork, bucktail jigs with trailer hooks, or a live-bait harness with a very large minnow.
LATE FALL October-November	Fish the river mouths. Concentrate on the remaining green weeds near drop-offs. Rock humps and bars also attract fish.	Use the same lures as early fall until water temperature drops to 50 degrees. Then switch to a live-bait rig with a large sucker minnow.
WINTER November-April	Very little is known about fishing through the ice in rivers. In lakes, the muskies remain in their late fall locations for a short period after the lake freezes over. Then they move down to the deeper breaks and become somewhat lethargic. Muskies feed only once every 25 to 30 days in mid-winter. In late winter just before ice-out, they become more active and move toward their spawning areas in shallow bays.	Use a tip-up with dacron line and a solid wire leader with a round-nose snap. A jig or plain hook with a large shiner or sucker minnow may be successful. Also try large jigs.

STREAM TROUT IN LAKES

SEASON	FISH LOCATION	LURES & TECHNIQUES
LATE SPRING May-June	Water temperature is the key. Brook trout prefer 52 to 56 degrees; brown trout prefer 60 to 65 degrees; and rainbow trout prefer 55 to 60 degrees. Look for areas where a layer of water at the preferred temperature merges with structure or shoreline. As surface temperatures climb, the trout will move deeper to find cooler water.	Troll with floating crank-baits. Also try spinners and cowbell attractors. Cast to rising trout with a #0 or #1 size in-line spinner lure. Keep the lure a good distance behind the boat. For shore fishing, use the same lures. A live-bait rig with an inflated night crawler or Eurolarvae can be productive too. Cheese, miniature marshmallows, fish eggs, and canned whole corn also work.
EARLY SUMMER June-July	The fish may go very deep in search of cooler water, then come to the surface during low-light periods to feed. Shore fishing becomes less productive. Fish can also be found near rock bars, points, sunken islands, or near inflowing water. Trout in fertile lakes will often suspend just above the thermocline. In lakes that are infertile, trout will move into the thermocline and suspend. Because there is no oxygen below the thermocline except near springs, trout must maintain an exact depth to survive. Use a depthfinder to locate the fish, and present your lure at the exact depth of the fish.	Now is the time for down-riggers and deep-running lures such as small crankbaits and spoons. Also try a spinner tipped with a dead minnow or a gob of night crawlers. Trout will often suspend just above or in the thermocline.
LATE SUMMER July-August	Look for the trout in the deep holes and near springs that bring in cooler water.	Use the same lures and techniques as early summer. Still fishing with a live-bait rig also works well.
EARLY FALL September	As the surface water cools, the fish will move up closer to shore.	Use floating injured-minnow lures, spinners, and cowbell attractors. Shore fishing is productive.
LATE FALL October	The fish will often be suspended near the surface in shallow water.	Trout season closes October 31st.
WINTER November-April	The fish can be found under the ice from 3 to 25 feet of water. They will often be suspended over deeper water off rock bars, sunken islands or other points extending from shore.	Season is from January to March. Trout may be taken on ice flies tipped with Eurolarvae, mousies, goldenrod grubs, scuds, etc. Techniques used for sunfish also work well here.

Where to Get Help

DNR Information Center, DNR Building, 500 Lafayette RD., St. Paul, MN 55155 Phone (612) 296-6157. Ask for these free publications: *Public Boat Launch Guide, Twin Cities Metropolitan Area; The Metro Area Rivers Guide* (Mississippi St. Croix, and Minnesota Rivers); *The Mississippi River;* information booklets or each major species of game fish; pamphlets listing fishing piers accessible to handicapped anglers; and lots more.

DNR Metro Area Fisheries, 1200 Warner Road, St. Paul, MN 55106. Phone (612) 772-7950. This office can provide extensive information on stocking pro grams, population survey reports, lake history, and development plans for lakes in the metro area. Ask for a free computer print-out detailing your favorite lake.

DNR Hinkley Area Fisheries, Box 398, 206 Power Ave. N., Hinkley, MN 55037 Phone (612) 1-384-7721. This office provides detailed information and computer print-outs on Chisago County lakes.

Hennepin County Park Reserve District, 12615 County Rd. 9, P.O. Box 47320 Plymouth, MN 55441-0320. Phone (612) 559-9000. Call for a free copy of their seasonal publication, "Time-Out," listing the facilities at each of their parks. There is no fee for using the boat launches but there is a daily parking fee. You can purchase an annual parking permit at the gatehouse at each park.

Hennepin County Sheriff's Water Patrol, 4141 Shoreline Drive, Spring Park, MN 55384. Phone (612) 471-8528. A contour map of Lake Minnetonka is available free of charge. It shows the location of public boat accesses, boat rentals, and other facilities. Send a self-addressed business-sized envelope with two 29-cent stamps.

Metropolitan Council, Mears Park Center, 230 E. 5th Street, St. Paul, MN 55101. Phone: 291-6359. Ask for the large full-color map showing the location of Regional Parks in the Twin Cities Metropolitan Area. It includes a list of activities at each park such as fishing, boat rental, camping, boat launch, swimming, etc. Send $1.00 for postage and handling.

MINNAQUA Program, sponsored by DNR and University of Minnesota Extension Service. Phone (612) 297-4919 to register for fishing workshops on metro lakes or to volunteer as an instructor. Spring workshops cover fishing basics, casting techniques, safety rules, protecting the resource, and cooking the catch. Ice fishing workshops are held in the fall. Handicapped anglers are encouraged to participate.

Minneapolis Parks and Recreation Board, Room 1, Flour Exchange Building, 310 4th Ave. So., Minneapolis, MN 55415. Phone (612) 348-5406. Several types of special permits are required for these lakes in addition to state licenses: Watercraft Permit; Motor Permit; Operator's Permit for Minors; and Ice House Permit. Applications are processed promptly.

Minnesota Bookstore, State of Minnesota, 117 University Ave., St. Paul, MN 55155. Phone (612) 297-3000 or toll free (world-wide) 1-800-657-3757. Contour maps are available for most lakes and rivers in Minnesota. A free catalog lists a large selection of Minnesota-related books and publications.

Directories

This information is accurate and complete at the time of printing. Changes are inevitable, however, so phone ahead to check if the service is still available.

BAIT SHOPS

ANOKA COUNTY

- Allen's Market, Co. Rd. 22 and Leyte St., Wyoming. 434-6153.

- Angler's Paradise, 809 W. Main St. (Hwy. 10), Anoka. 421-8996.

- Carlisle Store, 21831 Viking Blvd. NE (Co. Rd. 22), Wyoming. 462-5512.

- Coon Lake Market, 515 Lincoln Ave., East Bethel. 464-7614.

- Esau's Sporting Goods, 157th & Hwy. 65, Ham Lake. 434-5662.

- Tackle Box, 7860 Lake Drive, Lino Lakes. 784-5282.

- Trails End - Bass Pro, 7597 Hwy. 65 NE, Fridley. 784-9080.

- Trippel's Market, 1801 Main St., Centerville. 429-1678.

- Vados Bait, 7895 Hwy. 65 NE, Spring Lake Park. 784-6728.

CARVER COUNTY

- Cabin Fever, 1550 Arboretum (Hwy. 5), Victoria. 443-2022.

- Chanhassen Bait, 440 W. 79th St., Chanhassen. 934-0789.

- Holiday Store, 920 E. Hwy. 212, Chaska. 448-4882.

- In-Towne Marina, 8 E. Lake St., Waconia. 442-2096.

- La Marina, 300 E. Lake St., Waconia. 442-4925.

CHISAGO COUNTY

- Family Sports Center, Hwy. 8, Chisago City. 1-257-6143.

- Frankie's Bait, Hwy. 8 and Co. Rd. 77, Chisago City. 1-257-6334.

- Long's Bait Shop, 12790 Lake Blvd., Lindstrom. 1-257-6065.

- Sunrise Sporting Goods, I-35 and Co. Rd. 22, Wyoming. 462-4211.

DAKOTA COUNTY

- Hub's Bait House, under the river bridge, Hastings. 437-4358.

- John's Outdoor Sports, 1545 Vermillion St., Hasting. 437-7421.

- Langlais Nursery, 19770 Kenwood Trail, Lakeville. 469-2447.

- South Metro Bait, 1975 (Hwy. 13) Silver Bell Rd., Eagan. 454-0774.

HENNEPIN COUNTY

- B & D Bait, 1308 E. 66th St., Richfield. 866-5640.

- Bryn Mawr Bait & Tire, 328 S. Cedar Lake Rd., Minneapolis. 377-4743.

- Dred Scott Amoco, 10800 Rhode Island Ave. S, (Old Shakopee Rd. and Co. Rd. 18), Bloomington. 944-0010.

- Holiday Station, 9400-36th Ave. N., New Hope. 591-5960.

- Markham Sports, 18110 Hwy. 55, Hamel. 478-6721.

- R & R Bait Shop, 2630 Commerce Blvd., Mound. 472-1884.

- Rockford Coast to Coast, 7945 Hwy. 55 (Wright Co.), Rockford. 477-5820.

- Roy's Bait, 360 Hwy. 7, Excelsior. 474-0927.

- Shoreline Bait, 4030 Shoreline Dr., Spring Park. 471-7876.

- Spur General Store, 9200 Old Cedar Ave. South, Bloomington. 884-7366.

- Tackle Plus, 332 E. Lake St., Minneapolis. 827-4031.

- The Outpost, 11124 Hwy. 55, Plymouth. 544-7376.

- Vend-A-Bait (outside Tom Thumb Store), 8795 Columbine Rd. (Anderson Lake Pkwy. and Hwy. 169), Eden Prairie. 944-2181.

- Wayzata Bait, 15748 Wayzata Blvd. (Hwy. 12), Wayzata. 473-2227.

- Wosmek Bait & Tackle, 23220 Hwy. 55, Loretto. 478-2949.

RAMSEY COUNTY

- Angler's Bait Shop, 4610 Hwy. 61, White Bear Lake. 426-1142.

- South Metro Bait, 2463 W. 7th St., St. Paul. 454-0774.

- Bald Eagle Sports, 5960 Hwy. 61, Hugo. 429-9954.

- Beach's Shark Bait, 2251 Long Lake Rd. New Brighton. 784-6924.

- Gimp's Bait, 1239 Rice St., St. Paul. 487-9801.

- Hansen's Sporting Goods, 2037 East Co. Rd. E, White Bear Lake. 770-4120.

- High Bridge Boats & Bait, 350 W. Water Street, St. Paul. 290-0026.

- Joe's Sporting Goods, 935 N. Dale St., St. Paul. 488-5511.

- Lake Outfitters, 3625 Talmadge Circle, Vadnais Heights. 426-1936.

- Lake Owasso Marine, 2774 Victoria St., Roseville. 482-7710.

- Larry's Bait, 2626 White Bear Ave., Maplewood. 777-1731.

- Simon's Sport Shop, 2840 Hwy. 10, Mounds View. 784-2888.

- South Metro Bait, 2463 W. 7th St., St. Paul. Phone 454-0774.

SCOTT COUNTY

- J & D Sporting Goods, 15760 Hwy. 13, Prior Lake. 447-6096.

- River Valley Sports, 105 South Lewis St., Shakopee. 445-9109.

- The Sport Stop, 101 S. Lewis St., Shakopee. 445-5282.

- Vend-A-Bait (outside P.D.Q. Store), 14173 Commerce Ave. NE (Hwy. 42 & Hwy. 13), Prior Lake. 447-6656.

WASHINGTON COUNTY

- Blue Ribbon Bait, 1985 Geneva Ave. N., Oakdale. 777-2421.

- Bluff Bait, 806 South Main St. (Hwy. 95), Stillwater. 439-9204.

- Forest Lake Sports, 1007 Broadway, Forest Lake. 464-1200.

- Hanson's County Store, 19261 Manning Trail, Scandia. 433-3419.

- Kulvich's Bait, 303-21st St., Newport. 459-0408.

- Lake's Bait & Tackle, 1144 W. Broadway, Forest Lake. 464-8408.

- Little Bear Bait, 5051 Stewart Ave. (Hwy. 61 & 96 E.), White Bear Lake. 653-1326.

- Mike's Bait, 6625 Lake Blvd. (Hwy. 8), Forest Lake. 464-1557.

- Maui's Landing (Beanie's), 16777 N. 7th St., (below the Hudson bridge), Lakeland. 436-8874.

- Valley Bait, River Heights Plaza, 1400 Frontage Rd. (between Harty's and Norwest Bank), Stillwater. 439-5148.

BOAT RENTALS

ANOKA COUNTY

- **COON LAKE**
  Olson's Resort, East Bethel.
  434-5831. Boats only.

- **LINWOOD LAKE**
  Werner's Boat Rental, Linwood.
  462-2070. Boats only.

- **OTHER RENTALS**
  Blaine U-Haul Center, 9890 NE Hwy.
  65, Blaine. 780-0854. Boats, motors,
  and trailers.

  Anoka County Rent-All, 1531 Coon
  Rapids Blvd., Coon Rapids.
  755-7620. Canoes only.

CARVER COUNTY

- **SCHUTZ LAKE**
  Archie's Boat Rental, Excelsior. 474-
  8714. Boats only.

- **LAKE WACONIA**
  In Towne Marina, 8 E. Lake St.,
  Waconia. 442-2096. Boats, motors,
  and pontoons.

  La Marina, 300 E. Lake St., Waconia.
  442-4925 Boat, motor and pontoon.

CHISAGO COUNTY

- **CHISAGO & SOUTH LINDSTROM
  LAKES**
  Channel Boats, Chisago City.
  1-257-5663. Boats, motors, and
  pontoons.

  Rosehill Resort, Lindstrom.
  1-257-4040. Boats, motors, canoes,
  and pontoons.

- **GREEN LAKE**
  Lindberg's Landing, Chisago City.
  1-257-2631. Boats only.

- **NORTH CENTER LAKE**
  Blue Water RV Park, Lindstrom.
  1-257-2426. Boats only.

  Hillcrest Campgrounds, Lindstrom.
  1-257-5352. Boats only.

- **SOUTH CENTER LAKE**
  Dew Drop Inn, Center City.
  1-257-2204. Boats and motors.

  Whispering Bay Resort, Lindstrom.
  1-257-1784. Boats, motors, and
  pontoons.

- **ST. CROIX RIVER**
  Taylor Falls Canoe Rental, Taylor
  Falls. 1-462-7550, or, 1-465-6315.
  Canoes only. Shuttle service on St.
  Croix River.

- **OTHER RENTALS**
  Hallberg Marine, Wyoming Industrial
  Park, Wyoming. 462-4516. Boats,
  motors, trailers, and canoes.

DAKOTA COUNTY

- Burnsville U-Haul Center, 1720 W. Hwy.
  13, Burnsville. 894-6760. Boats, motors, and trailers.

HENNEPIN COUNTY

- **LAKE CALHOUN**
  Minneapolis Parks, Minneapolis.
  348-5364. Boats and canoes.

- **FISH LAKE**
  Fish Lake Park, Maple Grove.
  420-3423. Boats and canoes.

- **HYLAND LAKE**
  Hyland Lake Park, Bloomington.
  941-4362. Boats and canoes.

- **LAKE INDEPENDENCE**
  Baker Park Reserve, Medina.
  476-4666. Boats and canoes.

- **MEDICINE LAKE**
  French Regional Park, Plymouth.
  559-8891. Boats and canoes.

  Harty's Boats and Bait, Plymouth.
  546-6711. Boats, motors, and
  pontoons.

- **LAKE MINNETONKA**
  Gray's Bay Resort & Marina,
  Shorewood. 473-2550. Boats,
  motors, and canoes.

Howard's Point Marina, Shorewood. 474-4464. Boats and motors.

Minnetonka Boats, Mound. 472-1220. Boats, motors, and pontoons.

Rockvam Boat Yard, Spring Park. 471-9515. Boats and motors.

- **LAKE NOKOMIS**
  Minneapolis Parks, Minneapolis. 348-8941. Canoes only.

- **LAKE REBECCA**
  Lake Rebecca Park, Rockford. 476-4666. Boat and canoes.

- **LAKE SARAH**
  Shady Beach Resort, Maple Plain. 479-1636. Boats only.

RAMSEY COUNTY

- **BALD EAGLE LAKE**
  Lakeview Inn, Hugo. 426-0365. Boats, pontoons, and motors (weekends only).

- **LAKE OWASSO**
  Lake Owasso Marina, Shoreview. 482-7710. Boats, pontoons, electric motors, and canoes.

- **LAKE PHALEN**
  Lakeside Activity Center, St. Paul Parks. 771-7507 or 292-7445. Boats, canoes, and electric motors.

- **WHITE BEAR LAKE**
  Tally's White Bear Docking, White Bear Lake. 429-2633. Boats, motors, and pontoons.

- **MISSISSIPPI RIVER**
  High Bridge Boats and Bait, 350 W. Water St. Saint Paul. Boats and canoes. 290-0026

- **OTHER RENTALS**
  Nelson Marine, 3800 N. Hwy. 61, White Bear Lake. 429-4388. Boats, motors, and trailers.

Midway U-Haul Center, 883 University Ave., St. Paul. 227-9509. Boats, motors, and trailers.

SCOTT COUNTY

- **CLEARY LAKE**
  Cleary Lake Park, Prior Lake. 447-2171. Boat and canoes.

- **FISH LAKE**
  Fish Lake Acres Campground, Prior Lake. 492-3393 or 492-2251. Boats and canoes.

- **PRIOR LAKE**
  Wagon Ridge Marina, Prior Lake. 447-4300. Boats, motors, and pontoons.

- **SPRING LAKE**
  Craig's Resort, Prior Lake. 447-2338. Boats only.

WASHINGTON COUNTY

- **BIG CARNELIAN**
  Oswald's Resort, Stillwater. 439-3456. Boats and motors.

- **BIG MARINE LAKE**
  Shady Birch Resort, Marine on St. Croix. 433-3391. Boats and motors.

- **FOREST LAKE**
  Timm's Marina, Forest Lake. 464-3890, or 464-9965. Boats, motors, pontoons, and canoes.

- **SQUARE LAKE**
  Golden Acres Campgrounds, Stillwater. 439-1147 or 430-1374. Boats, motors, canoes, and pontoons.

- **ST. CROIX RIVER**
  Maui's Landing (Beanie's), 16777 N. 7th St., (below the Hudson bridge), Lakeland. 436-8874. Boat launch (fee); boats, motors, and pontoons.

LAKESIDE CABINS AND CAMPING FACILITIES

ANOKA COUNTY

- **CENTERVILLE LAKE**
  Rice Creek Chain of Lakes Regional Park, Centerville.
  757- 3920. Camping.

- **COON LAKE**
  Norquist Campgrounds, East Bethel.
  434-5533 or 434-5147. Camping.

CARVER COUNTY

- **LAKE AUBURN**
  Carver Park Reserve, Victoria.
  472-4911. Camping.

- **EAGLE LAKE**
  Baylor Park, Young America.
  1-467-3145. Camping.

- **LAKE ZUMBRA**
  Carver Park Reserve, Victoria.
  472-4911. Group camping only.

CHISAGO COUNTY

- **CHISAGO & SOUTH LINDSTROM LAKES**
  Rosehill Resort, Lindstrom.
  1-257-4040. Cabins.

- **GREEN LAKE**
  Lindberg's Landing, Chisago City.
  1-257-2631. Camping.

- **NORTH CENTER LAKE**
  Blue Waters Mobile Home Park, Lindstrom. 1-257-2426. Camping.

  Hillcrest Campgrounds, Lindstrom.
  1-257-5352. Camping.

- **SOUTH CENTER LAKE**
  Whispering Bay Resort, Lindstrom.
  1-257-1784. Camping.

- **NORTH LINDSTROM LAKE**
  Lakeview Motel, Lindstrom.
  1-257-4678. Lakeside motel rooms.

DAKOTA COUNTY

- **LAKE BYLLESBY**
  Lake Byllesby Regional Park, Randolph. 437-6608 or
  (507) 263-4447. Camping.

HENNEPIN COUNTY

- **HYLAND LAKE**
  Hyland Lake Park Reserve, Bloomington. 941-4362. Group camping only.

- **LAKE INDEPENDENCE**
  Baker Park Reserve, Maple Plain.
  476-4666. Camping.

- **LAKE MINNETONKA**
  Big Island Veteran's Camp, Excelsior.
  474-1958. Camping.

- **LAKE REBECCA**
  Lake Rebecca Regional Park, Rockford. 476-4666. Group camping only.

- **LAKE SARAH**
  Shady Beach Resort, Maple Plain.
  479-1636. Camping and cabins.

SCOTT COUNTY

- **CLEARY LAKE**
  Cleary Lake Regional Park, Prior Lake. 447-2171. Group camping.

- **FISH LAKE**
  Fish Lake Acres Campground, Prior Lake. 492-3393 or 492-2251. Camping.

WASHINGTON COUNTY

- **BIG CARNELIAN LAKE**
  Oswald's Resort, Stillwater.
  439-3456. Camping.

- **LAKE ELMO**
  Lake Elmo Regional Park Reserve, Lake Elmo. 439-6058. Camping.

- **FOREST LAKE**
  Timm's Marina & Campgrounds, Forest Lake. 464-3890 or 464-9965. Camping.

  Willow Point Resort. Forest Lake.
  464-2213. Cabins.

ICE HOUSE RENTAL

Most ice houses are equipped with gas stoves and electric lights. In some cases the owner will arrange to move the ice house to the lake of your choice.

CARVER COUNTY

- Cabin Fever Bait & Tackle, 1550 Arboretum (Hwy. 5), Victoria. 443-2022. Rents portable ice houses, gas augers, and depth finders.

- In Towne Marina, 8 E. Lake St., Waconia. 1-442-2096. Rents ice houses on Lake Waconia.

CHISAGO COUNTY

- Frankie's Live Bait, Hwy. 8, Chisago City. 1-257-6334. Rents ice houses on Chisago Lake.

DAKOTA COUNTY

- Angler's Paradise, 1975 (Hwy. 13) Silver Bell Road, Eagan. 454-0774. Rents portable ice houses.

HENNEPIN COUNTY

- Harty's Boat Rental, 1920 E. Medicine Lake Blvd., Plymouth. 546-3849. Rents ice houses on Medicine Lake.

- Roy's Live Bait, 360 Hwy. 7, Excelsior. 474-0927. Rents ice houses on Christmas and Minnetonka Lakes.

- Shoreline Bait & Tackle, 4016 Shoreline Drive, Spring Park. 471-7876. Rents ice houses on Lake Minnetonka.

- Tackle Plus, 332 E. Lake St., Minneapolis. 827-4031. Rents portable ice houses, gas augers, ice sticks, and related equipment.

- Wayzata Bait, 15748 Wayzata Blvd., Wayzata. 473-2227. Rents portable ice houses and ice houses on Lake Minnetonka.

- Minneapolis Parks — portable ice houses are permitted during daylight hours but must be removed each evening by dusk. Annual permits are required. Contact Permit Department, 310 So. 4th Ave., Minneapolis 55415.

RAMSEY COUNTY

- High Bridge Boats & Bait, 350 W. Water St., St. Paul. 290-0026. Rents portable ice houses.

WASHINGTON COUNTY

- Mike's Bait, 6625 Lake Blvd. (Hwy. 8), Forest Lake. 464-1557. Rents ice houses on Forest Lake.

Glossary

Back-trolling: trolling in the reverse direction (i.e., toward the stern of the boat). This method allows better boat control and slower speeds.

Backwater: area in a river where currents flow in a direction that is opposite to the main flow. Backwaters are created by points or other obstructions or by dams on rivers; they usually contain very fertile water with heavy weedbeds, brush, and flooded timber.

Bar: a long ridge of sand, gravel, or other material near the surface of the water, especially at the mouth of a stream.

Boat control: using the motion of the boat to control the direction and depth of the lure, as in trolling, back-trolling, or controlled drifting.

Break: place where there is a definite change in the depth, direction, or type of structure (rocks, stumps, etc.).

Breakline: a definite change in depth either sudden or gradual (weedline, drop-off, ledge, etc.).

Brushline: the inside or outside edge of a line of submerged brush.

Bulrushes: tall grasses with slender hollow stems; reeds.

Cabbage weeds: a family of plants known as pondweeds (potamogeten) whose broad leaf is preferred by most fish because it provides protection from the sun and predators.

Calendar periods (Seasonal patterns): the seasons of the year as defined by water temperature and the angle of light penetration. Patterns of fish movement are determined by these factors.

Chemical rehabilitation: chemicals not harmful to humans or animals are put into the water to kill all fish, particularly carp, suckers, and bullheads. The lake is then restocked with carefully selected species.

Cold front: the advancing edge of a cold air mass. A cold front brings an abrupt change from clear to stormy weather. The drop in temperature (usually with strong winds) and the clear skies that follow the cold front usually result in poor fishing.

Coontail (milfoil-moss): soft, clingy, deep-growing weeds that attract fish and are found in most fertile bodies of water.

Controlled drift: a system of boat control that requires the periodic use of a motor or oars to keep the lure moving with the current along a specific course, usually along the edge of a weedline or drop-off.

Current break: where faster water meets slower water in a river.

Depth finder: an electronic fishing aid that indicates the depth of bottom structure and solid objects such as weeds or fish; can also indicate the shape and density of underwater objects and bottom structure.

Drop-off: the point in a body of water where there is a definite increase in depth.

Drift: a system of boat control that requires placing the boat in a position that will allow the current or wind to move the boat along a specific course without the aid of oars or a motor.

Eurasian water milfoil weed: a fast-growing water plant that forms large, dense floating mats of vegetation that crowd out native plants and make recreational use of the water difficult.

Eurolarva: the larva of the blue-bottle fly (maggot), excellent for catching panfish and trout. (Plural *Eurolarvae*)

Fingerlings: young fish in their first summer of growth (length varies with species).

Flipping: line is stripped off the reel and the lure is "flipped" toward the target area.

Flat: an area in a body of water characterized by little or no change in depth.

Fry: very young fish from time of hatch to time they begin feeding.

Inside turn: an indentation or a deep cut of water running into shallower water, usually at the base (corner) of a point.

Live-bait rig: any rig designed to hold live bait that is cast, trolled, or still fished where the action of the live bait is intended to attract the fish (such as a Lindy Rig, or a plain hook).

Pattern: a consistently recurring behavior of the fish that indicates which fishing methods and locations would be most successful.

Point: an extrusion from the shoreline that extends into and under the water toward deeper water.

Riprap: rocks or concrete slabs that are placed on an embankment or sloping shoreline to prevent erosion.

Saddle: a site where structure narrows before widening again or where one piece of structure is linked to another.

Secchi disc: an 8-inch disc colored black and white that is lowered into the water to determine water clarity by measuring the depth at which the disc is no longer visible.

Slot limit: a special fishing regulation on some lakes that requires that all fish of a particular species within a specified range of lengths must be released.

Speed-trolling: a system of boat control in which a lure is trolled behind a boat moving at fast speeds; triggers strikes from fish that pass up slow-moving lures.

Striking short: a situation where fish are striking the end of the bait and avoiding the hook. The solution is a slower retrieve or a trailer hook.

Structure: any submerged object or change in the contour of the lake bottom that fish can use as a guidepost or cover as they move from one location to another (sunken islands, stumps, drop-offs, rock piles, etc.).

Summerkill: fish killed by oxygen depletion when sunlight fails to reach aquatic vegetation to produce new oxygen; often occurs after an extended period of calm, cloudy weather.

Sunken island: an underwater hump or hill protruding up from the bottom of the lake or river.

Suspended fish: fish that are hovering considerably above the bottom in open water.

Texas rig: a weedless plastic-worm rig coupled with a bullet weight; the shank of the fishhook is inserted through the head of the worm and the point is embedded in the body of the worm.

Thermocline: The middle layer of water in a lake where temperature stratification has occurred. The water is cooler than in the upper layer, but it may not contain adequate oxygen for the fish in late summer and fall. The epilimnion is the warmer upper layer. It contains plenty of oxygen, but the water may become too warm for the fish to be comfortable. The hypolimnion is the colder layer below the thermocline that lacks oxygen — and fish!

Trailer hook: an extra hook that trails behind the primary hook on single-hook lures such as jigs, spinnerbaits, buzzbaits, and spoons; used when the fish are striking short.

Trolling: a system of boat control that requires the use of a motor (gas or electric) to move the boat so as to pull a lure along a specific course.

Turnover: a mixing of water that occurs when the surface water is colder than the thermocline. The cold water sinks, and the warmer water rises from below. Fishing is not very productive.

Vertical jigging: an up-and-down method of jigging on a specific structure such as a drop-off or a defined object. Also a technique used for attracting suspended fish.

Water clarity: indicates the depth of light penetration that is adequate to sustain weed growth — usually measured with a Secchi disc.

Weedline: the edge of the weeds; where the densest vegetation ceases to grow. The inside weedline is the edge nearest to shore. The outside weedline is the edge nearest to deep water.

Winterkill: fish killed by oxygen depletion caused by thick ice and snow that prevent sunlight from reaching vegetation to produce new oxygen.

Yearling: a young fish from six months to two years old.

Contributors

Mark Allen is a master angler with an awesome record of tournament wins. Mark and his partner Gary Lake were top money winners in both the Minnesota-Wisconsin ProAm Bass Tournament series and the American Scholarship Tournament series in 1988 and 1989. In 1988, they were elected as the ProAm Sportsmen of the year. Mark also won the Green Lake (Spicer) Walleye tournament in both 1983 and 1984. He is on the promotion staff for Yamaha Motors, Ranger Boats, Northland Tackle, Berkley Line, Big John Thunder Bullets, Lone Tree Tackle, and Minn Kota Electric Motors.

Randy Amenrud has won countless honors in state, regional, and national competitions. His biggest catches include a 9 lb. 2 oz. largemouth bass from George Lake in Anoka; two 12 lb. walleyes from Gull Lake and Pelican Lake; and a 42 lb. muskie out of Rainy Lake. Randy is co-owner of Fishing Pro-Mo's, Inc., which specializes in designing promotions for clients such as Lund Boats, Mariner Motors, Northland Tackle, Normark Tackle, Blue Fox Tackle, Berkley Trilene Line, Repel Repellent, and many others. His most recent achievement was the 1991 Professional Walleye Trail Sportsman of the year award. Look for their Saturday TV Show "The Outdoor Sportsman" on Channel 5 at 1:00 p.m. featuring fishing, hunting, and other outdoor activities.

Todd Amenrud is a promotional representative for Fishing Pro-Mo's (see above). Todd is past owner of Amenrud's Woods & Water in Blaine and has ranked in many tournaments. In 1989, he and his father, Randy Amenrud, won the Father & Son Team of the Year Award sponsored by the Manufacturers Walleye Council.

Randy Barkley is the guy to call if you're looking for a good guide on Lake Minnetonka. For a year and a half while he was recuperating from a back injury, Randy spent every day fishing on Lake Minnetonka. His biggest catches were a 26 lb. northern and a 5 3/4 lb. smallmouth bass. Randy enjoys teaching kids to fish and welcomes them as part of his guide service.

Burk Berrisford is the owner of Little Bear Bait and Tackle located in White Bear Lake. He has been successfully tracking the fish on White Bear Lake since the early 1970's and shares his knowledge of the hotspots with his customers.

Larry Bollig is Assistant Manager at Burger Bros. Sporting Goods in Brooklyn Center and is one of the most talented and respected professionals in the fishing business. His customers prize his willingness to tell the truth about the effectiveness of products and about the claims made by the manufacturers. Larry has participated in numerous major walleye and bass tournaments since 1975 and has won or placed in most of them. Look for his popular and informative fishing seminars at the Burger Bros. stores.

Mike Bonn, owner of Blue Ribbon Bait in Oakdale, goes fishing at least 4 times a week all year long. Even during the dog days of mid-summer or the sub-zero weather of January, Mike says he can always find productive water. When the lakes aren't producing in the summer, he fishes the St. Croix River for walleyes and smallmouth bass. His best local catches are a 13 lb. northern pike from Olson Lake and an 8 lb. walleye from Silver Lake in North St. Paul.

Dave Brandeman is one of the nicest guys you will find in the fishing community, and he is also one of the most skilled anglers. Dave has fished "in the money" in bass tournaments more than 50 times. He won the Minnesota Bass Classic in 1977, the Bass Federation Championship in 1977, and the Tournament of Champions on Forest Lake in 1980. His biggest catches were a 6 lb. 11-1/2 oz. bass from the Horseshoe Chain in 1988 and a 6 lb. 9 oz. bass from South Center Lake in 1986.

Jeff Byrne can be found behind the counter of his shop, Cabin Fever Sporting Goods, in Victoria where he dispenses live bait as well as tips on how to use the equipment and where to find the big fish. Jeff studied sporting goods sales and management at Brainerd Vo-Tech and worked for Ken's Bait in Chaska for 6 years before opening his own shop. His largest catch was a 6 lb. 7 oz. largemouth bass from Bay Lake and a 10 lb. 3 oz. walleye from Saganaga Lake on the Gunflint Trail.

Pat Buchanan is co-owner and manager of B&D Bait & Tackle in Richfield and is skilled in repairing fishing reels. His passion is fishing, and he enjoys sharing his talent with others. Pat is very familiar with the Mississippi River and many lakes in the metro area, and he knows when each body of water will be productive.

Steve Carney operates the Metro Fishing Guide Service and can help you catch your limit on most metro lakes. Steve presents fishing seminars and workshops throughout the state for community parks and recreation departments. He shares his knowledge through his columns in *Minnesota Outdoor News, Dakota Outdoors*, and other newspapers. Steve is also on the promotion staff for Mercury Motors. For guide service or seminars, contact him at 920-4495.

Linda Condor has been a successful tournament angler for many years. She is also a guide on local lakes and offers workshops for couples that are guaranteed to improve fishing success. For guide service or workshops, call her at 612-439-2478.

Bob Conkey was owner of Bob's Bait in Mound near Lake Minnetonka. His biggest prize out of this lake was a 10 lb. 11 oz. walleye off Hardscrabble Point.

John Craig is an avid angler, knows most of the area lakes, and participates in the American Scholarship Tournament Circuit. His family owned Craig's Resort on Spring Lake for many years and he knows where the best spots are.

Steve Culhane has a long history of teaching people how to fish. He spent many years demonstrating his fishing knowledge as manager of the Fishing Department at Burger Bros., a Herman's Sporting Goods, and at the River Valley Sports Center in Shakopee. He also taught numerous fishing seminars at high schools in Shakopee, Richfield, and Prior Lake.

Dick Daily has lived on Turtle Lake since 1979 and has spent most of his leisure time learning the lake and finding the big ones. He has caught a 2 lb. 8 oz. crappie and has a 6 lb. 1/4 oz. bass from Turtle Lake hanging on his wall.

John Daily can give you more unique tips on catching fish than you would glean from most books. His dad was a guide on Lake Minnetonka, and John has fished metro lakes for more than 50 years. He is in demand as a fishing instructor at local educational institutions and fishing clubs. John has been employed by the Minnesota DNR since 1961 in all phases of fisheries management. He is now the aquaculture specialist who provides technical assistance to private hatcheries and directs the statewide hatchery license program.

Terry Dillard is an avid fisherman who regularly fishes more than 30 lakes in the metro area. He has caught 11 lb. plus northerns out of Demontreville Lake and Peltier Lake.

Troy Driscoll, a staff member at Blue Ribbon Bait in Oakdale, spends a lot of time learning area lakes and rivers. His biggest fish was a 6 lb. 4 oz. largemouth bass out of Phalen Lake and a 13 lb. northern pike out of Carver Lake.

John Dunlap has years of on-the-water experience learning the habits and characteristics of largemouth bass on local lakes. He is a tournament angler and knows how to catch big fish. John has been a member of the Vikings Bass Masters Bass Club for a number of years and served as its president.

Frankie Dusenka is co-owner of Frankie's Live Bait in Chisago City and has been an area guide since 1968. He is known throughout the state as the most knowledgeable resource on Chisago area lakes, and he encourages anglers to drop into his shop to find out where the big fish are biting. In addition, Frankie is also the owner of Freedom Enterprises, which creates fishing-related products. His latest invention is the Flip & Glow Bobber, a super-sensitive bobber that flips over and turns a different color when the fish hits the bait. He has also invented a plastic sleeve that fits over the ball bearing on a spinnerbait to keep weeds from gunking up the lure, especially the pesky milfoil weed.

Gary and Pete Erickson are a father and son fishing team and members of the North Metro Fishing Club. At every club tournament they fished, Gary and Pete placed in the top third. Gary Erickson, Pete's father, is on the sales staff at Capra's Sporting Goods in Blaine and loves to share his helpful hints with his customers.

Ken Evanoff has lived on Jane Lake for many years, and he can chart the subtle differences in fishing patterns from season to season and from high-water periods to low-water periods. His biggest trophies include a 7 lb. 3 oz. largemouth bass from Jane Lake and an 11 lb. 4 oz. walleye from the Mississippi River near Red Wing.

Dave Gardell owned Frank's Bait in Lakeville for many years. His biggest catch was a 30 lb muskie on his wall which he caught on 8 lb. line out of Leech Lake while angling for walleyes. His most memorable catch, however, was a 9 lb. northern he caught on Orchard Lake as a small child

Dave Genz is one of the most innovative and creative men in the fishing business. Owner of Winter Fishing Systems, Dave designs and manufactures products to make your ice fishing easier and more successful. His products include the Fishtrap, a portable ice house that requires no set-up time, and the Ice Box, a portable depth finder in a carrying case designed for winter use. Dave is also a fishing instructor and has been presenting seminars on most aspects of fishing since 1977. He was one of the first to present ice fishing seminars in the metro area and specializes in catching big panfish. In 1992, Dave participated in the World Ice Fishing Championship in Ontario, Canada. His team, Team USA, won a silver medal.

Bob Gibson has been fishing since he was old enough to hold a pole. When he was a kid, he spent hours working his lures in the bathtub to learn how each one performs. Then he would persuade his neighbors to take him to the shores of Lake Michigan and lagoons in the Chicago area to practice. Now Bob is the recreation program supervisor for Hennepin County Parks and is specifically responsible for organizing fishing events. He also organizes the annual fun-filled Carp Festival at the Coon Rapids Dam.

Dale Glader is the author of *Catching City Bass,* which is available in most local sporting goods stores. He has spent over 10 years on metro lakes developing methods that will produce big bass on overfished lakes. Most of the photographs in his book were taken on Bald Eagle Lake in Ramsey County.

Phil Gossard, owner of Chanhassen Bait & Tackle, has fished area lakes extensively, and his biggest fish was a 9 lb. northern from Lake Minnetonka. His shop offers a unique service much like the bridal registry in major department stores. Outdoor sports enthusiasts can come in and register a list of gifts they would like to receive for Christmas, birthdays, etc. Their friends and family can come in and select items off that list.

Dick Grzywinski is an expert angler and fishing guide (phone 612-771-6231). When you "fish with the Griz", you're not only guaranteed to catch fish, but you'll also learn about his special technique that will put fish in your boat for the rest of your life. His system, the Jig Rip technique, has been written up in numerous publications. Using this method, Griz has caught more than 100 walleyes that were over 10 pounds. He knows most of the metro lakes and captured a 27 lb. northern through the ice on Lake Phalen. His sponsors are Frankie's Live Bait, Northland Tackle, Lund Boats, Diawa Reels, Berkley Products, Freshwater Tackle, Yamaha Motors, and the Fishing & Hunting Library.

Glen Hallow, owner of the South Metro Bait & Tackle stores in Eagan and West St. Paul, assisted the city of Eagan in compiling information on how to fish area lakes. Glen also provides seminars for fishing clubs and is the owner of the Minnesota Pro Guide Service (phone 612-930-0036), which features 30 of the best tournament anglers in Minnesota. These guides can take you to most metro lakes as well as Mille Lacs and Leech Lake.

Chuck Hamer is well known as a dynamic speaker and excellent fishing instructor whose seminars drew standing-room-only crowds even on the coldest winter nights. Chuck is the creator of Tinsel Tail lures (jigs, spinnerbaits, spoons, etc.) for all species from trout to muskies. He is presently a manufacturer's representative for boats, skis, and docks.

Mike Hanson has fished area lakes most of his life and is a member of the Blaine In-Fisherman Club. He captured First Place honors at his club's monthly tournaments in 1989 and ranked in the top five in previous years. His biggest catches were a 9 lb. walleye from Rush Lake and a 1-3/4 lb. crappie from Linwood Lake.

Jim Hardman has lived on Lake Gervais since 1983 and knows the seasonal patterns for all species. His biggest trophy was a 6 lb. 2 oz. largemouth bass from this lake. Jim was on staff at Gimp's Live Bait in St. Paul and is studying for a career in fish and wildlife.

Joe Harty is the manager of Harty's Boat Rental which is owned and operated by the brothers and sisters of the Harty Family (Jim, Jerry, Judy, Bill, and Ann) and assisted by an army of nephews and nieces. Whichever Harty you find working, that person can tell you where the big fish are biting.

Larry Hayes has been employed at Tackle Plus in Minneapolis since 1972, and his specialty is repairing fishing reels. He can make your old reels work like new again and can tell you where all the fish are biting on area lakes.

Everal (Evie) Hedtke has fished area lakes for 50 years and found the hotspots long before the invention of fish locators and fancy boats. His largest fish was a 14 lb. northern pike from Parley Lake.

Tom Hedtke is past owner of Anchor's Bait &Tackle on Lake Waconia and is now a salesman at the Outpost, a fishing and hunting shop in Plymouth. He is also owner of Jordan Fluorescent Lures (jigs and ice flies). Look for them in local tackle shops.

Terry Hennon has been owner of the Sport Stop in Shakopee since 1979 and has one of the best taxidermy displays in the southern metro area. One of the tasks he enjoys the most in running an outdoor sports shop is teaching people how to use the equipment and how to find the fish from shore or from a boat.

Patty Holman has been catching trout and salmon on Square Lake for many years and frequently shares her knowledge of proper rigging and techniques.

Tim Holschlag is past president of the Minnesota Smallmouth Alliance, an organization dedicated to promoting Catch and Release as a means of conserving smallmouth bass. Tim has fished every smallmouth hotspot in 12 states and in the Canadian provinces of Quebec and Ontario. He is the author of *How to Fish Stream Smallmouth* and has written many articles for *Smallmouth Magazine* and other outdoor publications. Tom also conducts Moving Waters Guiding Service on the Mississippi, St. Croix, and Rum Rivers. Call him at (612) 781-3912.

Dick Kiefer is the Management Information Manager for the Hennepin County Park District located on Medicine Lake. He fishes this lake at every opportunity and knows the best panfish and bass shore fishing spots on the lake. Dick has also assisted the Lake Minnetonka Conservation District in developing a computer software program to track the growth and spread of the milfoil weed on the lake. This project will aid in the development of more effective treatment programs for this problem.

Jim Kirk is a young man with a headstart in the fishing business. Although he was only 16 at the time of our interview, he had already spent a number of years learning Twin Cities lakes and has been featured in the Outdoor Section of the *Minneapolis Tribune*. He caught a 15 lb. northern while shore fishing on Lake Calhoun and a 22 lb. carp from the shores of Wirth Lake. He is also a volunteer with the fishing program at Hospitality House teaching kids to fish at area lakes.

Gary Lake's skill in winning tournaments and bringing in big fish is legendary. Gary and his partner Mark Allen were top money winners in both the Minnesota-Wisconsin ProAm Tournament Series and the American Scholarship Tournament Series in 1988 and 1989. In 1988, they were selected as the ProAm Sportsmen of the year. In addition, Gary ranked 11th out of 100 contestants in the Don Shelby Invitational Tournament on Lake Minnetonka in 1989. He is a promotional representative for Berkley Line, Northland Tackle, Normark Lures, Blue Fox Tackle, Ranger Boats, and Minn Kota Electric Motors.

Kurt Larson has photographs of full stringers of huge walleyes taken from Lake Nokomis to convince skeptical metro anglers of the potential of this lake. Kurt is the fishing and outdoor equipment consultant for Bold Eagle, Inc. He was also host of the "Hooked on Fishing" show for cable TV, which featured local lakes.

Axel Lind has spent more than 30 years perfecting his skill on area lakes. On Linwood Lake, he caught a 3 1/2 lb. crappie, an 11 lb. northern, and a 6 lb. bass. He also caught northern pike weighing 16, 20, and 28 lbs., and he released all of them. Nice going Axel!

Dick McCarthy is an expert angler who lived near McCarrons Lake for 20 years and fished the lake every season. His biggest catches have been a 20 lb. northern from a Canadian lake and a 6 lb. 8 oz. bass from a lake in Wisconsin.

Kevin McDonald can be found on Lake Harriet during most of the season perfecting his technique for catching walleyes. Kevin is president of his company, Twin Cities Supply, as well as recreational consultant for Bold Eagle, Inc. He enjoys sharing his fishing skills with kids, and he leads youth groups on fishing trips to BWCA lakes.

Bob McLean, fishing manager of Jacks of Anoka for 18 years, is now a salesman for Rapid Sports Center in Coon Rapids. Since 1986, Bob has taught fishing classes for walleye, bass, sunfish, and crappies for the Anoka-Hennepin School District. Since 1986, he has competed in the prestigious Walleye Tournament sponsored by the Tackle Manufacturers Council.

Jim and Cindy Mase own the In Towne Marina on Lake Waconia and are eager to dispense good fishing advice along with boats and leeches. They are also founding members of the Lake Waconia Association which has played a major role in combating milfoil. In addition to providing community education programs on identifying and preventing the problem, the association also recruits volunteers to dive and uproot the milfoil from affected areas and raise money for treatment. Jim is one of the divers, and Cindy works with local government agencies and area educators to develop a curriculum for classroom use.

Ken Matheson is a master angler who has broad experience on the water, in the classroom, and in the fishing tackle retail business (18 years). Ken has taught fishing seminars and guided clients on local lakes. One year he spent every day on Turtle Lake charting the patterns of all species from May 1 to Labor Day. He completely redrew the Turtle Lake map for this book. Ken also developed the Bouncer, an ice fishing jig for panfish. To chart the effectiveness of this product throughout the ice fishing season, he fished every day on 3 to 5 different lakes for 101 continuous days. His research resulted in unique data that was used in *In-Fisherman Magazine*.

Bob Mehsikomer has an awesome list of credentials in the angling arena. He is the owner of Simply Fishing, Inc., which includes a multi-species TV and videotape series, a magazine, and a bass and muskie tournament circuit. He was winner of the Molson Export Big Fish Contest in 1988 and 1989, and winner of more than 40 Manitoba Master Angler Awards in 1988 and 1989 for northern pike, walleye, grayling, brook trout, and lake trout. He is currently recognized as the most successful muskie angler in the world and has caught and released more than 1,000 muskies. His most notable achievement was the World Record release of a 56-inch muskie (girth 25-1/2 inches; estimated weight 51-1/2 pounds) from Lake of the Woods in Canada. It was caught with a muskie lure he designed called The Awaker, now manufactured by Poe's Tackle Company.

Chet Meyers has been educating anglers since 1974 at Metro State University in Minneapolis where he is also a Professor of Philosophy. If you have an opportunity to participate in one of Chet's fishing classes, your skills will be enhanced for life. Chet has co-authored two books with Al Linder: *Catching Fish* and *BASS: A Handbook of Strategies*. He is a regular contributor to *Fishing Facts, Minnesota Sportsman, and In-Fisherman Magazine*.

Duane Melchnoir, a true "river rat" who fished the Minnesota River for more than 70 years, provided major input for the Rivers section of this book. He died in 1992 leaving behind a legacy of angling achievement. We appreciate his willingness to share angling techniques and the joy of fishing the Minnesota River.

Bud Miller lived on Spring Lake for 11 years and was president of the Spring Lake Association. He has also served as president of the State BASS Federation and the Minnetonka Bass Club and has participated in BASS tournaments for 20 years. Bud's biggest catch was an 11 lb. bass from Dale Hollow, Tennessee.

Bill Mosca is past owner of the Mosca Bait & Tackle Shop in Northfield. In 1987 when most of the water was drained from Byllesby Lake for repairs on the dam, Bill took photographs of the exposed river and lake bottom. He has used this unique information to draw a very precise map for this book showing the structural changes of the lake.

Dennis Nesbitt has been hauling in fish from Bryant Lake for more than 40 years. His biggest catches include a 7 lb. 4 oz. largemouth bass and a 31-inch tiger muskie that weighed more than pounds. Dennis is a firm believer in Catch and Release practices to ensure a future supply of trophy fish.

Butch Noterman, owner of the River Valley Sports Center in Shakopee, says he was born with a fishing rod in his hand. He has fished most of the lakes and rivers in a wide area and loves to share information about his favorite spots.

Shawn O'Hern lived on Fish Lake in Scott County for 15 years and learned every hotspot on the lake. His biggest catch was a 6 lb. largemouth bass which won him the Pepsi-Zebco Fishing Contest. On weekends, you'll find Shawn dispensing good information at The Sport Stop in Shakopee. His biggest catch in the metro area was an 18 lb. northern pike out of O'Dowd Lake.

Tina Outlaw is President of the Minnesota BASS N' Gal fishing club and has served as an officer in Women Anglers of Minnesota. She is also a successful tournament angler and ranked in the top 30 in the national BASS N' Gal tournament competition in 1986 and 1987. Tina enjoys sharing her skills with kids and is on the Advisory Board for the DNR MINNAQUA Program.

Art Perry's action-packed presentations at the January St. Paul Sportshow are guaranteed to help you become a better angler. Art is a member of the Lindy-Little Joe Fishing Team and is affiliated with the Babe Winkleman Good Fishing Team. His sponsors include Lindy-Little Joe, Fenwick Rods, Mariner Motors, the Alumnacraft Boat Company, and E-Z Load boat trailers. To schedule a seminar for your organization, call Art Perry at 612-533-7384.

Jim Picha is past owner of the Big Fish Bait & Tackle in New Prague and is a member of the New Prague Bass Busters. He has been very successful on the tournament trail for bass, walleyes and crappies. He won first place in a crappie tournament on Clear Lake and in a bass tournament on Lake Harriet. He also placed in the ProAm Bass Association Tournament and 16 other tournaments since 1985. His biggest challenge and source of enjoyment is sharing his skill with youngsters of all ages.

Joey Rauscher has lived on Lake Carnelian most of his life and is familiar with the location of most species in the lake. He is General Manager of Joe's Sporting Goods in St. Paul.

George Poppa owns Channel Boats on Chisago and South Lindstrom Lakes.

Mike Ring is past co-owner of Rice Creek Bait and now owns a carpet cleaning business in Circle Pines. Mike's most memorable fishing experience was on a winter night on Centerville Lake when he caught a 15 lb. northern, a 4 lb. walleye, and several slab crappies out of the same hole.

Brad Roel lives on Long Lake and has fished it 3 to 4 times a week every year since 1983. He is also a guide on Lake Minnetonka. Give him a call at (612) 476-0219.

Roger Rucci is one of the most interesting and dynamic speakers you'll find on largemouth bass and muskies. He is also a member of the Minnesota Pro Guide Service, Inc. (phone 930-0036) and is on the promotional staff of Fenwick Rods, Bottom Line Electronics, Mr. Twister, and Poe's Lures.

Chris Sager is the talented angler who hauled in a 33 1/2 lb. yellow tiger muskie out of Lake Calhoun in 1991 to break the state record. Since 1960, Chris has concentrated on learning the Minneapolis lakes and has caught walleyes over 10 pounds on both Lake Harriet and Lake Calhoun. Chris is a guide on area lakes so if you would like to fish his spots with him, call Let's Go Fishing at (612) 729-1603.

Ken Schak, an expert fisherman from Forest Lake, has been studying area lakes since the late 1970's and can give anglers some excellent advice on fishing Clear and Forest Lakes. His biggest trophy was a 7 lb. 6 oz. largemouth bass out of Forest Lake.

Mike Schuett started in the fishing business in 1967 at Joe's Sporting Goods in St. Paul. He now owns North Country Marketing, which is an agency representing Browning Arms, manufacturers of fishing and hunting equipment. Mike, who lives on Island Lake, is a successful walleye tournament angler and has ranked in most of the tournaments on Mille Lacs.

Orrin Sechter has fished metro lakes successfully for many years. The trait that sets him apart from most anglers is that Orrin can catch fish under tough conditions because he is willing to observe the subtle changes from day to day and adjust his choice of techniques and baits accordingly.

Brian Shaw, past manager of Mike's Bait in Forest Lake, is a talented angler who has spent a lifetime on area lakes. His "claim to fame" is a 35 lb. monster catfish out of the St. Croix River.

Duane Shodeen, regional fisheries supervisor for DNR Metro Region, deserves much of the credit for the excellent quality of fishing in the metro area. He oversees the fish management programs on over 200 lakes and river systems in the seven-county Metro Region. He is one of the hardest working employees of the State of Minnesota and also one of the nicest. He's never too busy to answer your questions about your favorite lake, and he presents the information in an easy to understand manner. Duane particularly enjoys working with the fishing clubs on projects to protect the habitat and improve the quality of metro fishing.

Jim Sivers has studied Lake Hiawatha for many years and was instrumental in redrawing the Hiawatha map in this book. He has pulled many one-pound crappies out of this lake over the years as well as a nine-pound northern.

Glen Simons has fished Staring Lake for over 40 years and knows where all the fish are.

Tim Sonenstahl, part owner of Wayzata Bait, is well known for his good humor and his knowledge of Lake Minnetonka and other area lakes. Tim is a guide on Lake Minnetonka and has given many seminars on how to fish this lake. He contributed much of the information in this book on how to fish the milfoil weed on Lake Minnetonka.

Brad Stanius is one of the most knowledgeable walleye anglers you could ever hope to meet. He has won every major walleye tournament in Minnesota at least once and has finished in the top ten in the prestigious national tournament of the Manufacturers Walleye Council (MWC) every year except one since 1985. Brad was a fishing guide in Grand Rapids for 8 years. After becoming a pharmacist, he owned a drugstore in Maplewood, served as Mayor of the city of White Bear, and is presently state representative from the White Bear area.

Roger Stein is the administrative naturalist for the Lowry Nature Center in the Carver Park Preserve. Roger presents seminars at the nature center on how to fish area lakes, and his fishing articles have appeared in the *Victoria Gazette*; *Minnesota Outdoor News;* and *Time-Out,* which is the publication of the Hennepin Parks Program.

Gary Swiers is a Lake Waconia angler who knows where the big ones are. He has caught an 11 lb. walleye, a 6 lb. bass, and plenty of big northerns and panfish out of this lake.

Bill (Tiny) Thomas has been directing customers to local hotspots at Roy's Live Bait in Excelsior since 1939. Frequently he goes out fishing in the early morning and then comes back to Roy's to report where the action is. He is convinced there are still plenty of trophy fish in area lakes and has been hauling them in to prove it.

Greg Thorne is a talented angler who has mastered most of the lakes and rivers in the metro area. Greg and his brother Paul own Thorne Bros Custom Rod and Tackle shop and the Fly Angler Shop, both in Fridley. They provide rod design and consulting services for leading fishing equipment manufacturers. Their custom rods, especially muskie rods, are known worldwide.

Bill Tomberlin is past owner of Bill's Bluff Bait in Stillwater. In addition to being a fishing whiz, Bill hosted the "Fishing Today" radio show on WTCN in Stillwater and wrote a fishing column for a Stillwater newspaper.

Dick Trombley was past DNR fisheries supervisor for the Hinckley area and was responsible for management of the lakes in the Chisago area. He is an avid bass angler and loves to fly fish for crappies and sunfish.

Terry Tuma is one of the busiest multi-talented anglers in the fishing business. He hosts the popular cable TV series "Fishing — An Inside Look" and also a radio show on KDHL Radio in Faribault. Terry has written many fishing articles for newspapers and magazines, and his seminars are always in demand. Give him a call at 612 469-4275 to schedule a seminar for your organization. Terry is the advertising manager and writer for *Outdoor News*, a weekly outdoor newspaper. He is also a consultant for tackle manufacturers, a field consultant for *In-Fisherman Magazine*, and a member of the Lindy-Little Joe Fishing Team.

Joe Unger is a guy to keep an eye on in the world of competitive fishing. He won the Leech Lake Mariner's Walleye Classic in 1989, and his latest trophy was an 8 lb. 1 oz. largemouth bass out of Lake Owasso in 1991. He has worked a number of years in the fishing equipment retail business and is now sales manager for Lake Country Boats in Forest Lake.

Skip Virchow fished Lake Phalen about 300 days per year for a number of years and knows the patterns of every species in this lake during all seasons and conditions. Skip was known as the "Friend of Lake Phalen" because he frequently stopped to show other anglers proper rigging and fishing techniques to improve their success.

George Wahl, owner of Wahl Tackle Company, is an expert muskie hunter and past president of Muskies, Inc. He also created the Eagle Tail Muskie Lure, a large bucktail lure with 2 single hooks instead of a treble hook. Look for it at local tackle shops.

Tim Walsh, owner of Mike's Bait in Forest Lake, is a skilled angler specializing in big northerns and slab crappies through the ice. He has a video of 2 lb. crappies out of a Minnesota lake. Tim is in demand as a speaker for small businesses and father-son events.

Ted Welch is the inventor, manufacturer, and distributor of Ted's EZE Fish Bottom Rigger which is designed to catch all species throughout the year, including the ice fishing season. It's particularly effective in fast current and produces better than other bottom riggers because it appears more natural to the fish. He has also designed a spinnerbait kit that includes 43 blade beads, and snap rings. Ted's biggest fish have been caught from shore. These include an 18 l northern, an 8 1/2 lb. bass, and a 6 lb. walleye from Lake Minnetonka as well as a 12 lb. northe from Lake Spurzem and a 12 lb. northern from Lake Rebecca.

Tom Zenanko's boundless energy and enthusiasm for fishing are contagious and his achiev ments are endless. He is the author of *Northern Pike Fishing, North Country Bassin'*, and *Walle Fishing Today* (updated). He has also produced 3 instructional videos: *Walleye Fishing Basic Introduction to Fishing*, and *Bigmouth Bassin'*. Tom is a frequent tournament winner and in 199 he won the Eagle/Minn Kota Western Walleye Pro/Am tournament on Lake Oahe in South Dakot He conducts seminars in major sport shows across the country and is the youngest angler ev inducted in the "Living Legends of American Sport Fishing".

Tom Zrust has been fishing since he was two years old, and you won't find a more talented al knowledgeable angler. He has won more than 100 bass, walleye, and muskie tournaments. a 3-year period, he won 6 total points championships, and all of them were on different major bas tournament circuits. Tom has been manager of the Burger Bros. store in Bloomington since 198

About the Author

"ishing sure beats housework — and anything else you can think of," says Sybil
mith who has been cranking out fishing guides and writing about fishing on metro
kes since 1982. Her first edition of the *Twin Cities Fishing Guide* sold over 70,000
pies and was followed by the *Brainerd-Whitefish Area Fishing Guide.*

or this edition of the *Twin Cities Fishing Guide*, Sybil interviewed more than 100
pert anglers, contacted numerous government agencies responsible for the
anning and management of fishing resources, and personally visited each of the
0 lakes to verify accesses and facilities.

uring the fishing season, Ms. Smith writes articles for the *St. Paul Pioneer Press*
what's new in Twin Cities fishing and teaches fishing seminars across the metro
ea. Give her a call if your fishing club or organization would like a presentation
where to find the big fish.

he is on the Lindy-Little Joe Fishing Team and has been featured in newspaper
d magazine articles and on radio and TV shows. She is also the owner of a
ok publishing company — FINS Publications.

ybil Smith was the first president of Women Anglers of Minnesota as well as past
esident of the Midwest Independent Publishers Association. She is also a
ember of the Minnesota's Fishing Roundtable — a DNR think tank that dis-
sses critical angling issues, identifies problems, and proposes solutions to
eserve good fishing in Minnesota.

FEEDBACK FROM READERS

e have tried to make this book as accurate and up-to-date as possible.
owever, lake conditions and facilities change from time to time. We wel-
me any suggestions you have for improving the next edition of this book.

ANOKA COUNTY

51. Centerville Lake
52. Coon Lake
53. Golden Lake
54. Ham Lake
55. Linwood Lake
56. Martin Lake
57. Moore Lake
58. Peltier Lake

CHISAGO COUNTY

59. Chisago &
    South Lindstrom Lakes
60. Comfort Lake
61. Green Lake
62. Kroon Lake
63. Little Lake
64. North Center Lake
65. North Lindstrom Lake
66. South Center Lake
67. Sunrise Lake

DAKOTA COUNTY

68. Lake Byllesby
69. Crystal Lake
70. Lake Marion
71. Orchard Lake

RAMSEY COUNTY

72. Bald Eagle Lake
73. Lakes Gervais &
    Kohlman
74. Island Lake
75. Lake Johanna
76. Long Lake
77. McCarrons Lake
78. Otter Lake
79. Lakes Owasso &
    Wabasso
80. Lake Phalen &
    Round Lake
81. Silver Lake
82. Snail Lake
83. Turtle Lake

WASHINGTON COUNTY

84. Battle Creek Lake
85. Big Carnelian Lake
86. Big Marine Lake
87. Bone Lake
88. Clear Lake
89. Lakes Demontreville
    Olson
90. Lake Elmo
91. Forest Lake
92. Jane Lake
93. Lily Lake
94. Square Lake
95. Tanners Lake
96. White Bear Lake

Maps were produced with a Macintosh™ computer.